I0886260

New Hollywood

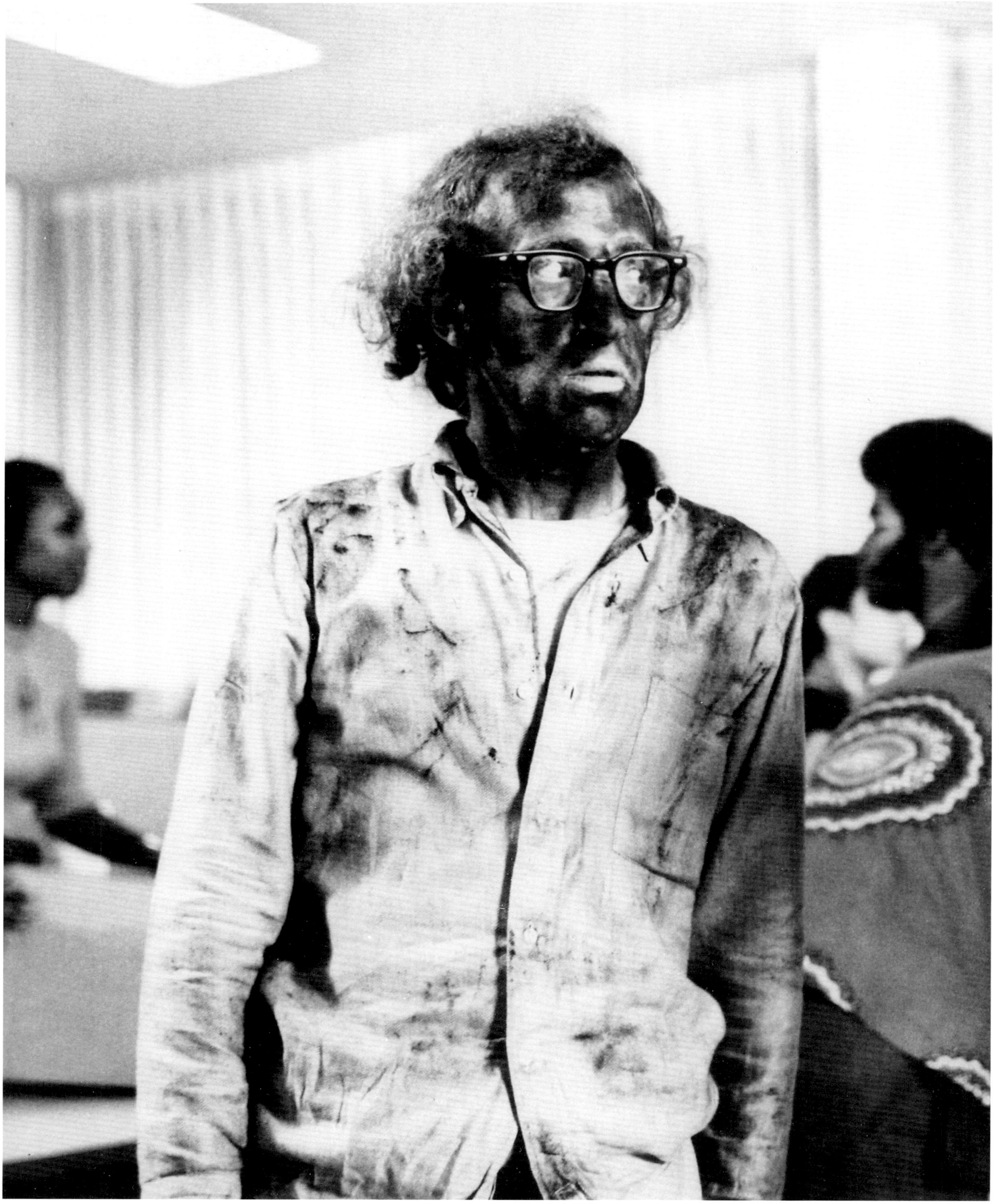

Renate Hehr

New Hollywood

Der amerikanische Film nach 1968
The American Film after 1968

Edition Axel Menges

Alle Abbildungen dieses Buches entstammen dem Archiv des Deutschen Filminstituts – DIF, Frankfurt am Main.

All illustrations of this book come from the archives of the Deutsches Filminstitut – DIF, Frankfurt am Main.

© 2003 Edition Axel Menges, Stuttgart/London
ISBN 3-930698-94-3

Alle Rechte vorbehalten, besonders die der Übersetzung in andere Sprachen.
All rights reserved, especially those of translation into other languages.

Druck/Printing: Druckhaus Münster GmbH, Kornwestheim
Bindearbeiten/Binding: Postkonfekt GmbH, Seeheim-Jugenheim

Lektorat/Editorial supervision: Dorothea Duwe
Englische Übersetzung/English translation: Michael Robinson
Gestaltung/Design: Axel Menges

Zum Thema

Ende der sechziger Jahre erregte der unerwartete Erfolg einer Reihe von amerikanischen Filmen Aufsehen, die ihre Wirkung ganz offensichtlich aus dem Bruch mit den Konventionen des klassischen Hollywood-Kinos bezogen. Als die ersten großen Meilensteine des neuen Trends gelten *Bonnie and Clyde* (1967) von Arthur Penn und *The Graduate* (1968, *Die Reifeprüfung*) von Mike Nichols. Beide Filme wurden überraschend zu Kassenhits, obwohl sie mit einem relativ bescheidenen Budget auskommen mußten und sich eigentlich nur an das begrenzte Marktsegment der jugendlichen Zuschauer richteten. 1969 wiederholte sich dasselbe mit *Easy Rider* von Dennis Hopper, einer Billigproduktion für den Jugendmarkt, die 400 000 $ kostete und in einem Jahr 19 000 000 $ einspielte. Diese Filme waren jedoch keine Einzelfälle. Gleichzeitig mit *The Graduate* kamen 1968 einige der innovativsten und unkonventionellsten Filme, die je von der amerikanischen Filmindustrie produziert worden waren, auf den Markt. Plötzlich schien es eine ungeahnte Ansammlung von Talenten und neuen Ideen zu geben, und Filmwissenschaftler und Kritiker sprachen von einer neuen Welle und dem Beginn eines neuen Filmzeitalters im amerikanischen Kino, für das der Begriff New Hollywood geprägt wurde.

Bei der Auseinandersetzung mit diesem Phänomen und mehr noch bei dem Versuch, es einzugrenzen, steht man früher oder später vor der Notwendigkeit zu definieren, was New Hollywood eigentlich war. Denn es zeigt sich, daß unter Filmhistorikern unterschiedliche und teilweise widersprüchliche Auffassungen über den Charakter, die Hauptakteure und die Dauer der Bewegung bestehen. Einige Veröffentlichungen der siebziger Jahre verstehen unter New Hollywood vor allem die sogenannte Jugendwelle, die nach dem Erfolg von *The Graduate* und *Easy Rider* einsetzte und nach 1971 wieder abflaute. Demnach handelte es sich um die kurzfristige Unterwanderung Hollywoods durch eine neue, von der linken Gegenkultur beeinflußte Generation von Filmemachern, die das amerikanische Mainstream-Kino revolutionieren wollten und schnell an den Grenzen des Systems scheiterten. Spätere Publikationen charakterisieren New Hollywood als die große Zeit der »Autorenfilmer«, als deren harter Kern in der Regel Robert Altman, Stanley Kubrick, John Cassavetes, Arthur Penn, Mike Nichols, Francis Ford Coppola und Martin Scorsese sowie gelegentlich Sam Peckinpah, Paul Mazursky und Michael Ritchie genannt werden. Diese Sichtweise impliziert, daß der Höhepunkt der Bewegung in den Jahren 1969 bis 1975 lag, in denen die meisten dieser Filmemacher ihre kreativste und erfolgreichste Phase hatten. Bei anderen Autoren entsteht der Eindruck, es handele sich vor allem um einen Generationswechsel, der durch das Vordringen der sogenannten »Movie Brats« bedingt war, zu denen neben Coppola und Scorsese unter anderem Brian De Palma, Peter Bogdanovich, George Lucas, Steven Spielberg, William Friedkin, Paul Schrader und John Milius gerechnet werden. Damit rückt ein späterer Zeitraum in den Mittelpunkt der Betrachtung, denn diese Gruppe konnte sich erst Mitte bis Ende der siebziger Jahre etablieren. Da insbesondere Bogdanovich, Spielberg und Lucas von anderer Seite vorgeworfen wird, sie hätten durch ihre Anpassung an erprobte Erfolgsrezepte die Rückkehr der Filmindustrie zu konventionellen Großproduktionen eingeleitet, stellt sich bei dieser Definition außerdem die Frage, ob, und wenn ja, bis wann ihre Filme New Hollywood zuzurechnen sind.

In den achtziger und neunziger Jahren erschienen einige Untersuchungen, die die allgemeinen inhaltlichen Merkmale von New Hollywood durch den Vergleich mit den Konventionen des klassischen Hollywood ergründen und neben den obengenannten Regisseuren auch die Werke anderer Filmemacher der Zeit berücksichtigen. Einige Arbeiten konzentrieren sich dabei auf formale und ästhetische Elemente. Andere führen die Erneuerungsstrategien des neuen Hollywood auf die sozialen, kulturellen und politischen Veränderungen der Zeit zurück und beziehen diese auf inhaltliche und stilistische Attribute. Daneben erschien im Laufe der Jahre eine Vielzahl von Studien, die sich mit verschiedenen Einzelaspekten, wie dem wirtschaftlichen und gesellschaftspolitischen Hintergrund, den künstlerischen und sozialen Wurzeln, den technischen und ästhetischen Neuerungen, den typischen Themen und Motiven, oder Auswirkungen des neuen Hollywood auf die spätere Filmproduktion beschäftigen. Aus heutiger Sicht erscheint New Hollywood als eine breite, ausgesprochen vielfältige Erneuerungsbewegung innerhalb des amerikanischen Mainstream-Kinos, die von den späten sechziger bis in die frühen achtziger Jahre dauerte und »ein ganzes Œuvre von Filmen – im Unterschied zum hin und wieder auftauchenden Meisterwerk – hervorbrachte, die risikobereit und qualitativ hochstehend waren«.

About this book

In the late sixties the unexpected success of a series of American films caused something of a stir; it was quite clear that they had made such an impact because they had broken with the classical Hollywood conventions. The first great milestones in this new trend are Arthur Penn's *Bonnie and Clyde* (1967) and Mike Nichols's *The Graduate* (1968). Both films became unexpected box-office hits, even though they had to work on relatively modest budgets and were actually aimed at the limited market segment of younger filmgoers. The same thing happened again in 1969 with Dennis Hopper's *Easy Rider*, a cheap production for the youth market that cost $400 000 and brought in $19 000 000 at the box office in a single year. But these films were no isolated cases. Some of the most innovative and unconventional films that the American film industry had ever produced came on to the market in 1968, at the same time as *The Graduate*. There suddenly seemed to be an entirely unexpected build-up of talents and new ideas. Film scholars and critics started talking about a new wave and the dawning of a new age in the American cinema. The phrase New Hollywood was coined to describe this.

In addressing this phenomenon, or even more in attempting to define it, sooner or later you will have to state what New Hollywood actually was. It turns out that film historians have different and to an extent contradictory views about the movement's character, its main protagonists and how long it lasted. Some seventies publications see New Hollywood as the so-called youth wave that started after the success of *The Graduate* and *Easy Rider*, then died off again after 1971. According to this theory, it was about a new generation of film-makers affected by left-wing alternative culture who wanted to revolutionize American mainstream cinema and were rapidly defeated by the limits of the system. Later publications identify New Hollywood as the great age of »auteur films«. The hard core here are usually Robert Altman, Stanley Kubrick, John Cassavetes, Arthur Penn, Mike Nichols, Francis Ford Coppola and Martin Scorsese, and occasionally Sam Peckinpah, Paul Mazursky and Michael Ritchie. This view implies that the movement peaked between 1969 and 1975, when most of these film-makers were going through their most creative and successful phase. Other writers give the impression that it is all about a change of generation brought about by the surge forward of the »Movie Brats«. These usually include Coppola and Scorsese, and then Brian De Palma, Peter Bogdanovich, George Lucas, Steven Spielberg, William Friedkin, Paul Schrader and John Milius. This makes a later period central to our considerations, as this group did not establish themselves until the mid to late seventies. Bogdanovich, Spielberg and Lucas in particular are reproached on the other hand with having taken the film industry back to conventional large-scale productions because they went along with tried-and-tested recipes for success. Thus this definition also raises the question of whether, and if so when, their films could be said to be part of New Hollywood.

Some eighties and nineties studies tried to get to the bottom of New Hollywood's general content characteristics by comparing them with the conventions of classical Hollywood, and including work by film-makers of the period other than those mentioned above. Some of these works concentrate on formal and aesthetic elements. Others relate New Hollywood's renewal strategies to the social, cultural and political changes of the period, and link these up with style and content attributes. As well as this, in the course of the years a number of studies have appeared addressing various individual aspects like the economic and socio-political background, artistic and social roots, technical and aesthetic innovations, typical themes and subject matter, or New Hollywood's effect on later film production. From today's point of view, New Hollywood seems like a broad, extremely diverse innovative movement within mainstream American cinema. It lasted from the late sixties to the early eighties and »produced a whole film œuvre – as distinct from the odd masterpiece that appeared now and then –, which was prepared to take risks and was of high quality«.

Anmerkungen zur Entstehung und Entwicklung von New Hollywood

Die Krise

Die Entstehung von New Hollywood traf mit einer tiefen Krise der amerikanischen Filmindustrie, zusammen, die seit dem Höhepunkt ihrer Entwicklung in den Jahren 1946 bis 1948 einen stetigen Niedergang erlebte. Die wesentlichen Ursachen lagen in der Auflösung des Studiosystems, dem Aufkommen des Fernsehens und gesellschaftlichen Veränderungen, auf die Hollywood falsch und zu spät reagierte.

Vor dem Zweiten Weltkrieg besaßen die acht größten Filmgesellschaften, Paramount, Metro Goldwyn Mayer, RKO, Warner Brothers, Twentieth Century Fox, United Artists, Columbia und Universal, ein Monopol bei der Produktion, dem Vertrieb und der Aufführung von Filmen, das seit den dreißiger Jahren von unabhängigen Produzenten und Kinobesitzern bekämpft wurde. 1948 erfolgte mit dem sogenannten Paramount Decree der erste einer Reihe von Gerichtsbeschlüssen, welche die Studios verpflichtete, sich von einem dieser Geschäftsbereiche zu trennen, woraufhin sie in den fünfziger Jahren nach und nach den größten Teil ihrer Filmtheater aufgaben. Hierdurch veränderten sich die Bedingungen für die Produktion von Filmen beträchtlich. Die bis dahin gängige Praxis der Blockbuchung, bei der die Kinobesitzer zur Abnahme des gesamten Programms einer Gesellschaft gezwungen waren, um die Kassenschlager zu bekommen, konnte nicht aufrechterhalten werden. Fortan mußte man jeden Film einzeln vermarkten, und das Risiko erhöhte sich. Die Folge war, daß die großen Filmgesellschaften die Zahl der Eigenproduktionen allmählich einschränkten und sich zunehmend auf den Vertrieb unabhängig produzierter Filme konzentrierten. Infolgedessen erhielten die Agenten eine neue Bedeutung, denn sie übernahmen nun die frühere Rolle der Studios, indem sie alle an einem Film Beteiligten zusammenbrachten und den Banken und Distributionsgesellschaften sogenannte Pakete aus Drehbuch, Regisseur und Schauspielern anboten, die natürlich besser verkäuflich waren, wenn sie bekannte Stars vorweisen konnten oder auf literarische Bestseller zurückgingen.

Der Rückgriff auf erprobte Erfolgsformeln verstärkte sich durch die wachsende Konkurrenz des Fernsehens, das sich in den fünfziger Jahren in den USA etablierte und einen Teil des traditionellen Familienpublikums abzog. Die Filmindustrie versuchte mit aufwendigen und entsprechend kostspieligen Großproduktionen zu kontern, die das Fernsehen nicht bieten konnte. Um das Risiko zu verringern, setzte man verstärkt auf bewährte Stars, Themen und Stoffe, die auf den Geschmack des Massenpublikums abzielten, wodurch wenig Raum für künstlerische Innovationen blieb. So waren viele Filme dieser Zeit konservativer und anspruchsloser als die meisten Werke des »goldenen Zeitalters« Hollywoods in den dreißiger und vierziger Jahren.

Der kommerzielle Erfolg von Filmen wie *Mary Poppins* (1964), *A Sound of Music* (1965, *Meine Lieder – meine Träume*) oder *Doctor Zhivago* (1966, *Doktor Schiwago*) schien diese Geschäftsstrategie zunächst zu bestätigen. In Wirklichkeit aber wurde das Filmgeschäft immer mehr zum Vabanquespiel. Häufig floß der größte Teil der Ressourcen einer Gesellschaft in eine einzige Großproduktion. Da ohnehin nur durchschnittlich 10 % der Erträge eines Films für Neuproduktionen übrigbleiben, stand immer weniger Kapital zur Verfügung. So konnte ein einziger großer Hit einer Filmgesellschaft zu immensen Profiten verhelfen, ein teurer Flop sie aber ebenso an den Rand des Bankrotts bringen, wie die meisten der Studios im Laufe der sechziger Jahre schmerzhaft erfahren mußten. Ein Umstand, der die Krise zunächst verschleierte, war das Geschäft mit dem Fernsehen, das durch die Gründung von Produktionsgesellschaften für Fernsehshows und –serien und den Verkauf alter Filmbestände für die Studios zu einer lukrativen Einnahmequelle wurde. Aufgrund des steigenden Bedarfs begannen die Fernsehgesellschaften in der zweiten Hälfte der sechziger Jahre mit der Produktion von eigenen abendfüllenden Filmen. 1968 war der Markt übersättigt, die Preise brachen ein. Mit Ausnahme von Disney und MCA erlitten alle großen Gesellschaften millionenschwere Verluste und mußten unter dem Druck der Banken ihre Produktionen drastisch einschränken.

Das neue Publikum

Das Debakel machte deutlich, daß die Krise der Filmindustrie nicht so sehr auf die Konkurrenz des Fernsehens zurückzuführen war, sondern der eigentliche Grund für die sinkenden Zuschauerzahlen in sozialen Veränderungen lag. Nach den unruhigen Zeiten der Depression und

Notes on the emergence and development of New Hollywood

The crisis

The emergence of New Hollywood coincided with a profound crisis in the American film industry, which had been in a state of constant decline since its heyday in the years 1946 to 1948. The principal causes were the break-up of the studio system, the rise of television and social changes that Hollywood responded to wrongly, and too late.

Before the Second World War the eight great film companies, Paramount, Metro Goldwyn Mayer, RKO, Warner Brothers, Twentieth Century Fox, United Artists, Columbia and Universal had a monopoly in the production, distribution and screening of films. Independent producers and cinema owners had been fighting this since the thirties. The so-called Paramount Decree, which was passed in 1948, was the first of a series of court decisions. It obliged the studios to give up one of these business fields, and in the fifties they did abandon most of their cinemas. This considerably changed film production conditions. The practice of block booking had been used until then. This meant that cinema owners had to take the whole of a company's programme in order to get the box-office hits; it was now no longer sustainable. Each film now had to be marketed separately, which considerably increased the risks involved. The consequence was that the large film companies gradually cut back the numbers of their own productions and concentrated increasingly on distributing films by independent producers. As a consequence of this, agents became more important, as they now took over the earlier role of the studio by bringing everyone involved in a film together and offering the banks and distribution companies so-called packages made up of screenplay, director and actors. These packages were of course easier to sell if they included famous stars or literary best sellers.

Recourse to tried-and-tested success formulae was further reinforced by increasing competition from television, which established itself in the USA in the fifties and took away part of the traditional film audience. The film industry tried coming back with elaborate and correspondingly expensive large-scale productions that television could not offer. To reduce the risk, they increasingly relied on established stars and themes as well as material aimed at mass tastes, which left little scope for artistic innovation. So the films made in this period were more conservative and less ambitious than most works from the »golden age« of Hollywood in the thirties and forties.

The commercial success of films like *Mary Poppins* (1964), *A Sound of Music* (1965) or *Doctor Zhivago* (1966) seemed to justify this commercial strategy at first. But in reality the film industry was becoming an increasingly risky game. Frequently the greatest part of a company's resources was invested in a single major production. As anyway only 10% of the profits on a film were available for new productions, there was less and less capital around, so one great hit could bring a film company enormous profits, but an expensive flop could also push them to the brink of bankruptcy, a painful lesson that most companies were forced to learn in the course of the sixties. One aspect that masked the crisis at first was business with television, which became a lucrative source of income through the foundation of production companies for TV shows and series, and the sale of old films. To meet increasing demand, the television companies started to make their own feature-length films in the second half of the sixties. The market was saturated by 1968, and prices collapsed. With the exception of Disney and MCA, all the big companies lost millions and had to restrict their productions drastically, under pressure from the banks.

The new audience

This debacle made it clear that the crisis in the film industry was not particularly caused by competition from television: the actual reason for the falling audience ratings was social change. After the unrest caused by the Depression and the Second World War, the average American was longing for normality. The economic upturn of the fifties brought relative prosperity that made it possible to start a family and set up a home of one's own. People preferred to move into the newly emerging suburbs, a long way away from the large cinemas in the city centres. Unlike television, which offered entertainment for all the family, without clashing with the business of the household, a cinema visit was hard to fit in with family life. Thus it had largely lost its social significance for this older generation.

des Zweiten Weltkriegs sehnten sich die Durchschnittsamerikaner nach Normalität. Der wirtschaftliche Aufschwung der fünfziger Jahre brachte einen relativen Wohlstand, der es ihnen ermöglichte, eine Familie zu gründen und sich ein Heim zu schaffen. Mit Vorliebe zogen sie in die neu entstehenden Vorstädte, weit weg von den großen Filmtheatern im Stadtzentrum. Anders als das Fernsehen, das Unterhaltung für die ganze Familie bot, ohne mit den Beschäftigungen zu Hause in Konflikt zu geraten, ließ sich das Kino nur schwer mit dem Familienleben vereinbaren. Für diese ältere Generation hatte es seine soziale Bedeutung somit weitgehend verloren.

Gleichzeitig entwickelten sich neue Publikumsschichten, die der Hollywood-Mainstream zunächst unbeachtet ließ: das traditionelle, kulturell orientierte, sogenannte »verlorene Publikum« und das jugendliche Publikum, das wie nie zuvor zu einem wesentlichen Wirtschaftsfaktor wurde.

In den fünfziger Jahren begannen die Jugendlichen, einen Lebensstil zu entwickeln, der sich von dem vorheriger Generationen grundlegend unterschied. Das Leben in den Vor- und Kleinstädten verschaffte den jungen Leuten einen gesicherten sozialen Rahmen. Sie hatten Geld, Autos, genug Freizeit, um sich mit Freunden zu treffen, und einen ungezwungenen Kontakt mit dem anderen Geschlecht. Andererseits empfanden sie die konservativen Strukturen als einengend und grenzten sich durch die Rock'n-Roll-Kultur von den Erwachsenen ab. Sie waren das typische Publikum der Autokinos, das in den fünfziger Jahren in den Vororten, Kleinstädten und auf dem Lande entstand. Das Kino bot die Gelegenheit, der Aufsicht der Eltern zu entkommen. Es war ein idealer Treffpunkt für Pärchen, diente den Jugendlichen dazu, sich mit ihrer Clique zu versammeln, und erfüllte damit weiterhin eine wichtige soziale Funktion.

Bis auf einige zaghafte Versuche in der zweiten Hälfte der fünfziger Jahren, mit Filmen der Jugendstars James Dean, Marlon Brando und Elvis Presley ein jüngeres Publikum zu erreichen, überließen die großen Filmgesellschaften diesen Markt vor allem den Produktionsfirmen von Low-Budget-Filmen. Zur größten dieser kleineren Gesellschaften entwickelte sich American International Pictures (AIP). Sie wurde 1956 gegründet und drehte im Drei-Wochen-Rhythmus jeweils zwei Filme mit einem Minibudget für die Doppelprogramme der Autokinos. Dabei setzte sie auf das Interesse der Jugendlichen für Sex, Autos, Jugendgangs und Nervenkitzel. Grob gestrickte Horrorgeschichten, Kriegs- und Gangsterfilme, Filme über private Autorennen, Motorradbanden und bizarre Science fiction bildeten das Kernstück des Programms. Ein unverzichtbares Element waren Sexszenen, die in den prüden fünfziger Jahren noch ausgesprochen gemäßigt aussahen. 1959 verschwanden die Doppelprogramme, und die AIP beschloß, das Budget zu erhöhen und in Farbe und Breitwand zu drehen. Der Film *Beach Party* (1963) zog ein ganzes Subgenre von Jugendpartyfilmen nach sich. Als die Sex- und Gewaltszenen der AIP-Filme den Protest von Eltern- und Lehrerorganisationen hervorriefen, versuchte die Firma, mit dem Edgar-Allen-Poe-Zyklus von Roger Corman, dem führenden Produzenten und Regisseur der Gesellschaft, eine gewisse Respektabilität zu erlangen.

Eine zweite Zuschauergruppe, die Hollywood weitgehend links liegenließ, war das intellektuelle, politisch und kulturell interessierte Publikum, das seine Weltsicht in den formelhaften Genrefilmen und den darin verbreiteten Werten nicht wiederfand. Diese intellektuelle Elite nahm die Veränderungen, die mit Amerika nach dem Zweiten Weltkrieg vorgegangen waren, bewußt wahr und empfand Unbehagen angesichts neuer politischer und sozialer Erscheinungen, wie der Atombombe, den gestörten Beziehungen zur UdSSR und China, dem Koreakrieg, der Kommunistenjagd der McCarthy-Ära, der sozialen Ungleichheit und der Anonymität und Beschränkung des individuellen Freiraums durch die zunehmende Verstädterung. Diese Schicht besuchte die Kunstfilmtheater, die seit den fünfziger Jahren vermehrt in den Großstädten und Universitätsvierteln entstanden. Sie gingen aus der Not der kleineren Kinos hervor, sich auf dem Markt zu behaupten. In Anbetracht der Verteuerung und Verknappung der A-Filme konzentrierten sie sich in ihren Programmen auf die Wiederaufführung von klassischen Hollywood-Filmen und auf unabhängige Produktionen. Daneben griffen sie zunehmend auf ausländische Filme zurück, die zum ersten Mal ungehinderten Zugang zum US-Markt hatten und überwiegend von kleineren, spezialisierten Firmen vertrieben wurden. Auf diese Art wurden Filme wie die der italienischen Neorealisten und der französischen Nouvelle Vague, von Michelangelo Antonioni, Ingmar Bergman oder Akira Kurosawa in den USA bekannt. Sie eröffneten den amerikanischen Zuschauern, die an die Konventionen des klassischen Hollywood gewöhnt waren, eine neue Dimension des Kinos, veränderten die Sehgewohnheiten des Publikums und beeinflußten die künstlerischen Vorstellungen der amerikanischer Filmemacher.

In den sechziger Jahren verbanden sich die kritische Intelligenz und die jugendliche Subkultur zu einer wachsenden Gegenkultur. Das kulturelle und ideologische Bindeglied dieser beiden

At the same time, new audience segments developed that mainstream Hollywood ignored at first: the traditional, culturally oriented, so-called »lost audience« and the young audience that was a crucial economic factor as it had never been before.

In the fifties, young people started to develop a lifestyle that was fundamentally different from that of earlier generations. Life in the suburbs and small towns gave young people a secure social framework. They had money, cars, enough free time to meet their friends and make free and easy contact with the opposite sex. But they also found the prevailing conservative structures too restrictive, and erected the barrier of Rock'n'Roll culture between themselves and their parents. They were the typical audience for the drive-in cinemas that sprang up in the suburbs, small towns and rural areas in the fifties. The cinema offered an opportunity to get away from parental supervision. It was an ideal meeting place for couples, young people used it to get together with their clique, and thus it also fulfilled an important social function.

With the exception of a few tentative attempts in the mid to late fifties to reach a younger audience with films by young stars like James Dean, Marlon Brando and Elvis Presley, the big film companies left this market to firms who produced low budget films. American International Pictures (AIP) became one of the largest of these smaller firms. It was founded in 1956 and made two mini-budget films every three weeks for the double bills in drive-in cinemas. These exploited young people's interest in sex, cars, youth gangs and kicks. Crude horror stories, war and gangster films, films about private motor races and bizarre science fiction made up the core of the programme. An essential element was sex scenes, which looked extremely restrained in the prudish fifties. The double bills disappeared in 1959, and AIP decided to increase its budget and shoot in colour and wide screen. The film *Beach Party* (1963) triggered a whole sub-genre of youth parties films. When the sex and violence in AIP films led to protests from parents' and teachers' organizations, the company tried to acquire a certain respectability with the Edgar Allan Poe cycle by Roger Corman, the company's leading producer and director.

A second group of filmgoers that Hollywood largely ignored was the audience with intellectual, political and cultural interests, who were not interested in the world view propagated in formulaic genre films and the values they promoted. This intellectual élite consciously accepted the changes that had happened in America since the Second World War and were uncomfortable with new social and political phenomena like the atomic bomb, damaged relationships with the USSR and China, the Korean War, the Communist witch-hunts of the McCarthy era, social inequality and the anonymity and curtailment of individual freedom caused by increasing urbanization. This group went to the art cinemas that had increasingly appeared in big cities and university areas since the fifties. These emerged because small cinemas found it so difficult to survive. Given the increasing cost and shortage of A movies, their programmes concentrated on re-screening classic Hollywood films and independent productions. As well as this, they increasingly turned to foreign films, which had free access to the US market for the first time, and were mainly distributed by small specialist firms. In this way films made by the Italian neo-Realists and the French Nouvelle Vague, by Michelangelo Antonioni, Ingmar Bergman or Akira Kurosawa became known in the USA. They opened up a new dimension of the cinema for American audiences, who were used to the classical Hollywood conventions, changed the way they looked at things and influenced American film-makers' artistic ideas.

In the sixties the critical intelligentsia and the youth subculture combined to form a growing alternative culture. The cultural and ideological link between these two groups was the Beat Generation, the small group of literary figures that formed in fifties New York and San Franzisko around Alan Ginsberg, Jack Kerouac, William S. Burroughs and Neal Cassidy. The Beat Poets did not just become the literary mouthpiece of intellectual bohemian society in the second half of the decade. They also helped to trigger the emergence of the hippie movement, formulating and practising their essential ideas: the rejection of the establishment, of traditional moral and social ideas, of urbanization and the constraining structures of modern labour, replacing them with the conviction that in a mass society real freedom lay in developing one's own individuality. Spontaneity and subjectivity were seen as the most important criteria for action. As well as this, there was a move towards sexual liberality, and new experiences were sought. Being constantly on the move, both geographically and in the sense of inner movement through drugs, was intended to work against mental inertia and physical decay, and to bring eternal youth. People studied the religions of the Far East, or »fled« into unspoiled nature. The hippie movement grew up in the early sixties in East Village in New York and in the Haight Ashbury district of San Fransciso. It consisted mainly of students and ex-students who hoped to realize their

Gruppen bildete die Beat-Generation, jener kleine Kreis von Literaten, die sich in den fünfziger Jahren in New York und San Francisco um Alan Ginsberg, Jack Kerouac, William S. Burroughs und Neal Cassady formierten. Die Beat-Poeten entwickelten sich in der zweiten Hälfte des Jahrzehnts nicht nur zum literarischen Sprachrohr der intellektuellen Bohème. Sie beeinflußten auch die Entstehung der Hippiebewegung, deren wesentliche Ideen sie formulierten und praktizierten: die Ablehnung des Establishments, der herkömmlichen moralischen und sozialen Vorstellungen, der Verstädterung und der zwanghaften Strukturen der modernen Arbeitswelt, die Überzeugung, daß in einer Massengesellschaft die wirkliche Freiheit in der Entwicklung der eigenen Individualität liege. Spontaneität und Subjektivität galten als die wichtigsten Kriterien des Handelns. Darüber hinaus strebte man nach sexueller Freizügigkeit und suchte nach neuen Erlebnissen und Erfahrungen. Ständiges In-Bewegung-Sein sowohl im geographischen als auch im Sinne innerer Bewegung durch Drogen sollte dem geistigen Stillstand und dem körperlichen Verfall entgegenwirken und eine ewig währende Jugend nach sich ziehen. Man beschäftigte sich mit fernöstlichen Religionen oder trat die »Flucht« in die unberührte Natur an. Anfang der sechziger Jahre bildete sich in East Village in New York und im Bezirk Haight Ashbury in San Franzisko die Hippiebewegung heraus. Hauptsächlich setzte sie sich aus Studenten und Exstudenten zusammen, die durch das Zusammenleben in Kommunen und »Großfamilien« ihre Ideale von Frieden, freier Liebe und einem einfachen, ursprünglichen Leben zu verwirklichen hofften. Zusammen mit der konsumorientierten Popkultur, die sich seit Anfang der sechziger Jahre mit der Musik der Beatles und der Rolling Stones von England aus über die ganze Welt verbreitete, prägten ihre Ideen das Selbstgefühl einer ganzen Generation, die durch ihre Begeisterung für Rockmusik, informelle und phantasievolle Kleidung, lange Haare, die Bemalung mit Körperfarben und auffälligen Schmuck, eine legere Sprache und formlose Umgangsformen die Befreiung des Körpers und die Abgrenzung gegen die Zwänge und Rituale der Erwachsenenwelt demonstrierte. Verstärkt wurde dies durch den politischen Protest, der sich im Rahmen von zwei großen sozialen Bewegungen artikulierte: der Bürgerrechtsbewegung der Schwarzen, die in der zweiten Hälfte der fünfziger Jahre, ausgehend vom Süden des Landes, einen Aufschwung erlebte, und der Protestbewegung gegen den Vietnamkrieg, deren Hochburg ab 1963 die Universitäten waren. Mit der Ausweitung des Rassenkonflikts auf die Städte und der zunehmenden Intervention der USA in Vietnam in der zweiten Hälfte der sechziger Jahre erfaßten die Ideen der Gegenkultur immer größere Teile der Jugendlichen und des intellektuellen Mittelstands. Tausende von Protestaktionen im ganzen Land, Massendemonstrationen wie die jährlichen Märsche auf Washington und Straßenschlachten mit der Polizei und der Nationalgarde, offenbarten einen tiefen Riß zwischen dem liberalen Amerika, das eine unübersehbare Kraft erlangt hatte, und der konservativen, sogenannten »schweigenden Mehrheit«, wie sie Vizepräsident Spiro T. Agnew titulierte. Da die Protestbewegung überwiegend von jungen Leuten getragen wurde, basierte diese Spaltung zum Teil auf einem Generationenkonflikt. Doch sehr viel ausgeprägter war der Konflikt zwischen zwei Kulturen mit unterschiedlichen Wertvorstellungen und Lebensstilen.

Der alternative Markt

Während die Studios weiter auf konventionelle Produkte für das traditionelle Familienpublikum setzten, entwickelte sich eine Art alternativer Markt, der die kulturellen Bedürfnisse dieser wachsenden Zuschauergruppe aufnahm. Eine Folge der Auflösung des Studiosystems war, daß sich bereits in den fünfziger Jahren eine Vielzahl von unabhängigen Produktionsgesellschaften etablieren konnte, die teilweise mit den »Mayors« zusammenarbeiteten, häufig aber am Rande oder außerhalb des Hollywood-Mainstreams funktionierten. Auf diese Weise entzogen sie sich der direkten Kontrolle durch die Studiobosse und erlangten einen gewissen Grad an künstlerischer Unabhängigkeit. Von ihnen gingen die wesentlichen Impulse für eine künstlerische Erneuerung des Hollywood-Films aus. Ein Ausdruck dessen war das neue Phänomen der Kultfilme, darunter eine Reihe von Hollywood-Filmen, die bewußt oder unbewußt die alten Formeln unterliefen, jedoch bezeichnenderweise nicht zu den großen Kassenerfolgen ihrer Zeit gehörten, aber auch unabhängige Produktionen, wie John Cassavetes' Regiedebüt *Shadows* (*Schatten*), das 1960 in Venedig den Kritikerpreis erhielt, jedoch von Hollywood vollkommen ignoriert wurde, sowie die frühen Filme späterer Starregisseure des neuen Hollywood, wie Martin Scorseses *Who's That Knocking at My Door?* (1968, *Wer klopft denn da an meine Tür?*), Brian De Palmas *Greetings* (1968, *Grüße*) und *Hi, Mom* (1970) oder George Lucas' *THX-1158* (1970).

ideals of peace, free love and a simple, natural life by living in communes and »composite families«. Along with a consumer-oriented Pop culture, which had spread all over the world from England with the music of the Beatles and the Rolling Stones, their ideas shaped the self-perception of a whole generation who were demonstrating the liberation of their bodies and their rejection of the constraints and rituals of the adult world through their enthusiasm for rock music, informal and imaginative clothing, long hair, body painting and ostentatious jewellery, casual language and informal manners. This was reinforced by the political protests articulated as part of two major social movements: the black civil rights movement, which experienced an upturn in the second half of the fifties, starting in the south, and the protest movement against the Vietnam War, with its stronghold in the universities from 1963 onwards. The ideas of the alternative culture attracted increasing numbers of young people and the intellectual middle classes in the second half of the sixties as racial conflicts spread to the cities and the USA intervened increasingly in Vietnam. Thousands of protest campaigns nationwide, mass demonstrations like the annual marches on Washington and street battles with the police and the National Guard revealed a deep gulf between liberal America, which had acquired power that could not be ignored, and the conservative, so-called »silent majority«, as Vice-President Spiro T. Agnew called them. As the protest movement was supported largely by young people, this split was based partly on a generational conflict. But the conflict between two cultures with different world views and life-styles was considerably more pronounced.

The alternative market

While the studios continued to rely on conventional products for the traditional family audience, a kind of alternative market developed that started to address the cultural needs of this growing group of filmgoers. One consequence of the breakdown of the studio system was that a large number of independent production companies were able to set themselves up even in the fifties. They worked partly with the major studios, but frequently functioned on the fringe of or outside the Hollywood mainstream. In this way they avoided direct control by the studio bosses and acquired a certain degree of artistic autonomy. They were responsible for key initiatives that led to an artistic renaissance for the Hollywood movie. One expression of this was the new phenomenon of cult films, including a number of Hollywood films that consciously or unconsciously undermined the old formulae but were not among the great box-office successes of their day, and also independent productions like John Cassavetes's directorial début *Shadows* (1960), which won the 1960 Critics' Prize in Venice, but was completely ignored by Hollywood, and also early films by later New Hollywood star directors like Martin Scorsese's *Who's That Knocking at My Door?* (1968), Brian De Palma's *Greetings* (1968) and *Hi, Mom* (1970) or George Lucas's *THX-1158* (1970).

It is symptomatic that both *Bonnie and Clyde* and *The Graduate* succeeded on the periphery of mainstream Hollywood, while Columbia made *Easy Rider* more or less by chance. *The Graduate* was financed and distributed by Embassy, a small production company, while *Bonnie and Clyde* had to win through against resistance from the co-producer, Warner-Seven Arts. Most critics dismissed the film after its première at the Montreal film festival as an ordinary gangster film with unduly brutal scenes of violence. So Warner Bros. promptly decided to banish it to the drive-in cinemas. Finally Warren Beatty successfully insisted on a re-launch. Although the film disappeared from the cinemas again after a short time, its fame stubbornly persisted. The soundtrack climbed up the hit parade, and Fay Dunaway's costumes created a new fashion style. Finally it was launched yet again, with considerable fanfares, the critics revised their opinions and the film became a box-office hit, winning a number of prizes, including two Oscars.

Easy Rider is the direct successor to a number of films that were made by AIP under Roger Corman in the second half of the sixties. In 1966 he shot the motor-bike epic *The Wild Angels* with Peter Fonda in the lead. This film made it to the Venice Film Festival. It took $ 5 000 000 at the box office with production costs of $ 350 000, and was one of AIP's great commercial successes. Then Corman made the drugs film *The Trip* in 1967, again with Peter Fonda, dealing with a stressed businessman's trip on LSD. In the same year AIP produced *Psych-Out*, one of the few films dealing with the hippie scene, directed by Richard Rush and with the then unknown Jack Nicholson in the lead, and *Hell's Angels on Wheels* both of which reflect the mood of young people at the time precisely and unpretentiously. The cameraman Lazlo Kovacs, who

Symptomatisch ist, daß sowohl *Bonnie and Clyde* als auch *The Graduate* ihren Erfolg am Rande des Hollywood-Mainstreams errangen, während *Easy Rider* eher zufällig bei Columbia entstand. *The Graduate* wurde von Embassy, einer kleineren Produktionsgesellschaft, finanziert und vertrieben, während *Bonnie and Clyde* sich gegen den Widerstand des Koproduzenten Warner-Seven Arts behauptete. Der Film wurde nach der Uraufführung auf dem Filmfestival in Montreal von den meisten Kritikern als ein gewöhnlicher Gangsterfilm mit übermäßig grausamen Gewaltszenen abgetan. Daraufhin beschloß Warner Bros., ihn in die Autokinos zu verbannen. Schließlich konnte Warren Beatty einen Neustart erwirken. Obwohl der Film schon nach kurzer Zeit wieder aus den Kinos verschwand, hielt sich sein Ruhm hartnäckig. Der Soundtrack erklomm die Hitparaden, und die Kostüme von Faye Dunaway kreierten einen neuen Modestil. Schließlich wurde er noch einmal im großen Stil gestartet, die Kritiker revidierten ihre Meinung, der Film entwickelte sich zu einem Kassenschlager und gewann eine Reihe von Preisen, darunter zwei Oscars.

Easy Rider steht in direkter Nachfolge einer Reihe von Filmen, die unter der Leitung von Roger Corman in der zweiten Hälfte der sechziger Jahre bei AIP entstanden. 1966 drehte er das Motorrad-Epos *The Wild Angels* (*Die wilden Engel*) mit Peter Fonda in der Hauptrolle. Der Film schaffte es bis zu den Filmfestspielen in Venedig und wurde mit einem Einspielergebnis von 5 Millionen $ bei Produktionskosten von 350 000 $ zu einem der großen kommerziellen Erfolge der AIP. Wiederum mit Peter Fonda machte Corman 1967 den Drogenfilm *The Trip*, der vom LSD-Trip eines gestreßten Geschäftsmannes handelt. Im gleichen Jahr produzierte AIP unter der Regie von Richard Rush mit dem noch unbekannten Jack Nicholson in der Hauptrolle *Psych-Out*, einen der wenigen Filme, der von der Hippieszene handelt, und *Hell's Angels on Wheels* (*Die wilden Schläger von San Franzisko*), die genau und unprätentiös die Stimmung der damaligen Jugend wiedergeben. Bei beiden Filmen arbeitete der Kameramann Lazlo Kovacs mit, der später durch *Easy Rider* berühmt wurde. 1968 spielte Dennis Hopper die Hauptrolle in dem Motorradfilm *The Glory Stompers* (*Die teuflischen Engel*). Die AIP erzielte mit diesen und anderen Filmen, die sich mit der Jugendkultur befaßten, wie *Riot on Sunset Strip* (1967, *Wir ... die Wilden vom Sunset Strip*) oder *Wild in the Streets* (1968, *Wild in den Straßen*), gute Gewinne. *Easy Rider* wurde nur deshalb nicht von AIP produziert, weil Arkoff, der Leiter der AIP, mit einer Zusage zögerte, als Peter Fonda ihm das Drehbuch anbot, da es Dennis Hoppers erste Regiearbeit sein sollte. Daraufhin ging Fonda zu Columbia, wo der Produzent Bert Schneider das Budget mit den Einspielergebnissen der AIP-Motorradfilme verglich und sofort akzeptierte.

1. Lelia Goldoni (Lelia), Rupert Crosse (Rupert) und Hugh Hurd (Hugh) in *Schatten* von John Cassavetes, 1960.
2. Robert De Niro (Jon Rubin) und Roz Kelly (Photographin) in *Grüße* von Brian De Palma, 1968.

1. Lelia Goldoni (Lelia), Rupert Crosse (Rupert) and Hugh Hurd (Hugh) in *Shadows* by John Cassavetes, 1960.
2. Robert De Niro (Jon Rubin) and Roz Kelly (photographer) in *Greetings* by Brian De Palma, 1968.

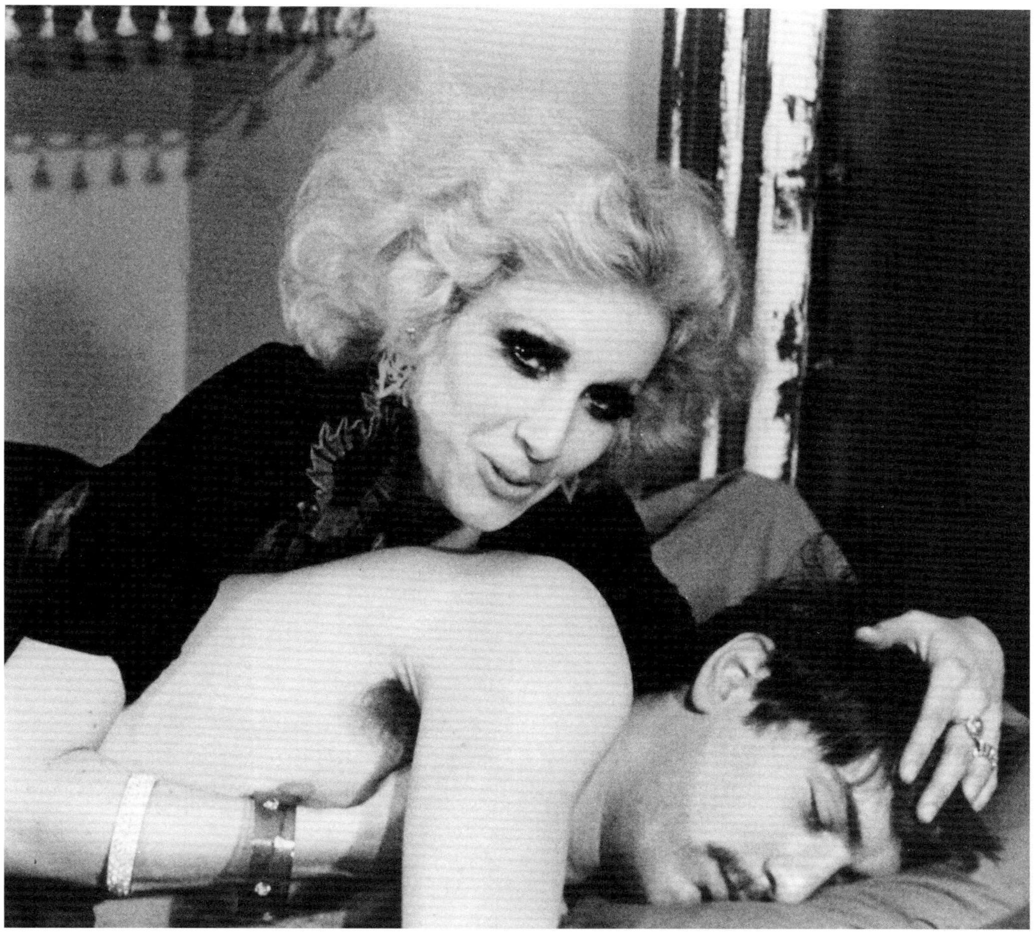

later also became famous for *Easy Rider*, worked on both these films. In 1968, Dennis Hopper played the lead in the biker film *The Glory Stompers*. AIP made good profits with these and other films addressing youth culture, like *Riot on Sunset Strip* (1967) or *Wild in the Streets* (1968). AIP did not produce *Easy Rider*, only because Arkoff, the director of AIP, hesitated to take it up when Peter Fonda offered him the screenplay, as it was to be Dennis Hopper's first work as a director. So Fonda went to Columbia, where the producer Bert Schneider compared the budget with the AIP biker films' box-office profits and immediately accepted.

All three films are in the style of the European art film, especially that of the Nouvelle Vague, and were received by critics and audiences as something completely new. But the main reason for their success was that they chimed with the late sixties »Zeitgeist«. The story of the two appealing, romantic outlaws Bonnie and Clyde, who fight the establishment in the manner of Robin Hood and are destroyed by betrayal, hit the tone and spirit of the left-wing alternative culture with their mixture of comedy and tragedy. *The Graduate* conveys the same critical attitude to the values of middle-class society, here from the point of view of a young student who is trying to find himself. He sees himself confronted with the emotional emptiness of his well-to-do family home and the dual standards and treachery of the adult world. With the girl he loves, he escapes into an uncertain future, while the two drop-outs from *Easy Rider* embody the anti-heroism of the alternative culture: lonely rebels looking for freedom who are destroyed by the hostile world around them.

The first wave

A process of reorganization and concentration was under way in the film industry in the late sixties. The studios were either taken over by large conglomerates as in the case of Paramount and United Artists, swallowed up by large entertainment groups like Universal and Warner, or expanded into other areas themselves, like Twentieth Century Fox, Columbia and MGM. The last of the old studio bosses disappeared with reorganization. They were replaced by a new kind of manager. Most of them were financial experts or lawyers who knew very little about the

Der Stil aller drei Filme steht in der Tradition des europäischen Kunstfilms, insbesondere der Nouvelle Vague, und wurde von Kritikern und Zuschauern als vollkommen neuartig empfunden. Doch der Hauptgrund für ihren sensationellen Erfolg war, daß sie den Zeitgeist der späten sechziger Jahre trafen. Die Geschichte der zwei sympathischen, romantischen Outlaws Bonnie und Clyde, die in Robin-Hood-Manier gegen das Establishment kämpfen und durch Verrat untergehen, traf mit ihrer Mischung aus Komik und Tragik den Ton und das Lebensgefühl der linken Gegenkultur. *The Graduate* vermittelt die gleiche kritische Einstellung gegenüber den Werten der bürgerlichen Gesellschaft, hier von der Warte eines jungen Studenten, der sich auf der Suche nach einer Lebensperspektive mit der emotionalen Leere seines wohlhabenden Elternhauses, der Doppelmoral und dem Verrat der Erwachsenenwelt konfrontiert sieht. Zusammen mit dem Mädchen, das er liebt, entflieht er in eine ungewisse Zukunft, während die beiden Aussteiger aus *Easy Rider* die Verkörperung des Antihelden der Gegenkultur sind: einsame Rebellen auf der Suche nach Freiheit, die von einer feindseligen Umwelt zerstört werden.

Die erste Welle

Ende der sechziger Jahre setzte in der Filmindustrie ein Prozeß der Reorganisation und Konzentration ein. Die Studios wurden entweder von großen Mischkonzernen übernommen, wie im Fall von Paramount und United Artists, von Großunternehmen der Unterhaltungsindustrie geschluckt, wie Universal und Warner, oder sie expandierten selbst in andere Branchen, wie Twentieth Century Fox, Columbia und MGM. Mit der Reorganisation verschwanden die letzten der alten Studiobosse. An ihre Stelle trat eine neue Art von Managern. Die meisten waren Finanzexperten oder Rechtsanwälte, die wenig vom Filmgeschäft verstanden, dafür jedoch um so mehr von der elementaren Logik eines Unternehmens. Die Devise lautete: Kostensenkung, Einführung neuer Marketingmethoden, Diversifizierung des Produkts und Erschließung neuer Publikumsschichten. Nachdem sich die Konzentration auf Standardprodukte als verfehlte Geschäftsstrategie erwiesen hatte, war man für neue Ideen offen, und es entstand ein relativer Freiraum für Experimente. Im Gegensatz zu den ehemaligen Filmmoguln fühlten sich deren Nachfolger den früher erfolgreich Gewesenen oder langjährigen Freundschaften gegenüber nicht verpflichtet. Eher neigten sie dazu, neue Talente zu fördern. Viele neue Regisseure erhielten so nicht nur Zugang zum Hollywood-Mainstream, sondern es fand auch ein Generationswechsel bei den Drehbuchautoren, Kameraleuten und Produzenten statt.

Nach dem Erfolg von *Bonnie and Clyde* und *The Graduate* witterte Hollywood einen gewinnträchtigen Trend und propagierte eine amerikanische »neue Welle«. Dabei richteten sich die

3. *Die wilden Engel* von Roger Corman, 1966.
4. Faye Dunaway (Bonnie Parker) und Warren Beatty (Clyde Barrow) in *Bonnie und Clyde* von Arthur Penn, 1967.
5. Anne Bancroft (Mrs. Robinson) und Dustin Hoffman (Benjamin Braddock) in *Die Reifeprüfung* von Mike Nichols, 1968.
6. Peter Fonda (Wyatt »Captain America« Earp) und Dennis Hopper (Billy) in *Easy Rider* von Dennis Hopper, 1969.

3. *The Wild Angels* by Roger Corman, 1966.
4. Faye Dunaway (Bonnie Parker) and Warren Beatty (Clyde Barrow) in *Bonnie and Clyde* by Arthur Penn, 1967.
5. Anne Bancroft (Mrs. Robinson) and Dustin Hoffman (Benjamin Braddock) in *The Graduate* by Mike Nichols, 1968.
6. Peter Fonda (Wyatt »Captain America« Earp) and Dennis Hopper (Billy) in *Easy Rider* by Dennis Hopper, 1969.

film business, but were correspondingly well informed about elementary commercial logic. The motto was: cut costs, introduce new marketing methods, diversify the product and gain access to new segments of the public. Concentrating on standard products turned out to be a misguided business strategy, so they were open to new ideas, and this led to a relatively large degree of scope for experiments. Unlike the earlier film moguls, they did not feel any sense of commitment to former successes or long-standing friendships, and were more inclined to promote new talent. This meant that not only did many new directors gain access to mainstream Hollywood, but there was also a change of direction among screenplay writers, cameramen and producers.

After the success of *Bonnie and Clyde* and *The Graduate*, Hollywood scented a profitable trend and propagated an American »new wave«. Here hopes were invested first of all in directors like Arthur Penn and Mike Nichols who had gained a reputation for ambitious material and artistic innovation. This included established film-makers like Sidney Lumet, Stanley Kubrick, Martin Ritt and George Roy Hill as well as promising young talents who had had their first successes, like Sydney Pollack, William Friedkin or Stuart Rosenberg, but also people who had had earlier difficulties with realizing their ideas within the studio system, like for example John Cassavetes, Sam Peckinpah and Robert Altman. As well as this, Hollywood employed directors who had previously become famous in Europe like Roman Polanski, John Schlesinger, Richard Lester and Michelangelo Antonioni. Also, a number of newcomers who had already proved themselves in the theatre, on television or in other functions in the film industry were given a chance, like the comics Woody Allen, Paul Mazursky and Mel Brooks, Alan J. Pakula, who had worked for many years as a producer, and the television director Michael Ritchie, whom Robert Redford engaged for his *Downhill Racer* (1969) project because he had liked one of his television films.

Hollywood discovered the youth market with the surprise success of *Easy Rider* in 1969, and increasingly went over to promoting projects by young directors of the next generation. In the next two years many novice directors like Hal Ashby, James Bridges, Haskell Wexler, Douglas Trumbell, Paul Williams, Charles Eastman, Philip Kaufman, Jerry Schatzberg, Bill Norton, Stan Dragoti and Stuart Hagman were given the opportunity to make films largely independently of studio influence with budgets of one to two million dollars. Of course there were high hopes of the makers of *Easy Rider*. The producers Bob Rafelson, Bert Schneider and Steve Blauner founded BBS, with financial backing from Columbia; Jack Nicholson, Peter Bogdanovich and Henry Jaglom were also involved in this. Columbia engaged Richard Rush, while

Hoffnungen zunächst vor allem auf Regisseure, die sich, wie Arthur Penn und Mike Nichols, den Ruf erworben hatten, eine Vorliebe für anspruchsvolle Stoffe und künstlerische Innovationen zu haben. Dazu zählten bereits etablierte Filmemacher, wie Sidney Lumet, Stanley Kubrick, Martin Ritt und George Roy Hill sowie vielversprechende junge Talente, welche erste Erfolge vorzuweisen hatten, wie Sydney Pollack, William Friedkin oder Stuart Rosenberg, aber auch Leute, die zuvor auf Schwierigkeiten gestoßen waren, ihre Ideen innerhalb des Studiosystems zu verwirklichen, wie beispielsweise John Cassavetes, Sam Peckinpah und Robert Altman. Außerdem holte sich Hollywood Regisseure, die zuvor in Europa Berühmtheit erlangt hatten, wie Roman Polanski, John Schlesinger, Richard Lester und Michelangelo Antonioni. Daneben erhielten eine Reihe von Newcomern eine Chance, die sich aber alle schon im Theater, im Fernsehen oder in anderen Funktionen im Filmgeschäft bewährt hatten, wie die Komiker Woody Allen, Paul Mazursky und Mel Brooks, Alan J. Pakula, der lange Jahre als Produzent gearbeitet hatte, und der Fernsehregisseur Michael Ritchie, den Robert Redford für sein Projekt *Downhill Racer* (1969, *Schußfahrt*) verpflichtete, weil ihm einer seiner Fernsehfilme gefallen hatte.

Mit dem Überraschungserfolg von *Easy Rider* im Jahre 1969 entdeckte Hollywood den Jugendmarkt und ging verstärkt dazu über, die Projekte von jungen Nachwuchsregisseuren zu fördern. In den folgenden beiden Jahren bekamen viele Regieneulinge, wie Hal Ashby, James Bridges, Haskell Wexler, Douglas Trumbell, Paul Williams, Charles Eastman, Philip Kaufman, Jerry Schatzberg, Bill Norton, Stan Dragoti und Stuart Hagman, Gelegenheit, mit Budgets von ein bis zwei Millionen Dollar Filme zu drehen, die vom Studioeinfluß weitgehend unabhängig waren. Besonders große Erwartungen wurden naturgemäß in die Macher von *Easy Rider* gesetzt. Mit finanzieller Rückendeckung von Columbia gründeten die Produzenten Bob Rafelson, Bert Schneider und Steve Blauner die BBS, zu der außerdem Jack Nicholson, Peter Bogdanovich und Henry Jaglom gehörten. Außerdem verpflichtete Columbia Richard Rush, während Universal sich Dennis Hopper, Peter Fonda und Monte Hellman sicherte, der bei AIP zusammen mit Jack Nicholson die beiden ungewöhnlichen Western *Ride in the Whirlwind* (1965, *Ritt im Wirbelwind*) und *The Shooting* (1967, *Das Schießen*) gedreht hatte.

Das Ergebnis war eine Fülle von Filmen, die sich thematisch und gestalterisch über die Konventionen der Hollywood-Standardprodukte hinwegsetzten, welche allerdings nach wie vor das Gros der Filmproduktion ausmachten. Trotzdem belegten 1969 gleich mehrere innovative Filme erste Plätze auf der Liste der kommerziell erfolgreichsten Filme, die von *Butch Cassidy & the Sundance Kid* (*Zwei Banditen*) von George Roy Hill angeführt wurde, dicht gefolgt von *Midnight Cowboy* (1969, *Asphalt-Cowboy*) von John Schlesinger (Platz 3), *Easy Rider* (Platz 4) und *Bob & Carol & Ted & Alice* (Platz 6) von Paul Mazursky sowie in einigem Abstand von *The Sterile Cuckoo* von Alan Pakula (Platz 15). Weitere erfolgreiche Filme des Jahres waren Arthur Penns Hippieballade *Alice's Restaurant*, Sam Peckinpahs *The Wild Bunch* (*Sie kannten kein Gesetz*) und das Depressionsdrama *They Shoot Horses, Don't They?* (*Nur Pferden gibt man den Gnadenschuß*) von Sydney Pollack. Dieselben Filme dominierten die Nominierungslisten für die wichtigsten Filmpreise der USA, und erstmals erhielt mit *Midnight Cowboy* ein Film des neuen Hollywood den Oscar für den besten Film und die beste Regie. Die Erfolgsserie von New Hollywood ging 1970 weiter mit *M.A.S.H*. von Robert Altman, *Little Big Man* von Arthur Penn, *Catch-22* von Mike Nichols, *Woodstock* von Michael Wadleigh und *Five Easy Pieces* (*Ein Mann sucht sich selbst*) von Bob Rafelson. 1971 wurde *French Connection* (*Brennpunkt Brooklyn*) von William Friedkin nicht nur zu einem der größten Kassenerfolge des Jahres, sondern erhielt neben anderen Auszeichnungen auch den Oscar für den besten Film und die beste Regie. Unter den erfolgreichsten Filmen des Jahres waren außerdem Stanley Kubricks *Clockwork Orange* (*Uhrwerk Orange*), *Carnal Knowledge* (*Die Kunst zu lieben*) von Mike Nichols, *The Last Picture Show* (*Die letzte Vorstellung*) von Peter Bogdanovich und *Klute* von Alan J. Pakula.

Zu dieser Zeit war bereits zu erkennen, daß sich die Erwartungen in den Jugendmarkt nicht erfüllten. Einige Filme der jungen Nachwuchsregisseure liefen zwar recht gut, keiner jedoch konnte den Erfolg von *Easy Rider* auch nur annähernd wiederholen. Im übrigen war der Markt durch die Fülle der Jugendfilme, die plötzlich in die Kinos kamen, schnell übersättigt. Daneben gab es Fehler bei der Vermarktung, so daß viele interessante Filme, von denen heute einige Kultstatus haben, wie Monte Hellmans *Two-Lane Blacktop* (1971, *Asphaltrennen*) und Haskell Wexlers *Medium Cool* (1968), sang- und klanglos untergingen. Zudem kümmerten sich die jungen Filmemacher wenig um die vorgefundenen Sehgewohnheiten, so daß ihre Filme für ein Massenpublikum nur schwer zugänglich waren. Das herausragendste Beispiel bildet Dennis Hoppers zweiter Film *The Last Movie*, der nur unter Schwierigkeiten zustande kam und des-

Universal snapped up Dennis Hopper, Peter Fonda and Monte Hellman. Hellman had been involved with Jack Nicholson at AIP in making the two unusual Westerns *Ride in the Whirlwind* (1965) and *The Shooting* (1967).

The result was a large number of films that ignored Hollywood conventions creatively and in terms of subject matter, though standard products did still represent the majority of film productions. Nevertheless, in 1969, several innovative films immediately went to the top of the list of the most successful films commercially. This started with George Roy Hill's *Butch Cassidy and the Sundance Kid*, closely followed by John Schlesinger's *Midnight Cowboy* (3rd place), *Easy Rider* (4th place) and Paul Mazursky's *Bob & Carol & Ted & Alice* (6th place), and at some distance by Alan Pakula's *The Sterile Cuckoo* (15th place). Other successful films in the same year were Arthur Penn's hippie ballad *Alice's Restaurant*, Sam Peckinpah's *The Wild Bunch* and the depression drama *They Shoot Horses Don't They?* by Sydney Pollack. The same films dominated the nominations for the most important American film awards, and a New Hollywood film, *Midnight Cowboy*, won Oscars for best picture and best direction for the first time. The New Hollywood run of success continued the next year (1970) with Robert Altman's *M.A.S.H.*, Arthur Penn's *Little Big Man,* Mike Nichols' *Catch 22*, Michael Wadleigh's *Woodstock* and Bob Rafelson's *Five Easy Pieces*. In 1971, William Friedkin's *French Connection* was not only one of the year's greatest box-office successes, but won Oscars for best picture and best direction, as well as a number of other awards. Among the year's other most successful films were Stanley Kubrick's *Clockwork Orange*, *Carnal Knowledge* by Mike Nichols, *The Last Picture Show* by Peter Bogdanovich and Alan J. Pakula's *Klute*.

It was already clear by this time that the expectations placed in the youth market were not being fulfilled. Some of the films by the younger generation of directors were quite successful, but none of them even came close to repeating the success of *Easy Rider*. Also the market was rapidly saturated by the large number of youth films that came into the cinemas. There were also marketing errors, which meant that many interesting films that later acquired cult status, like Monte Hellman's *Two-Lane Blacktop* (1971) and Haskell Wexler's *Medium Cool* (1968) sank without trace. The young film-makers were not bothered about the audience's usual approach to looking at films either, so that their work was accessible to a mass audience only with difficulty. The best example of this is Dennis Hopper's second film, *The Last Movie* (1971), which was made under considerable difficulties, and has a plot whose thread gets lost amid a number of subjective and experimental elements.

But a much more important factor was that after 1968 the broad alternative culture of the sixties was starting to run out of steam, and the spirit of the »Swinging Sixties« was being replaced by more sober notes. The assassination of Martin Luther King in April 1968 and the days of street battles between demonstrators and police at the Democratic Party Congress in Chicago in August of the same year led to a radicalization of protest against the Vietnam War and to radical groups who were prepared to resort to violence like the Weatherman or Black Panther splitting off, with whom the majority of moderate protesters could not identify. The hippie movement reached its peak in the so-called »Summer of Love« of 1967, when they made a pilgrimage to San Francisco in their hundred thousands. »Dropping out« of society, which usually lasted only for a short time, became a fashionable phenomenon. Haight Ashbury was populated by over 100 000 homeless teenagers. The hippie lifestyle fell even further into disrepute as a result of acts of violence, the increasing numbers of drug addicts and the fact that the scene was being undermined by organized crime. At the same time hippie culture started to be commercialized: records, posters, psychedelic clothing, love beads, joss sticks, jeans, waterbeds, cosmetics and hair accessories in the hippie style were mass produced and sold. The hippie movement divided up into those who were interested in mysticism, who moved to the country to try out alternative lifestyles, and those with political interests who got involved in the New Left movement. The protest generation had grown up and was looking at new, very much more concrete problems like environmental pollution, the re-definition of traditional institutions like marriage and family or protests against a corrupt state.

So the younger generation of directors drew their image from a movement that was in decline. And precisely because most of their films reflect this, they seem like a farewell to the hopes of the sixties and thus to the film-makers themselves. Scarcely any of the newcomers to whom every door in Hollywood had seemed to be open for time were able to establish themselves. Many directed only one or at best two films. For others, years passed before they had another opportunity to make a film: this applied to Stan Dragoti, Bill Norton, Paul Williams, Peter Fonda and Dennis Hopper. The same thing happened to the most promising talents of the

sen Handlungsstrang sich in einer Vielzahl von subjektiven und experimentellen Elementen verliert.

Sehr viel wichtiger aber war, daß nach 1968 die breite Bewegung der Gegenkultur der sechziger Jahre Auflösungserscheinungen zeigte und das Lebensgefühl der »Swinging Sixties« von Ernüchterung überlagert wurde. Die Ermordung von Martin Luther King im April 1968 und die tagelangen Straßenschlachten zwischen Demonstranten und Polizei anläßlich des Parteitags der Demokraten im August gleichen Jahres in Chicago führten zu einer Radikalisierung des Protests gegen den Vietnamkrieg und zur Abspaltung radikaler, gewaltbereiter Gruppen, wie der Weatherman oder der Black Panther, mit denen sich die große Mehrheit der gemäßigten Protestler nicht mehr identifizieren konnte. Die Hippiebewegung erreichte ihren Höhepunkt im sogenannten »Summer of Love« des Jahres 1967, als Hunderttausende nach San Franzisko pilgerten. Der zumeist nur zeitweise »Ausstieg« aus der Gesellschaft entwickelte sich zu einer Modeerscheinung. In Haight Ashbury bevölkerten über 100 000 obdachlose Teenager den Stadtteil. Der Lebensstil der Hippies geriet durch Gewaltakte, die Zunahme von Drogenabhängigen und die Unterwanderung der Szene durch das organisierte Verbrechen immer mehr in Verruf. Gleichzeitig begann die Kommerzialisierung der Hippiekultur: Schallplatten, Poster, Kleidung in psychedelischen Farben, Liebesperlen, Räucherstäbchen, Blue Jeans, Wasserbetten, Kosmetik und Haar-Accessoires im Hippiestil wurden als Massenware produziert und verkauft. Die Hippiebewegung teilte sich in mystisch Interessierte, die auf das Land zogen, um alternative Lebensformen auszuprobieren, und politisch Interessierte, die sich in der New-Left-Bewegung engagierten. Die Protestgeneration war erwachsen geworden und beschäftigte sich mit neuen, viel konkreteren Problemen, wie der Umweltverschmutzung, der Neudefinition traditioneller Institutionen, wie Ehe und Familie, oder dem Protest gegen einen korrumpierten Staat.

Somit bezogen die jungen Nachwuchsregisseure ihr Image aus einer Bewegung, die sich im Niedergang befand. Und gerade weil die meisten ihrer Filme dies reflektieren, wirken sie wie ein Abgesang auf die Hoffnungen der Sechziger und damit auf die Filmemacher selbst. Von den Newcomern, denen zuvor alle Türen Hollywoods offenstanden, konnte sich kaum einer etablieren. Viele führten nur bei einem oder bestenfalls zwei Filmen Regie. Bei anderen dauerte es Jahre, bis sie erneut Gelegenheit erhielten, einen Film zu machen, wie im Fall von Stan Dragoti, Bill Norton, Paul Williams, Peter Fonda und Dennis Hopper. Ebenso erging es den vielversprechendsten jungen Talenten jener Zeit, die sich in der BBS zusammengefunden hatten. Die Gesellschaft löste sich 1972 auf, und Bob Rafelson und Henry Jaglom konnten erst Mitte der siebziger Jahre ihren nächsten Film drehen, wobei der letztere sich von Hollywood entfernte und zu einem bekannten Vertreter des amerikanischen Independent Film wurde. Jack Nicholson führte zwar 1975 und 1990 zwei weitere Male Regie, konzentrierte sich jedoch im übrigen auf seine Karriere als Schauspieler. Lediglich Peter Bogdanovich hatte keine Schwierigkeiten, weiter als Regisseur zu arbeiten, da sich seine Projekte zunehmend an traditionellen Erfolgsformeln ausrichteten.

Das neue Hollywood in den siebziger Jahren

Das Scheitern der Jugendwelle zwang die Manager an der Spitze der Filmkonzerne, ihre Geschäftsstrategie zu überdenken. Die Kassenhits der Jahre 1970 und 1971, *Love Story*, *Airport* und *The Fiddler on the Roof* (*Anatevka*) machten deutlich, daß das Massenpublikum große, konventionelle Unterhaltungsfilme sehen wollte. Daneben hatte der kommerzielle und künstlerische Erfolg einer Reihe von innovativen Filmen aber auch gezeigt, daß ein relativ großes, intellektuelles, von der Gegenkultur beeinflußtes Publikum vorhanden war, das nicht außer acht gelassen werden durfte. Folglich erschien es lohnend, auf ein gemischtes Programm aus aufwendigen, kommerziell orientierten Produktionen und kleineren, anspruchsvolleren Filmen zu setzen. Diese Geschäftsstrategie erwies sich als erfolgreich. Bereits 1972 zeichnete sich ein neuer Boom ab. Die wöchentlichen Zuschauerzahlen in den Kinos stiegen, waren allerdings nach wie vor weit entfernt von denen des goldenen Zeitalters. 1974 gelang es der Filmindustrie endlich, den alten Umsatzrekord aus dem Jahr 1946 zu übertreffen. Bereits 1975 konnten alle acht großen Filmgesellschaften wieder Dividenden an ihre Aktionäre zahlen. Bis Ende der siebziger Jahre erreichten sie ein Wachstum von rund 140%. Eine weitere Entwicklung, die zur Überwindung der Krise beitrug, war die Erholung des Geschäfts mit dem Fernsehen. Die Preise für die Lizenzvergabe von Kinofilmen erreichten 1972 wieder dasselbe Niveau wie vor der Krise und stiegen bis Ende der siebziger Jahre um ein Vielfaches an, so daß für Neuproduktionen ein zusätzliches finanzielles Potential entstand.

day who had come together in BBS. The company wound itself up in 1972, and Bob Rafelson and Henry Jaglom did not make their next films until the mid seventies. Jaglom in fact left Hollywood and became a well-known exponent of the American independent film. Jack Nicholson did direct twice more in 1975 and 1990, but concentrated otherwise on his acting career. Only Peter Bogdanovich had no difficulty in continuing to work as a director, as his projects increasingly turned to traditional success formulae.

New Hollywood in the seventies

The failure of the youth wave forced the managers at the top of the film groups to rethink their commercial strategies. The box-office hits of 1970 and 1971, *Love Story*, *Airport* and *Fiddler on the Roof* showed that the mass audience wanted to see big, conventionally popular films. As well as this, the commercial and artistic success of a number of innovative films had also made it clear that there was a relatively large, intellectual audience influenced by the alternative culture that could not be ignored. Consequently it seemed worthwhile to go for a mixed programme made up of elaborate, commercially oriented productions and smaller, more demanding films. This commercial strategy proved successful. A new boom started as early as 1972. Weekly audience figures in the cinemas rose, but were still a long way from those achieved in the golden age. In 1974 the film industry finally managed to beat the old turnover record dating from 1946. All the eight major film companies were able to pay dividends to their shareholders again by 1975. By the late seventies they had reached a growth rate of about 140%. Another development that helped them to weather the crisis was the recovery of television deals. Prices for cinema film licences reached the same level they had been at before the crisis in 1972, and increased many times until the late seventies, creating an additional financial potential for new productions.

This development created favourable conditions for those film-makers who were interested in realizing their personal projects and experimenting with new ideas. They were now able to establish themselves in the mainstream. All the directors who had been successful in the first wave of New Hollywood remained in business throughout all the ups and downs of the seventies. Robert Altman, Sidney Lumet, John Cassavetes, Alan J. Pakula, Sydney Pollack, Sam Peckinpah, Woody Allen, Paul Mazursky and George Roy Hill all experienced career peaks in the seventies and became the most important New Hollywood figures. Others like Hal Ashby, Michael Ritchie, James Bridges, Robert Benton, Philip Kaufman and Jerry Schatzberg acquired enough respect in the first New Hollywood wave to be able to work regularly, and with the exception of Schatzberg, who concentrated on small films with artistic ambitions, they all made a big breakthrough later. As well as this there were a number of other directors who contributed remarkable films to Hollywood's artistic renaissance like the choreographer and Broadway director Bob Fosse, Martin Ritt, Roman Polanski, the Czech director Milos Forman, the Briton John Boorman and also Alan Rudolph, who made his directorial début in 1977 after years as an assistant director with Robert Altman. Together they are the »auteur film-makers« of mainstream American cinema to a greater or lesser extent, who found conditions in the sixties that made it possible for them to develop their own style and their own subject-matter. A large number of films owe their existence to their creativity. They are not only among the most interesting that Hollywood ever produced, all classics to a large extent, but were also commercially very successful.

The successes of this older generation of film-makers prepared the way for the so-called whiz kids, who largely came from the universities, like Francis Ford Coppola, Martin Scorsese, George Lucas, Brian De Palma, Paul Schrader, Terrence Malick and John Milius. Unlike the directors of the fifties, who learned their trade in the theatre or in television, they discovered how to make film from film itself, and had a grip on the whole bandwidth of technique. They also studied film history, the creative possibilities and stylistic directions taken by film, and had a solid theoretical background that was influenced by auteur theory and the Nouvelle Vague in the sixties, which in its turn suggested going back to the qualities of the classical American directors. Although they, like the older film-makers, were mainly influenced by the ideas of the alternative culture, and had an approach that was critical of society and the media, they were above all film freaks, whose main interest lay in exploring the possibilities of the medium to the full and revolutionizing them. This links them with other film-makers of their generation who did not come from the universities, but started in television, or who first worked as film scholars

Diese Entwicklung schuf günstige Bedingungen für diejenigen Filmemacher, die daran interessiert waren, ihre persönlichen Projekte zu verwirklichen und mit neuen Ideen zu experimentieren. Sie konnten sich nun innerhalb des Mainstreams etablieren. Alle, die in der ersten Welle von New Hollywood Erfolge verzeichnen konnten, blieben mit allen Höhen und Tiefen die siebziger Jahre hindurch im Geschäft. Robert Altman, Sidney Lumet, John Cassavetes, Alan J. Pakula, Sydney Pollack, Sam Peckinpah, Woody Allen, Paul Mazursky, Mel Brooks und George Roy Hill erlebten in den siebziger Jahren einen Höhepunkt ihrer Karriere und wurden zu den wichtigsten Trägern des neuen Hollywood. Andere, wie Hal Ashby, Michael Ritchie, James Bridges, Robert Benton, Philip Kaufman und Jerry Schatzberg, erwarben sich in der ersten Welle von New Hollywood genügend Ansehen, um regelmäßig arbeiten zu können, und mit Ausnahme von Schatzberg, der sich auf kleinere, künstlerisch anspruchsvolle Filme konzentrierte, schafften alle später den großen Durchbruch. Daneben gab es eine Reihe anderer Regisseure, die mit bemerkenswerten Filmen zur künstlerischen Erneuerung Hollywoods beitrugen, wie der Choreograph und Broadway-Regisseur Bob Fosse, Martin Ritt, Roman Polanski, der tschechische Regisseur Milos Forman, der Brite John Boorman sowie Alan Rudolph, der nach Jahren als Regieassistent bei Robert Altman 1977 sein Regiedebüt gab. Sie alle bilden in mehr oder weniger starkem Maße die »Autorenfilmer« des amerikanischen Mainstream-Kinos, welche in den siebziger Jahren Bedingungen vorfanden, die es ihnen ermöglichten, ihren eigenen Stil und ihre eigene Thematik zu entwickeln. Ihrer Kreativität entsprang eine große Zahl von Filmen, welche nicht nur zu den interessantesten gehören, die Hollywood je hervorgebracht hat, und zum großen Teil längst Klassiker sind, sondern häufig auch kommerziell außerordentlich erfolgreich waren.

Die Erfolge dieser älteren Generation von Filmemachern bereiteten das Feld für die sogenannten Whiz-Kids, die überwiegend von den Hochschulen kamen, wie Francis Ford Coppola, Martin Scorsese, George Lucas, Brian De Palma, Paul Schrader, Terrence Malick und John Milius. Im Gegensatz zu den Regisseuren der fünfziger Jahre, die sich das Handwerk am Theater oder beim Fernsehen aneigneten, lernten sie Filmemachen am Film selbst und beherrschten die gesamte Bandbreite der Technik. Daneben studierten sie Filmgeschichte, die gestalterischen Möglichkeiten und Stilrichtungen des Films und hatten einen soliden theoretischen Hintergrund, der in den sechziger Jahren unter dem Einfluß der Autorentheorie und der Nouvelle Vague stand, die wiederum auf die Qualitäten der klassischen amerikanischen Regisseure verwies. Obwohl sie wie die älteren Filmemacher zum größten Teil von den Ideen der Gegenkultur beeinflußt waren und einen gesellschafts- und medienkritischen Ansatz hatten, waren sie vor allem Filmfreaks, deren vorrangiges Interesse darin bestand, die Möglichkeiten des Mediums auszuloten und zu revolutionieren. Das verbindet sie mit anderen Filmemachern ihrer Generation, die zwar nicht den Hochschulen entstammen, sondern beim Fernsehen begannen oder zunächst als Filmwissenschaftler und Filmkritiker arbeiteten, wie Peter Bogdanovich und William Friedkin, oder Werbe- und Dokumentarfilme drehten, wie Michael Cimino, aber ebenso von den technischen Möglichkeiten des Mediums fasziniert waren.

Ihr Aufstieg ging nicht ohne Umwege vor sich. In den sechziger Jahren galt ein Abschluß an der Hochschule wenig. Um Arbeit in der Filmindustrie zu bekommen, brauchte man eine Mitgliedskarte der Gewerkschaft und Beziehungen, denn Hollywood bestand nach wie vor aus Cliquen. Außerdem ging die Zahl der Eigenproduktionen der Studios stark zurück, und sie boten nicht mehr den Trainingsgrund für Filmemacher wie früher. Wie schon die Gruppe, aus der *Easy Rider* hervorging, fanden auch mehrere dieser Regisseure in ihren Anfängen ein Experimentierfeld bei Roger Corman, der sich durch das Talent auszeichnete, junge Filmemacher zu entdecken und zu fördern, wobei seine Motive nicht ganz uneigennützig waren, denn die jungen Filmemacher brannten derart darauf, Regie zu führen, daß sie fast umsonst arbeiteten. Corman verhalf Francis Ford Coppola mit *Dementia 13* (1963), Peter Bogdanovich mit *Targets* (1968, *Bewegliche Ziele*), Martin Scorsese mit *Boxcar Bertha* (1972, *Boxcar Bertha – Die Faust des Rebellen*) und John Milius mit *Dillinger* (1973) zu ersten Regieaufträgen. Zudem übernahm er den Vertrieb von Brian De Palmas *Sisters* (1973, *Die Schwestern des Bösen*).

Daneben versuchten die Absolventen der Hochschulen, im Filmgeschäft Fuß zu fassen, indem sie zunächst in anderen Funktionen arbeiteten. Einige etablierten sich anfangs als Drehbuchautoren, darunter Francis Ford Coppola, Paul Schrader, John Milius, Michael Cimino und Terrence Malick. Die daraus entstandenen Verbindungen nutzten sie, um ihre ersten Filme drehen zu können. Martin Scorsese und Brian De Palma erwarben sich zuerst mit kleinen, unabhängig finanzierten Filmen einen gewissen Bekanntheitsgrad, ehe sie ihre ersten Regieangebote bekamen. George Lucas war noch Student an der Hochschule, als er Coppola traf.

7. Tim O'Kelly (Bobby Thompson) in *Bewegliche Ziele* von Peter Bogdanovich, 1968.

7. Tim O'Kelly (Bobby Thompson) in *Targets* by Peter Bogdanovich, 1968.

and critics like Peter Bogdanovich and William Friedkin, or who made commercials and documentaries like Michael Cimino, but were equally fascinated by the technical possibilities of the medium.

Their rise was not without its detours. In the sixties, a film school qualification did not mean very much. To get work in the film industry you needed an Equity card and connections, as Hollywood was entirely run by cliques, as ever. Also the number of in-house productions declined considerably, and they no longer provided a training ground for film-makers as they used to. Like the group from which *Easy Rider* emerged, several of these directors also found an experimental field in their early days with Roger Corman, who had a talent for discovering and promoting young film-makers, though his motives were not entirely selfless, as the young directors were so keen to make films that they worked for almost nothing. Corman helped Francis Ford Coppola, with *Dementia 13* (1963), Peter Bogdanovich, with *Targets* (1967), Martin Scorsese, with *Boxcar Bertha* (1972) and John Milius, with *Dillinger* (1973), to get their first directorial commissions, and also undertook to distribute Brian De Palma's *Sisters* (1973).

The university graduates also tried to get a foothold in the film business by working in other capacities at first. Some established themselves as screenplay writers, including Francis Ford Coppola, Paul Schrader, John Milius, Michael Cimino and Terrence Malick, and used the connections that emerged to make their first films. Martin Scorsese and Brian De Palma first established themselves with small, independently produced films before their first directing commissions. George Lucas was still a university student when he met Coppola Coppola later funded his first film projects. The only one who made it without a great deal of trouble was Steven Spielberg. He started to make shorts that caused a stir and got him a seven-year contract as a television director with MCA/Universal. His first big success was the television film *Duel* (1971), and he was able to go on to make his first cinema film *The Sugarland Express* in 1974. But for most of these film-makers the big breakthrough did not come until the mid to late seventies.

The film that drew attention to the »whiz kid« generation was Coppola's *The Godfather* (1972). This became the first New Hollywood blockbuster and is still one of the 100 greatest box-office hits of the American cinema. In contrast with the new film-makers' predominant preference for small, personal films, this is a large epic work lasting for almost three hours, aiming deliberately at commercial success. This gave rise to a trend that was to become a typical feature of seventies Hollywood: the attempt to combine artistic ambition and entertainment in large-scale productions, and reach a mass audience in this way. This concept regularly worked out in subsequent years. Friedkin had already shown in *The French Connection* (1971) that he was able to turn a plot in which

Später förderte Coppola dessen ersten Filmprojekte. Der einzige, der sich relativ mühelos durchsetzte, war Steven Spielberg. Er begann zunächst, Kurzfilme zu drehen, die Aufsehen erregten und ihm 1968 einen Siebenjahresvertrag als Fernsehregisseur bei MCA/Universal einbrachten. Seinen ersten großen Erfolg konnte er mit dem Fernsehfilm *Duel* (1971) verbuchen, woraufhin er 1974 mit *The Sugarland Express* seinen ersten Kinofilm drehen konnte. Für die meisten dieser Filmemacher kam der große Durchbruch jedoch erst Mitte bis Ende der siebziger Jahre.

Der Film, der die Aufmerksamkeit auf die »Wunderkindergeneration« lenkte, war Coppolas *The Godfather* (1972, *Der Pate*), welcher zum ersten Blockbuster des neuen Hollywood wurde und nach wie vor zu den 100 größten Kassenhits des amerikanischen Kinos zählt. Im Gegensatz zu der damals unter den neuen Filmemachern vorherrschenden Vorliebe für kleine, persönliche Filme handelte es sich hier um ein großes episches Werk von fast drei Stunden Länge, das bewußt auf kommerziellen Erfolg angelegt war. Damit begann ein Trend, der zu einer typischen Erscheinung des Hollywood-Films der siebziger Jahre wurde: der Versuch, in Großproduktionen künstlerischen Anspruch und Unterhaltung zu verbinden und damit ein Massenpublikum zu erreichen. In den folgenden Jahren sollte sich dieses Konzept immer wieder bewähren. Friedkin, der bereits in *The French Connection* (1971) gezeigt hatte, daß er eine Handlung, in der über lange Passagen kaum etwas passiert, in einen Spannungsreißer verwandeln kann, lieferte 1973 mit *The Exorcist* (*Der Exorzist*) einen weiteren Blockbuster des neuen Hollywood. 1974 belegte *The Godfather: Part II* (*Der Pate: Teil II*) einen der vorderen Plätze auf der Liste der kommerziell erfolgreichsten Filme. Der Trend setzte sich 1975 mit *Jaws* (*Der weiße Hai*) von Steven Spielberg fort, der in den folgenden Jahren einen Kassenhit nach dem anderen produzierte, während George Lucas mit *Star Wars* (1977, *Krieg der Sterne*) den erfolgreichsten Film aller Zeiten herausbrachte, dessen Einnahmen erst 1997 von *Titanic* übertroffen wurden.

Die enormen Gewinne aus dieser relativ geringen Zahl von Blockbustern führten dazu, daß die Wunderkindergeneration als die Retter von Hollywood gefeiert wurden. Allerdings kam es auch vor, daß die Rechnung nicht aufging: Coppolas *Apocalypse Now* (1979) schaffte es gerade eben, die Kosten einzuspielen, obwohl er bei Kritikern und Publikum ein großer Erfolg war. Spielbergs Kriegspersiflage *1941* (1979) lief zwar recht gut, wuchs sich aber dennoch zu einem kommerziellen Desaster aus, da das Einspielergebnis weit unter den Kosten lag. Scorseses Versuch, mit dem Musical *New York, New York* (1977) in die Sphäre der Blockbuster einzudringen, scheiterte ebenso an den Kinokassen wie Coppolas Vorstoß in das Genre mit *One From The Heart* (1982, *Einer mit Herz*). Als die größte kommerzielle Katastrophe des neuen Hollywood gilt jedoch Michael Ciminos *Heaven's Gate* (1980, *Heaven's Gate – Das Tor zum Himmel*), der United Artists in eine tiefe Krise stürzte und zum Aufkauf der Gesellschaft durch MGM führte.

Die meisten dieser jüngeren Generation der »movie brats«, wie sie auch genannt wurden, beteiligten sich zwar an der Jagd nach dem Blockbuster, empfanden aber gleichzeitig die damit verbundenen künstlerischen Konzessionen als unbefriedigend und unternahmen immer wieder Versuche, in kleineren, weniger kommerziell orientierten Filmen ihre persönlichen Themen und künstlerischen Vorstellungen zu verwirklichen. Andere, wie Paul Schrader und Alan Rudolph, ließen sich dagegen nie auf konventionelle, am Massengeschmack orientierte Stoffe ein und beschränkten sich dafür auf kleinere und mittlere Budgets, wobei Rudolph, der zwar dem Alter nach zur Generation der »movie brats« gehört, von seiner Konzeption her aber eher Robert Altman nahesteht und wie dieser im Laufe seiner Karriere eine schwierige Gratwanderung zwischen künstlerischem Anspruch und kommerziellem Erfolg vollzogen hat.

Die Vielzahl der kleineren persönlichen Filme, die nur möglich waren, weil es auch ein Publikum dafür gab, sind ein entscheidendes Merkmal des amerikanischen Kinos der siebziger Jahre. Dies führte zu einer nie dagewesenen Bandbreite an Themen und stilistischer Vielfalt, die wichtige Impulse für eine Erneuerung des Mainstream-Kinos gaben. Gleichzeitig bewirkten sie die Diversifizierung des Produkts, nach welchem die Filmindustrie verlangte.

Im Spannungsfeld zwischen Kunst und Kommerz

So unterschiedlich der Hintergrund und die thematischen Vorlieben dieser Filmemacher sein mögen, verbindet sie doch eines: die Auffassung, daß der Film ein Medium des persönlichen künstlerischen Ausdrucks ist. Darin kommt ein neues Selbstverständnis zum Ausdruck, das entscheidend von dem des klassischen Hollywood abweicht. Traditionell kam dem Regisseur innerhalb des Studiosystems die Funktion des technischen Leiters zu. Er wurde als Handwer-

8. Barbara Hershey (»Boxcar« Bertha Thompson) und David Carradine (»Big« Bill Shelly) in *Die Faust des Rebellen* von Martin Scorsese, 1972.

8. Barbara Hershey (»Boxcar« Bertha Thompson) and David Carradine (»Big« Bill Shelly) in *Boxcar Bertha* by Martin Scorsese, 1972.

hardly anything happens for long periods into nail-biting experience, and in 1973 he delivered another New Hollywood blockbuster in the form of *The Exorcist*. In 1974 *The Godfather: Part II* occupied one of the highest places in the list of the most successful commercial films. The trend continued in 1975 with Steven Spielberg's *Jaws*. He came up with one box-office hit after another in subsequent years, and George Lucas produced the most successful film of all time with *Star Wars* in 1977. Its takings were not exceeded until *Titanic* in 1997.

The enormous profits made by this relatively small number of blockbusters meant that the whiz-kid generation were celebrated as the saviours of Hollywood. Though again, things did not always work out: Coppola's *Apocalypse Now* (1979) only just managed to break even, even though it was a major success critically and at the box office. Spielberg's war satire *1941* (1979) went quite well but turned out to be a commercial disaster as the box-office takings came in well under the costs. Scorsese's attempt with the musical *New York, New York* (1977) to break into the sphere of the blockbusters was just as much a failure at the box office as Coppola's move into the genre with *One From The Heart* (1982). But the greatest New Hollywood disaster was Michael Cimino's *Heaven's Gate* (1980), which plunged United Artists into a major crisis and led to the purchase of the company by MGM.

Most of this younger generation of »movie brats«, as they were also known, were involved in the quest for the blockbuster, but at the same time found the associated artistic concessions unsatisfactory and constantly made attempts to address their own personal themes and realize their artistic ideas in smaller, less commercially oriented films. Others, like Paul Schrader and Alan Rudolph, never allowed themselves to be drawn into working on conventional material aimed at mass tastes, restricting themselves instead to small and medium-sized budgets. Rudolph, who belonged to the »movie brat« generation by virtue of his age but was closer to Robert Altman in terms of ideas, walked a fine line in the course of his career between artistic ambition and commercial success.

The large number of small personal films that could only be made because there was an audience for them are a key feature of seventies American cinema. This led to an unprecedentedly wide range of themes and stylistic diversity that gave an important boost to the renaissance of mainstream cinema. At the same time they led to diversification of the product that the film industry was asking for.

ker betrachtet, der die vorgegebenen Szenen nach bewährtem Muster abfilmte und in der Regel kaum Kontrolle über den Schnitt und damit das endgültige Aussehen des Films hatte, die dem Produzenten und den Studiobossen oblag.

Die Aufwertung des Regisseurs begann in den fünfziger Jahren in Europa mit den Filmen der italienischen Neorealisten sowie Filmen von Ingmar Bergman und Akiro Kurosawa, dessen *Rashomon* auf dem Filmfestival von Venedig im Jahre 1951 für Furore sorgte. 1954 veröffentlichte François Truffaut einen Essay über die »politique des auteurs«, in welchem er sich dafür aussprach, daß der Film als eine eigenständige Kunstgattung angesehen werden müsse, in der dem Regisseur die Rolle des kreativen Subjekts zukäme. In der Folge entstand die französische Nouvelle Vague, die mit jedem ihrer Filme das Kino neu zu erfinden schien. Anfang der sechziger Jahre führte Andrew Sarris die theoretischen Ansätze der Nouvelle Vague als »auteur theory« in den USA ein. Ihr Einfluß machte das Filmemachen dort erstmals zum Objekt seriöser Kritik und prägte die Vorstellungen einer ganzen Generation junger Nachwuchsregisseure.

Die Studios reagierten darauf, indem sie Produktionen von Filmemachern, wie Arthur Penn und Mike Nichols, unterstützten, die an kleineren und anspruchsvolleren Filmen interessiert waren, weil diese ein ständiges, wenn auch beschränktes Publikum fanden und Ansehen bei den Kritikern genossen. Als sich die ersten großen Erfolge dieser und anderer Regisseure des neuen Hollywood einstellten, wurde die Autorentheorie plötzlich zum Mainstream. Das Credo lautete, daß ein Film von der Vision eines Individuums geprägt sein müsse, was jedoch nicht bedeutete, daß die Regisseure nun freie Hand hatten. Die Vertreter der Studios mischten sich nach wie vor in die künstlerische Gestaltung ein. Insbesondere sahen diejenigen Filmemacher, denen es vor allem auf die Inhalte ankam, ihre künstlerische Freiheit durch das Hollywood-System, das für sie der Inbegriff des Establishments war, ernsthaft gefährdet und waren bestrebt, sich so weit wie möglich aus seinem Dunstkreis zu entfernen. Um ihre Position zu verbessern, versuchten einige Regisseure, sich finanziell unabhängig zu machen. Coppola gründete 1969 seine eigene Produktionsgesellschaft Zoetrope mit Sitz in San Franzisko, die sich allerdings hauptsächlich mit Geldern von Warner finanzierte. Schon nach einem Jahr hörte die Gesellschaft kurzzeitig auf zu funktionieren, weil Warner mit keinem der vorgelegten Projekte einverstanden war und die Rückzahlung der Vorschüsse verlangte. Nicht zuletzt aus diesem Grunde akzeptierte Coppola das Angebot, die Regie von *The Godfather* zu übernehmen. Mit den Gewinnen reaktivierte er die Gesellschaft und finanzierte unter anderem George Lucas' *American Graffiti* (1973). Sein Hang zu Mammutprojekten ließ ihn jedoch wiederholt alles auf eine Karte setzen, so daß es ihm nie gelang, sich aus der Abhängigkeit der Großen zu befreien. Coppola, Bogdanovich und Friedkin bildeten 1972 außerdem kurzzeitig in einem Gemeinschaftsunternehmen mit der Paramount die Director's Company mit dem Ziel, ihre kreative Autonomie durch die Aufteilung der Gewinne aus den Filmen aller drei zu sichern. Die Gesellschaft funktionierte jedoch nie richtig, weil die drei Regisseure mit anderweitigen Projekten ausgelastet waren. Robert Altman gründete 1970 seine Produktionsgesellschaft Lion's Gate, mit der er einige seiner eigenwilligsten Arbeiten, wie *Brewster McCloud* (1970, *Nur fliegen ist schöner*), *Three Women* (1977, *Drei Frauen*) und *Quintet* (1979, *Quintett*), produzierte. Für Paul Mazursky stellten seine Gewinne aus *Bob & Carol & Ted & Alice* (1969) eine Möglichkeit dar, sich eine relative finanzielle Unabhängigkeit zu bewahren und selbst über seine Projekte zu entscheiden. John Cassavetes, dem seine Unabhängigkeit aus Prinzip wichtig war, finanzierte seine Filme teilweise aus seinen Einnahmen als Schauspieler und gründete dafür die Faces Distributing Corporation, mit der er *A Woman under the Influence* (1974, *Eine Frau unter Einfluß*), *The Killing of a Chinese Bookie* (1976, *Die Ermordung eines chinesischen Buchmachers*) und *Opening Night* (1977, *Die erste Vorstellung*) ohne Studiobeteiligung produzierte.

In der Directors Guild of America (DGA), die 80 % der Filmemacher repräsentierte, bildete sich ab 1966 eine Front heraus, die für das Recht des Regisseurs auf den Director's Cut, das heißt die volle künstlerische Kontrolle über das Endprodukt, kämpfte. Ein Kuriosum, das aus diesem Streit hervorging, ist das Recht des Regisseurs, seinen Namen zurückzuziehen und durch das Pseudonym Alan Smithee ersetzen zu lassen, wenn er vom Schnitt des Films ausgeschlossen wird und sich vom Endresultat distanzieren will. Die ersten, die davon Gebrauch machten, waren 1967 Don Siegel und Robert Totten für den Film *Death of a Gunfighter* (*Frank Patch – deine Stunden sind gezählt*). Nach jahrelangen Verhandlungen kam es im Dezember 1973 schließlich zum Abkommen über das kreative Mitspracherecht zwischen der DGA und dem Verband der Produzenten, der Association of Motion Picture and Television Producers (AMPTP), das dem Regisseur eine grundsätzliche Mitbestimmung bei allen inhaltlichen und gestalterischen Fragen einräumt und die Produzenten verpflichtet, im voraus festzulegen, wer

In the field of tension between art and commerce

However diverse the background and thematic preferences of these film-makers may be, they have one thing in common: they see film as a medium for personal artistic expression. This expresses a new self-perception that deviates considerably from classical Hollywood. Traditionally the director was the technical manager within the studio system. He was seen as a craftsman who filmed the prescribed scenes according to a tried-and-tested pattern and usually had next to no control over editing and thus the way the film finally looked, which was the territory of the producers and studio bosses.

The status of the director started to be enhanced in Europe in the fifties with films by the Italian neo-Realists, Ingmar Bergman and Akiro Kurosawa, whose *Rashomon* caused a furore at the 1951 Venice Film Festival. In 1954, François Truffaut published an essay on the »politique des auteurs«, in which he stated that film must be seen as an artistic genre in its own right, with the director in the role of the creative subject. This led to the French Nouvelle Vague, who seemed to reinvent the cinema with each of their films. In the early sixties, Andrew Sarris introduced the theoretical ideas of the Nouvelle Vague to the USA as »auteur theory«. This influence made film-making there the object of serious criticism for the first time, and the ideas of a whole new generation of young directors were shaped by it.

The studios reacted to this by supporting the work of directors like Arthur Penn and Mike Nichols, who were interested in smaller, more ambitious films because these reached a constant, if limited audience and met with critical approval. When these and other New Hollywood directors registered their first major successes, the auteur theory suddenly became mainstream. The belief was that a film had to be shaped by the vision of an individual, but this did not mean that directors now had a free hand. The studio people continued to interfere in artistic matters. Film-makers who were particularly concerned about content felt that their artistic freedom was seriously under threat from the Hollywood system, which they saw as the epitome of the establishment, and tried to distance themselves from its influence as much as possible. To improve their position, some directors tried to make themselves financially independent. Coppola founded his own production company Zoetrope, based in San Fransisco, in 1969, though it was largely financed by Warner money. The company ceased to function after just one year, because Warner did not agree with any of the proposed projects and insisted that their advances be returned. Not least for this reason, Coppola accepted the offer to take over direction of *The Godfather*. He reactivated the company with the profits, and financed films including George Lucas's *American Graffiti* (1973). But his taste for mammoth projects led him to put all his money repeatedly on one horse, so that he never successfully escaped being dependent on the major studios. As well as this, Coppola, Bogdanovich and Friedkin formed the Directors' Company, as a joint venture with Paramount, for a short time in 1972. Its aim was to secure creative autonomy for the three of them by sharing the profits from their films. But the company never worked properly because the three directors were fully occupied with other projects. Robert Altman founded his Lion's Gate production company in 1970, using it to produce some of his most quirky works like *Brewster McCloud* (1970), *Three Women* (1977) and *Quintet* (1979). Paul Mazursky's profits from *Bob & Carol & Ted & Alice* (1969) gave him a fair amount of financial independence and freedom to make decisions about his own projects. John Cassavetes, for whom independence was important on principle, financed his films partly from his earnings as an actor, founding the Faces Distributing Corporation, with which he produced *A Woman Under the Influence* (1974), *The Killing of a Chinese Bookie* (1976) and *Opening Night* (1977) without studio participation.

A movement formed within the Directors Guild of America (DGA), which represented 80% of film-makers, from 1966. This fought for the director's right to make the director's cut, i. e. full artistic control over the end product. One curiosity that emerged from this dispute is the director's right to withdraw his name and have it replaced by the pseudonym Alan Smithee if he is excluded from the cutting process and wants to distance himself from the end product. The first to make use of this were Don Siegel and Robert Totten for the film *Death of a Gunfighter* in 1967. After years of negotiation an agreement about the right to a share in creative decisions was finally reached in December 1973 between DGA and the Association of Motion Picture and Television Producers (AMPTP). This fundamentally entitled the director to participation in all creative questions and those relating to content and obliged the producer to determine in advance who would decide about the end product. From then on contractual clauses about artistic copyright made an anachronism of the commissioned director and the »director's cut« became

über das Endprodukt entscheidet. Von da an machten Klauseln über künstlerisches Urheberrecht in Verträgen aus dem Auftragsregisseur einen Anachronismus, und der »Director's Cut« wurde die Regel. Lob und Tadel für einen Film richteten sich zunehmend auf den Regisseur. Anders als früher, als ein Film sich vor allem durch die Namen der Schauspieler verkaufen ließ, war es nun der gute Name des Regisseurs, der eine Finanzierung erwirkte, der die Stars für ein Projekt gewann und einen Film vermarkten. konnte. Auf diese Art erfand Hollywood seine eigene Version der Autorentheorie in Form eines neuen Mythos, den des Regisseurs als Superstar.

Obwohl jedoch verkündet wurde, daß das Medium nun definitiv den Regisseuren gehöre, schlug sich dies keinesfalls auf deren Einkommen und künstlerische Unabhängigkeit nieder, denn sie sahen sich nach wie vor den Gesetzen des Marktes unterworfen. Die Kosten für die Produktion von Filmen stiegen in den siebziger Jahren derart an, daß die Filmemacher zwangsläufig darauf angewiesen waren, mit einer der großen Gesellschaften zusammenzuarbeiten, um eine Finanzierung für ihre Filme zu erhalten. Außerdem änderten sich die Marketingstrategien und erhielten einen zunehmenden Stellenwert für den Erfolg eines Films. In den Jahren 1972 bis 1974 verdoppelten sich die Ausgaben für Fernsehwerbung von rund 32 Mill. auf 60 Mill. Dollar. Werbeabteilungen oder Publicity-Agenturen wurden beauftragt, bereits während der Dreharbeiten alles zu tun, um den Film ins Gespräch zu bringen und ihm ein Image zu verleihen. Interviews mit den Stars und dem Regisseur, Fernsehauftritte in Talk-Shows, Artikel in Zeitungen und Zeitschriften dienten dazu, die Diskussion über einen Film anzufachen, ganz gleich, ob im positiven oder im negativen Sinne, wie die Kontroversen um *The Last Tango in Paris* (1972, *Der letzte Tango von Paris*) von Bernardo Bertolucci zeigten, die den Film zu einem Kassenhit machten. Es wurden Marktforschungsabteilungen eingerichtet, die das Publikumsverhalten untersuchten und in Voraufführungen die Reaktion der Zuschauer testeten. Man nahm die Tradition der dreißiger Jahre wieder auf, die Premieren zu sozialen Ereignissen zu stilisieren, und schließlich wurde der Film in großem Stil mit 500 bis 1000 Kopien und begleitet von einer massiven Anzeigenkampagne auf den Markt gebracht. Bezeichnend ist, daß zwar die Zahl der Kinos abnahm, es aber immer mehr Erstaufführungskinos gab, die sich bis in die Vorstädte hinein ausbreiteten.

Daneben gewann die Vermarktung von Filmen über Nebenprodukte, wie Spielzeug, Schallplatten, Bücher, Videospiele, Poster, T-Shirts usw., zunehmende Bedeutung. Diese Vermarktungsstrategien wurden in der zweiten Hälfte der siebziger Jahre zu einer gängigen Praxis bei großen, auf ein Massenpublikum abzielenden Produktionen. Der erste Film, der mehr Gewinne aus Nebenprodukten schöpfte als aus verkauften Kinokarten, war schließlich 1977 *Star Wars*. Diese Entwicklung bewirkte, daß die Filmemacher, selbst wenn sie dazu in der Lage waren, ihren Film mit unabhängigen Mitteln zu finanzieren, auf das Vertriebsnetz der Studios angewiesen waren, denn nur diese konnten eine angemessene Werbekampagne und eine landesweite und internationale Verbreitung in Erstaufführungskinos sichern, die allein die Chance boten, die Kosten zu amortisieren. Dies bedeutete, daß die Regisseure sich zwangsläufig mit den großen Filmgesellschaften arrangieren mußten. Und diese ließen Experimente nur in dem Maße zu, wie sie ihre Gewinnaussichten nicht beeinträchtigt sahen.

Die geltende Regel lautete: Die künstlerische Freiheit eines Regisseur mißt sich am Erfolg seines letzten Films. Die Erfahrung zeigte, daß die Einmischung der Finanziers um so größer war, je mehr Kapital auf dem Spiel stand, und gerade bei teuren Filmen Zugeständnisse an den Massengeschmack gemacht werden mußten, während diejenigen Regisseure, die aufwendige Produktionen vermieden und auf den Einsatz kostspieliger Stars verzichteten, mit kleineren Arbeiten einen relativen Erfolg erzielten und, wie Robert Altman, Paul Mazursky, Woody Allen oder John Cassavetes, am unabhängigsten arbeiten konnten. So basieren die kommerziell erfolgreichsten Produkte des neuen Hollywood oftmals auf einer modernisierten Fassung klassischer Erfolgsformeln, während die kleineren Filme origineller, innovativer und letztlich interessanter sind. Doch in jedem Fall mußten die Filmemacher den schwierigen Balanceakt zwischen kommerziellem Erfolg und künstlerischer Originalität vollziehen, der ein Hauptmerkmal des neuen Hollywoods der siebziger Jahre ist.

the norm. Praise and blame for a film were increasingly attached to the director. And so unlike earlier days, when a film was sold largely on the names of the actors, it was now the good name of the director that attracted finance, won stars over to a project and could sell a film. In this way Hollywood invented its own version of the auteur theory in the form of a new myth: the director as superstar.

But although it had been proclaimed that the medium now definitely belonged to the director, this in fact had no effect at all on their income or their artistic independence, as they were subject to market forces. Film production costs rose so much in the seventies that film-makers had to work with one of the big companies to be able to finance their films. As well as this, marketing strategies changed and were increasingly important for the success of a film. From 1972 to 1974 spending on television advertising doubled from about 32 million to 60 million dollars. Advertising departments or publicity agencies were commissioned to do everything they could to get a film talked about and to create an image for it while it was still being shot. Interviews with the stars and the director, television appearances on talk-shows, articles in newspapers and magazines were introduced to stimulate discussion about a film. It did not matter whether this was positive or negative, as shown by the controversy surrounding Bernardo Bertolucci's *Last Tango in Paris* (1972), which made the film a box-office hit. Market research departments were set up to examine audience behaviour and test spectator response in preliminary screenings. The thirties tradition of making premières into social events was revived, and finally the film was launched in style, with 500 to 1000 copies available and accompanied by a massive advertising campaign. It is significant that the number of cinemas went down, but there were more and more première cinemas, extending right out into the suburbs.

As well as this, merchandise like toys, records, books, video games, posters, T-shirts etc. became increasingly important in film marketing. These marketing strategies became common practice in the second half of the seventies for large productions aimed at a mass audience. The first film to make more profit from merchandise than sold cinema tickets was *Star Wars* in 1977. This development meant that the film-makers, even if they were in a position to finance their own films independently, had to depend on the studios' distribution networks, as only they could guarantee a suitable advertising campaign and nation-wide and international distribution in première cinemas that offered the only chance of paying off costs. This meant that directors had to come to terms with the big film companies. And the latter would only permit experiments to the extent that they did not see them as a threat to their profit prospects.

The effective rule was: a director's artistic freedom is measured against the success of his last film. Experience showed that the financiers interfered more the more capital was at stake. Very expensive films in particular had to make concessions to popular taste, while directors who were prepared to go without elaborate productions and expensive stars, and had relatively great success with small works, like Robert Altman, Paul Mazursky, Woody Allen or John Cassavetes, could work the most independently. Thus New Hollywood's commercially most successful products are often based on an updated version of classic success formulae, while the smaller-scale films are more original, more innovative and ultimately more interesting. But in any case directors had to walk a successful line between commercial success and the artistic originality, a feat that is one of the hallmarks of New Hollywood in the seventies.

Erneuerungsstrategien

Die USA in den siebziger Jahren – Desintegration und Rebellion

Inhaltlich waren die Filme des neuen Hollywood entscheidend von den Ideen der Gegenkultur geprägt, die Ende der sechziger Jahre die Grenzen der Subkultur überschritten, um in den Mainstream einzugehen, den sie das kommende Jahrzehnt hindurch bestimmten. Darin vermischten sich das politische Engagement der Protestbewegung mit der Auflehnung gegen herkömmliche gesellschaftliche Strukturen, Lebensformen und Wertvorstellungen. Die Bürgerrechtsbewegung hatte die rassistische Ungleichheit und die soziale Benachteiligung von Minderheiten ins öffentliche Bewußtsein gerückt und erschütterte den Glauben an die Chancengleichheit, die angeblich jedem die Möglichkeit bietet, mit Fleiß, Beharrlichkeit und Durchsetzungsvermögen sein Glück zu machen. Angesichts der Zwänge der anonymen Massengesellschaft und der damit verbundenen Einschränkung der persönlichen Freiheit erschien der Mythos von Amerika als dem Land der unbegrenzten Möglichkeiten, das dem Individuum die freie Entfaltung seiner Persönlichkeit garantiert, zunehmend unglaubwürdig. Der Vietnamkrieg, dessen Ziele der Öffentlichkeit immer uneinsichtiger waren, warf die Frage nach der Berechtigung der amerikanischen Einmischung in externe Konflikte auf, und das Bekanntwerden von Massakern, wie in My Lai, zog die moralische Überlegenheit der amerikanischen Armee ernsthaft in Zweifel. Die Erfahrung des gewaltsamen Vorgehens der Ordnungskräfte gegen friedliche Protestaktionen und die damit verbundene Beschneidung der Grundrechte des Individuums ließen den Staat repressiv erscheinen. Der Watergate-Skandal, der die amerikanische Öffentlichkeit seit 1972 bewegte und 1974 den Rücktritt von Präsident Nixon erzwang, erschütterte endgültig die Glaubwürdigkeit und moralische Integrität der politischen Führer, die bis dahin als die Verkörperung der amerikanischen Ideale und Werte betrachtet wurden. Hinzu kam das Trauma der Niederlage in Vietnam, wo ein kleines, mit archaischen Mitteln kämpfendes Land die Weltmacht USA trotz seiner haushohen waffentechnischen Überlegenheit niedergerungen hatte. Im Gegensatz zum Zweiten Weltkrieg, aus dem die Veteranen als siegreiche Helden zurückgekehrt waren, erinnerten die Heimkehrer aus dem Vietnamkrieg, von denen viele schwere körperliche und psychische Schäden davongetragen hatten, an die tiefen Wunden, die dieser Krieg im amerikanischen Selbstbewußtsein zurückgelassen hatte. Diese Entwicklung rief in der linken Protestbewegung ein tiefsitzendes Mißtrauen gegenüber dem sogenannten Establishment, dem Machtgeflecht von Wirtschaft, Politik und Wissenschaft, hervor und bestärkte die Auffassung, daß der amerikanische Traum ein Opfer des Machtstrebens und der Profitgier skrupelloser Geschäftemacher und Politiker geworden sei. Die Undurchschaubarkeit

9. Ossie Davis (Joseph Winfield Lee), Telly Savalas (Jim Howie) und Burt Lancaster (Joe Bass) in *Mit eisernen Fäusten* von Sydney Pollack, 1967.
10. Paul Newman (Butch Cassidy) und Katherine Ross (Etta Place) in *Zwei Banditen* von George Roy Hill, 1969.
11. Jason Robards (Cable Hogue) und Stella Stevens (Hildy) in *Abgerechnet wird zum Schluß* von Sam Peckinpah, 1970.

9. Ossie Davis (Joseph Winfield Lee), Telly Savalas (Jim Howie) and Burt Lancaster (Joe Bass) in *The Scalphunters* by Sydney Pollack, 1967.
10. Paul Newman (Butch Cassidy) and Katherine Ross (Etta Place) in *Butch Cassidy and the Sundance Kid* by George Roy Hill, 1969.
11. Jason Robards (Cable Hogue) and Stella Stevens (Hildy) in *The Ballad of Cable Hogue* by Sam Peckinpah, 1970.

Renewal strategies

The USA in the seventies – disintegration and rebellion

In terms of content, a major influence on New Hollywood cinema were the ideas of the alternative culture that had cut across the boundaries of the subculture in the sixties. These then passed into mainstream culture, which they were to define throughout the coming decade. Here the political commitment of the protest movement was mixed with resistance to traditional social structures, life-styles and values. The civil rights movement had shifted racial inequality and social neglect of minorities into the public consciousness and shook the belief in equality of opportunity that allegedly offers everyone the opportunity to engineer his or her own happiness through hard work, persistence and the ability to assert themselves. Given the constraints of the anonymous mass society and the associated restrictions on personal freedom, the myth of America as the land of unlimited opportunities that guaranteed each individual the freedom to develop his or her own personality seemed increasingly incredible. The Vietnam War, whose aims became ever more opaque to the public, raised the question of America's right to involve itself in external conflicts, and the revelation of massacres like the one in My Lai cast serious doubt on the moral superiority of the American army. Experience of violence by the forces of law and order against peaceful protest campaigns and the associated infringement of basic human rights made the state seem repressive. The Watergate scandal, which occupied the American public from 1972 and forced Richard Nixon to resign in 1974, undermined the credibility and moral integrity of the political leadership once and for all; hitherto they had been seen as the embodiment of American ideals and values. On top of this came the trauma of defeat in Vietnam, where a small country fighting with archaic resources had beaten down a world power in the shape of the United States, despite its total superiority in terms of arms technology. In contrast with the Second World War, from which the veterans returned as victorious heroes, men returning from the Vietnam War, many of whom had sustained severe physical and psychic damage, were reminders of the deep wounds that this war had left in the American psyche. This development fuelled a profound mistrust by the left-wing protest movement of the so-called establishment, the power structure made up of economics, politics and science, and reinforced the view that the American dream was a victim of the desire for power and greed for profit of unscrupulous speculators and politicians. The baffling nature of the modern world and apparently omnipresent corruption added fuel to the fear that technological progress could be abused and expressed itself in criticism of civilization and pessimism about the future. The alternative culture turned its criticism against the idealized image of the »American Way of Life«, which was shaped by middle-class life-styles in the small towns and suburbs. Under the influence of the women's movement the patriarchal structures of the sacred American institutions and their basic pillars, family and religion, were laid bare and puritanical moral concepts unmasked as repressive and insincere. Against this were set the claims of alternative, more open life-styles and liberal sexual morality, as defined by the hippie culture's ideas of »self-realization« and »free love«. In the course of the sexual revolution the view of the role of the sexes changed. This led among other things to the emergence of the gay rights movement, which started with the so-called Stonewall Riots on 27 July 1969. The apparent demolition of traditional social structures and values led to a general lack of direction in the conservative camp as well as in the left-wing alternative culture, and to the search for a new national and personal identity.

The disintegration of American society inevitably affected the conventions of the classical Hollywood film, which reproduced conservative values and the traditional myths of mass culture in an idealized form, reduced to ritual within the genres. This led to a series of genre formulae that were repeated in a number of variations and soon became a myth themselves. Given the social changes of the sixties and seventies, these seemed increasingly incredible, as the gulf between legend and reality had become all too apparent. As a consequence of this, New Hollywood's renewal strategies were directed mainly at the traditional genres. A growing critical awareness of the genre formulae had already started to show in the transitional period from classical Hollywood to New Hollywood. The classical genres, stories and heroes continued to exist, but these conventions were increasingly treated ironically, and parodied or caricatured. In the sixties and seventies a large number of films parodied the genre clichés, including many that can be labelled as New Hollywood: in *The Scalphunters* (1968) Sydney Pollack turned the Western convention upside down by giving a rough and ready trapper an extraordinarily cultivated former black slave as a companion. The heroes in George Roy Hill's Western

der modernen Welt und die scheinbar allgegenwärtige Korruption schürte die Furcht vor dem Mißbrauch des technischen Fortschritts und äußerte sich in Zivilisationskritik und Zukunftspessimismus. Die Gegenkultur weitete ihre Kritik auf das idealisierte Bild des »American Way of Life« aus, das vom Lebensstil des Mittelstands in den Vor- und Kleinstädten geprägt war. Unter dem Einfluß der Frauenbewegung wurden die patriarchalischen Strukturen der geheiligten amerikanischen Institutionen und deren Grundpfeiler, Familie und Religion, offengelegt und die puritanischen Moralbegriffe als repressiv und verlogen entlarvt. Dem setzte man den Anspruch auf alternative, offenere Lebensformen und eine liberale Sexualmoral entgegen, die von der Vorstellung der »Selbstverwirklichung« und der »freien Liebe« der Hippiekultur geprägt war. Im Zuge der sexuellen Revolution veränderte sich die Auffassung über die Rolle der Geschlechter, was unter anderem zur Entstehung der Homosexuellenbewegung beitrug, die ihren Ausgangspunkt im sogenannten Stonewall-Aufstand vom 27. Juli 1969 hat. Die offensichtliche Auflösung der herkömmlichen gesellschaftlichen Strukturen und Wertvorstellungen führte nicht nur in der linken Gegenkultur, sondern auch im konservativen Lager zu einer allgemeinen Orientierungslosigkeit und der Suche nach einer neuen nationalen und persönlichen Identität.

Der Prozeß der Desintegration der amerikanischen Gesellschaft berührte zwangsläufig auch die Konventionen des klassischen Hollywood-Films, der die konservativen Wertvorstellungen und traditionellen Mythen der Massenkultur in idealisierter Form reproduzierte und in den Genres ritualisierte. Daraus entstand eine Reihe von Genreformeln, die in verschiedenen Variationen wiederholt und selbst zu einem Mythos wurden. Angesichts der sozialen Veränderungen der sechziger und siebziger Jahre erschienen diese zunehmend als unglaubhaft, da die Kluft zwischen Legende und Wirklichkeit zu offensichtlich geworden war. Infolgedessen richteten sich die Erneuerungsstrategien von New Hollywood hauptsächlich auf die traditionellen Genres. Bereits in der Übergangsperiode des klassischen Hollywood zu New Hollywood zeigte sich ein wachsendes kritisches Bewußtsein gegenüber den Genreformeln. Die klassischen Genres, Geschichten und Helden bestanden weiter, doch diese Konventionen wurden zunehmend ironisch, parodistisch und als Karikatur betrachtet. In den sechziger und siebziger Jahren gab es eine große Zahl von Filmen, welche die Genreklischees parodierten, darunter viele, die New Hollywood zugerechnet werden können: In *The Scalphunters* (1967, *Mit eisernen Fäusten*) stellte Sidney Pollack die Westernkonventionen auf den Kopf, indem er einem rauhbeinigen Trapper einen außerordentlich kultivierten ehemaligen schwarzen Sklaven an die Seite stellte. Die Helden in George Roy Hills Western *Butch Cassidy and the Sundance Kid* (1969, *Zwei Banditen*) agieren innerhalb der bekannten Verhaltensmuster des Genres, sind sich der Mythen jedoch bewußt und beziehen so gleichzeitig eine Position der ironischen Distanz. Sam Peckinpah drehte *The Ballad of Cable Hogue* (1970, *Abgerechnet wird zum Schluß*), eine für ihn ungewohnt heitere Fabel über die Pioniere des Westens. Robert Altman parodiert in *The Long Goodbye* (1973, *Der Tod kennt keine Wiederkehr*) die Detektivfilme der schwarzen Serie. *Prime Cut* (1971, *Die Professionals*) von Michael Ritchie ist eine Satire auf die Macho-Mythen des Gangsterfilms mit Lee Marvin als Gangster im Kampf gegen einen durchgeknallten Schurken, der nicht nur seine Feinde durch den Fleischwolf dreht und zu Würstchen verarbeitet, sondern auch einen schwunghaften Mädchenhandel betreibt. Woody Allen karikiert in *Take The Money and Run* (1969, *Woody, der Unglücksrabe*) die Konventionen der Gangsterfilme, indem er in einem Pseudo-Dokumentarfilm den Werdegang des vollkommen unbedarften Gangsters Virgil Stockwell, gespielt von ihm selbst als schmächtiger, schüchterner und übernervöser Brillenträger, Revue passieren läßt. In seinem Science-fiction-Film *Sleeper* (1973, *Der Schläfer*) erzählt er in Form einer Slapstick-Komödie die Geschichte eines Mannes, der 1973 versehentlich eingefroren, nach 200 Jahren wieder aufgetaut wird und sich in einer veränderten Welt zurechtfinden muß, während *Love and Death* (1975, *Die letzte Nacht des Boris Gruschenko*) die Kostümfilme à la *Doktor Schiwago* parodiert. Mel Brooks spezialisierte sich in den siebziger Jahren auf Genreparodien. In seinen Filmen *Blazing Saddles* (1973, *Is' was Sheriff?*), *Young Frankenstein* (1974, *Frankenstein Junior*), *Silent Movie* (1976) und *High Anxiety* (1977, *Mel Brooks' Höhenkoller*) benutzt er die klassischen Standardtypen, Szenarien und Handlungsformeln und führt sie ad absurdum, indem er die Klischees überzieht, so daß sie als solche sichtbar werden und nur noch komisch wirken.

Außerdem zeigte sich bis Mitte der siebziger Jahre eine ausgeprägte Tendenz zur kritischen Revision der Genreformeln durch die bewußte Konfrontation der Filmmythen mit der Realität, um sie als Mythen zu entlarven und in Frage zu stellen. Daneben bestand vor allem unter den sogenannten Whiz-Kids aber auch ein starkes Interesse an der Modernisierung und Weiterentwicklung der klassischen Genres, indem man sich bewußt auf deren Konventionen stützte,

12. Gene Hackman (»Mary Ann«) und Lee Marvin (Nick Devlin) in *Die Professionals* von Michael Ritchie, 1971.
13. Elliot Gould (Philip Marlowe) in *Der Tod kennt keine Wiederkehr* von Robert Altman, 1973.
14. Woody Allen (Virgil Stockwell) in *Woody, der Unglücksrabe* von Woody Allen, 1969.
15. Gene Wilder (Dr. Frankenstein), Peter Boyle (Monster) und Marty Feldman (Igor) in *Frankenstein Junior* von Mel Brooks, 1974.

12. Gene Hackman (»Mary Ann«) and Lee Marvin (Nick Devlin) in *Prime Cut* by Michael Ritchie, 1971.
13. Elliot Gould (Philip Marlowe) in *The Long Goodbye* by Robert Altman, 1973.
14. Woody Allen (Virgil Stockwell) in *Take The Money and Run* by Woody Allen, 1969.
15. Gene Wilder (Dr. Frankenstein), Peter Boyle (Monster) and Marty Feldman (Igor) in *Young Frankenstein* by Mel Brooks, 1974.

Butch Cassidy and the Sundance Kid (1969) act within the genre's familiar behaviour patterns, but they are aware of the myths, and so they occupy a position of ironic distance at the same time. Sam Peckinpah made *The Ballad of Cable Hogue* (1970), a fable about the pioneers of the West that was unusually light-hearted for him. In *The Long Goodbye* (1973), Robert Altman parodied black series detective films. *Prime Cut* (1971) by Michael Ritchie is a satire on the macho myth of the gangster film, with Lee Marvin as a gangster fighting against an out-and-out villain who not only puts his enemies through the mincing machine and makes them into sausages but is also a thriving white slave trader. In *Take the Money and Run* (1969), Woody Allen caricatures the conventions of gangster films by making a pseudo-documentary reviewing the career of the completely untalented gangster Virgil Stockwell, whom he plays himself as weedy, shy, excessively nervous, and bespectacled. Then in his science fiction film *Sleeper* (1973) he uses slapstick comedy to tell the story of a man who is accidentally frozen in 1973, then thawed out after 200 years, when he has to make his way in a changed world, while *Love and Death* (1975) parodies costume dramas à la *Dr. Zhivago*. Mel Brooks specialized in genre parodies in the seventies. His films *Blazing Saddles* (1973), *Young Frankenstein* (1974), *Silent Movie* (1976) and *High Anxiety* (1977) use standard types, scenarios and action formulae and reduce them to absurdity by stretching the clichés so that they are revealed as such, and seem merely amusing.

As well as this, a marked tendency emerged up to the mid seventies to revise the genre formulae critically by deliberately confronting the film myths with reality, in order to reveal them as myths, and question them. But the so-called whiz kids in particular were extremely interested in modernizing the classical genres and developing them further by deliberately using their conventions as a support but linking this with new content, subject matter and techniques. This also included upgrading genres or sub-genres like horror films, science-fiction films, music films, youth comedies or biker films of the AIP that up to then had largely appeared in the form of low-budget productions. Determined to reach a younger audience, the film-makers took up their basic formulae and polished them to establish them in the mainstream cinema. They also varied and mixed features of different genres, going so far as to create sub-genres and new genres whose conventions they largely established themselves. But the key renewal feature was that in many cases the film-makers found the classical formulae unsuitable for reflecting their views, and so turned to other traditions like the underground film or the European art film.

16. Ben Johnson (Tector Gorch), Warren Oates (Lyle Gorch), William Holden (Pike Bishop) und Ernest Borgnine (Dutch Engstrom) in *Sie kannten kein Gesetz* von Sam Peckinpah, 1969.
17. Dustin Hoffman (Jack Crabb) in *Little Big Man* von Arthur Penn, 1970.
18. Marlon Brando (Robert Lee Clayton) und Jack Nicholson (Tom Logan) in *Duell am Missouri* von Arthur Penn, 1975.
19. Jim Davis (Julie Blocker), Jason Robards (Ewing) und James Kline (Ralph Cole) in *Eine Farm in Montana* von Alan Pakula, 1978.

16. Ben Johnson (Tector Gorch), Warren Oates (Lyle Gorch), William Holden (Pike Bishop) and Ernest Borgnine (Dutch Engstrom) in *The Wild Bunch* by Sam Peckinpah, 1969.
17. Dustin Hoffman (Jack Crabb) in *Little Big Man* by Arthur Penn, 1970.
18. Marlon Brando (Robert Lee Clayton) and Jack Nicholson (Tom Logan) in *The Missouri Breaks* by Arthur Penn, 1975.
19. Jim Davis (Julie Blocker), Jason Robards (Ewing) and James Kline (Ralph Cole) in *Comes a Horseman* by Alan Pakula, 1978.

diese jedoch mit neuen Inhalten, Motiven und Techniken verband. Dazu zählte auch die Aufwertung von Genres oder Subgenres, die wie der Horrorfilm, der Science-fiction-Film, der Musikfilm, die Jugendkomödie oder die Motorradfilme der AIP bis dahin weitgehend in Form von unabhängigen Low-Budget-Produktionen verbreitet waren. Im Bestreben, ein jugendliches Publikum zu erreichen, griffen die Filmemacher deren Grundformeln auf und polierten sie, um sie im Mainstream-Kino zu etablieren. Außerdem variierten und mischten sie die Merkmale verschiedener Genres bis hin zur Schaffung von Subgenres und neuen Genres, deren Konventionen sie entscheidend prägten. Der wesentlichste Faktor der Erneuerung war jedoch, daß die Filmemacher in vielen Fällen die klassischen Formeln als ungeeignet empfanden, ihre Sicht der Dinge wiederzugeben, und sich auf andere Traditionen wie die des Undergroundfilms oder des europäischen Kunstfilms besannen.

Westernfilme – Abgesang auf den Mythos der offenen Grenzen

Die kritische Auseinandersetzung mit dem amerikanischen Selbstverständnis führte Ende der sechziger Jahre zu einer Renaissance des Western. Der Grundkonflikt der klassischen Western beruht auf dem Widerspruch von sozialer Ordnung / Zivilisation versus Anarchie / Wildnis, personifiziert durch den mutigen und rechtschaffenen Pionier, der im Kampf gegen die Unbilden der Natur und mordlustige Indianer eine Ranch errichtet, eine Familie gründet und die Zivilisation in die Wildnis trägt. Der typische Westernheld ist ein guter Ritter, ein Mann der Tat mit einem scheinbar naturgegebenen Gerechtigkeitsgefühl jenseits des Gesetzes, der den Schwachen beisteht und ihnen bei der Durchsetzung der zivilisatorischen Werte hilft. Er ist aber auch ein Einzelgänger, mehr mit der Natur verwachsen als mit der menschlichen Gemeinschaft, der nach Beendigung seiner Mission mit unbekanntem Ziel weiterzieht.

Dem versuchten die neuen Western, ein realistisches Bild entgegenzusetzen. In dieser revidierten Vision der Besiedlung des Westens zieht die weiße Zivilisation in Gestalt von Glücksrittern und geschäftstüchtigen Prostituierten, marodierenden Abenteurern und Banditen, skrupellosen Geschäftsleuten aus dem Osten und anonymen Gesellschaften in den Wilden Westen ein. Der damit verbundene gesellschaftliche Fortschritt erscheint äußerst fragwürdig, denn im Gegensatz zu den klassischen Western kommen mit ihnen nicht die Werte der zivilisierten Gesellschaft, sondern Profitstreben, Gewalt, Korruption, Machtgier und eine verlogene Doppelmoral. In Robert Altmans *McCabe and Mrs. Miller* (1971) bringen findige Kleinunternehmer mit der Errichtung eines Bordells, eines Spielsalons und eines Badehauses erste Ansätze zivilisier-

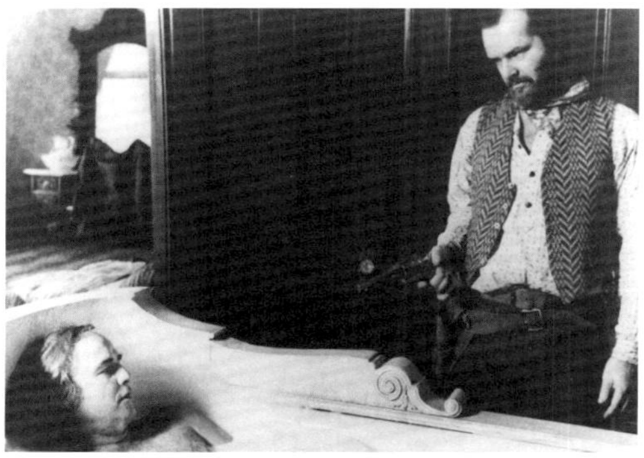

Westerns – a farewell to the myth of open borders

Critical examination of American self-perception led to a renaissance of the Western in the late sixties. The basic conflict within the classical Western is based on the contradiction between social order / civilization versus anarchy / wilderness, personified by the courageous and upright pioneer who sets up a ranch while fighting the rigours of nature and the bloodthirsty Indians, then starts a family and brings civilization to the wilderness. The typical Western hero is a good horseman, a man of action with an apparently nature-endowed sense of justice beyond the law that sustains the weak and helps them to establish civilized values. But he is also a loner, more in tune with nature than human society. When his mission is complete, he will move on, with no particular destination in mind.

The new Westerns tried to confront this with a realistic image. In this revised version of the settlement of the West, white civilization moves into the Wild West in the guise of fortune-hunters and prostitutes with a good business sense, looting adventurers and bandits, unscrupulous businessmen from the East and anonymous commercial enterprises. The social progress associated with this seems extremely questionable, as unlike the classical Western it does not involve the values of civilized society but profiteering, violence, corruption, craving for power and insincere double standards. In Robert Altman's *McCabe and Mrs Miller* (1971) ingenious small businessmen bring civilized values to a primitive mining village by setting up a brothel, an eating house and a bath-house. Their success whets the appetite of the owners of the powerful mining company, which has McCabe killed by hired hitmen, without either the law and the villagers raising a finger to prevent it. In *The Wild Bunch* (1969) by Sam Peckinpah the railroad company hires a gang of cowardly, unkempt bounty hunters who behave worse than the bandits they are intended to render harmless. The ranchers in Peckinpah's *Pat Garret and Billy the Kid* (1973), Arthur Penn's *The Missouri Breaks* (1976), Alan J. Pakula's *Comes a Horseman* (1978) and Michael Cimino's *Heaven's Gate* (1980) are coolly calculating businessmen who run their property like a modern business, though they are not averse to taking the law into their own hands and committing murder to further their interests. They are backed by respectable citizens, the state and financial sharks from the East. Unlike the classical Western where violence serves law and order and is thus seen as justifiable, here it is an instrument of advancing capitalism that is turned against the community, signifying a lapse into barbarism.

The myth of the cavalry as the heroic saviours of civilization did not survive in the new Western either. They appear either as a dilettante, inexperienced unit who move around awkwardly on strange terrain, as in *The Wild Bunch* and Sydney Pollack's *Jeremiah Johnson* (1972), or as

ten Lebens in ein primitives Bergarbeiterdorf. Ihr Erfolg weckt den Appetit der Besitzer der mächtigen Bergbaugesellschaft, die McCabe von gedungenen Killern töten läßt, ohne daß das Gesetz und die Dorfbewohner einen Finger rühren, sie daran zu hindern. In *The Wild Bunch* (1969, *Sie kannten kein Gesetz*) von Sam Peckinpah heuert die Eisenbahngesellschaft eine Horde von feigen, verwahrlosten Kopfgeldjägern an, die sich schlimmer gebärden als die Banditen, die sie unschädlich machen sollen. Die Rancher in Peckinpahs *Pat Garret and Billy the Kid* (1973), Arthur Penns *The Missouri Breaks* (1976, *Duell am Missouri*), Alan J. Pakulas *Comes a Horseman* (1978, *Eine Farm in Montana*) und Michael Ciminos *Heaven's Gate* (1980, *Heaven's Gate – Das Tor zum Himmel*) sind scharf kalkulierende Geschäftsmänner, die ihren Besitz wie ein modernes Unternehmen verwalten, allerdings nicht vor Selbstjustiz und Mord zurückschrecken, um ihre Interessen durchzusetzen. Rückendeckung erhalten sie von den ehrbaren Bürgern, dem Staat und den Finanzhaien aus dem Osten. Anders als im klassischen Western, wo die Gewalt im Dienste von Recht und Ordnung steht und damit eine Legitimation erhält, ist sie hier ein Instrument des vordringenden Kapitalismus, das sich gegen die Gemeinschaft richtet, und bedeutet einen Rückfall in die Barbarei.

Auch der Mythos der Kavallerie als heldenhafte Retterin der Zivilisation hatte in den neuen Western keinen Bestand. Sie tritt entweder als dilettantische, unerfahrene Truppe auf, die sich ungeschickt auf fremdem Terrain bewegt, wie in *The Wild Bunch* und Sydney Pollacks *Jeremiah Johnson* (1972), oder als eine grausame Bande von Mördern an wehrlosen Indianern. *Little Big Man* (1970) von Arthur Penn schildert die Schlacht am Little Big Horn, bei der die weißen Truppen unter der Führung von General Custer eine vernichtende Niederlage erlitten, aus der Sicht des 121jährigen Trappers Jack Crabb. Seine Version der Ereignisse entlarvt Custer als einen geltungssüchtigen, selbstherrlichen, eitlen Dummkopf und die angeblichen Siege seiner Truppen als Überfälle auf friedliche Indianerlager, bei denen sie alles niederbrennen und wehrlose Frauen und Kinder ermorden. In diesen Western kommt die gängige Sichtweise der Zeit zum Ausdruck, die die indianische Lebensweise im Gegensatz zur Wettbewerbsgesellschaft der Weißen als eine ganzheitliche, moralischere Lebensform begreift und in Umkehrung der klassischen Formel die Indianer als die Opfer eines Ausrottungsfeldzugs zeigt. In der Darstellung der weißen Zivilisation als kolonialistisch, barbarisch, heuchlerisch und lebensverachtend sind die Parallelen zu Vietnam offensichtlich.

Die Kirche, eine weitere Säule des amerikanischen Selbstverständnisses, wird als moralische Instanz ebenfalls in Frage gestellt. In dem Film *McCabe and Mrs. Miller* besteht die Kirchengemeinde hauptsächlich aus Raufbolden und Freudenmädchen. Der Prediger Pendrake aus *Little Big Man* erweist sich als sexuell verklemmter, auf sein leibliches Wohl bedachter Spießer, der seinem Schützling Jack die vermeintlichen christlichen Tugenden mit der Peitsche einzubleuen versucht und ihn so für immer davon kuriert. In *The Ballad of Cable Hogue* tritt ein dubioser Prediger in Erscheinung, der seine wirren religiösen Theorien vor allem dazu benutzt, einsame Frauen zu verführen, während in *The Wild Bunch* die Kirche in Gestalt eines salbadernden Pastors präsent ist, der vor einer Gemeinde aus bornierten Spießern gegen den Sittenverfall wettert. In all diesen Filmen zeigt die Institution Kirche eine verlogene Doppelmoral, die sie hinter rigiden puritanischen Moralvorstellungen verbirgt. Zur Durchsetzung moralischer Werte erweist sie sich als ungeeignet.

Darüber hinaus setzen sich die Western zunehmend mit dem Konflikt zwischen dem ursprünglichen Leben der Pionierzeit und dem Vordringen der Zivilisation auseinander, das zwangsläufig die Freiheit des Individualisten beschränkt und seinen Lebensstil gefährdet. Während die klassischen Western in der Regel in den goldenen Tagen des Wilden Westens in der zweiten Hälfte der 19. Jahrhunderts spielen, als noch alle Möglichkeiten offen schienen, beschäftigt sich das Genre nun immer häufiger mit dem Ende dieser Ära um die Jahrhundertwende. Viele Western der Zeit wirken wie ein Abgesang auf den Wilden Westen und den Mythos der offenen Grenzen. Die Helden von *Butch Cassidy and the Sundance Kid* (1969, *Zwei Banditen*) sind sympathische Outlaws, die angesichts des Vordringens des technischen Fortschritts und des Gesetzes aus dem amerikanischen Westen nach Bolivien flüchten, um ihr Banditenleben fortsetzen zu können. Der Untergang des traditionellen Lebensstils des Westens und die Bemühungen seiner Helden, ihn wider alle Vernunft aufrechtzuerhalten, ist eines der beständigen Themen Sam Peckinpahs, für das er am Ende von *The Ballad of Cable Hogue* ein Symbol setzt, wenn der Held vergeblich versucht, ein führerlos dahinrollendes Auto mit bloßen Händen zu stoppen, und dabei umkommt. Peckinpahs Westernhelden stehen vor dem Dilemma, ihr Freiheitsideal einem zweifelhaften gesellschaftlichen Fortschritt zu opfern oder von ihm vernichtet zu werden. Diese beiden Haltungen werden in *Pat Garret and Billy the Kid* mit-

20. James Coburn (Sheriff Patrick J. Garrett), Kris Kristofferson (William H. »Billy the Kid« Bonney) und R. G. Armstrong (Deputy Sheriff Bob Ollinger) in *Pat Garret und Billy the Kid* von Sam Peckinpah, 1973.
21. Christopher Walken (Nathan D. Champion) in *Das Tor zum Himmel* von Michael Cimino, 1980.
22. Robert Redford (Jeremiah Johnson) und Stefan Gierasch (Del Gue) in *Jeremiah Johnson* von Sydney Pollack, 1972.

20. James Coburn (Sheriff Patrick J. Garrett), Kris Kristofferson (William H. »Billy the Kid« Bonney) and R. G. Armstrong (Deputy Sheriff Bob Ollinger) in *Pat Garret and Billy the Kid* by Sam Peckinpah, 1973.
21. Christopher Walken (Nathan D. Champion) in *Heaven's Gate* by Michael Cimino, 1980.
22. Robert Redford (Jeremiah Johnson) and Stefan Gierasch (Del Gue) in *Jeremiah Johnson* by Sydney Pollack, 1972.

a brutal gang murdering defenceless Indians. *Little Big Man* (1970) by Arthur Penn presents the battle of Little Big Horn, in which the white troops under General Custer suffered a humiliating defeat, seen through the eyes of a 121-year-old trapper called Jack Crabb. His version of events reveals Custer as a vain, autocratic idiot with a craving for recognition, and the alleged victories by his troops as ambushes on peaceful Indian camps, in which Custer's men burn everything down and murder defenceless women and children. This Western expresses the view that was current at the time, which sees the Indian way of life, in contrast with the competitive white society, as an integrated, more moral life-style. It reverses the classical formula, showing the Indians as victims of an extermination campaign. Representing white civilization as colonialist, barbaric, hypocritical and contemptuous of life in this way establishes obvious parallels with the Vietnam War.

The Church, another pillar of the America's conception of itself, is also questioned as a moral authority. In *McCabe and Mrs Miller* the church congregation consists mainly of ruffians and women of easy virtue. Preacher Pendrake in *Little Big Man* turns out to be a sexually repressed petit bourgeois obsessed with creature comforts who tries to lash the supposed Christian virtues into his protégé Jack with a whip and so turn him off from them for ever. In *The Ballad of Cable Hogue* a dubious preacher appears who uses his muddled religious theories mainly to seduce lonely women, while in *The Wild Bunch* the Church is present in the form of a pretentiously waffling pastor who denounces the decline of morality to a congregation of bigoted petits bourgeois. The Church as an institution demonstrates insincere double moral standards in all these films, hiding behind rigidly puritanical ideas of morality and showing itself as totally unsuited to establishing moral values.

Westerns also address the conflict between the primitive life of the pioneering days and the progress of civilization, inevitably restricting the freedom of the individualist and threatening his life-style. Classical Westerns are usually set in the golden age of the Wild West in the second half of the nineteenth century, when all the options seemed to be open. The genre now deals more frequently with the end of this era around the turn of the century. Many Westerns of this period seem like a farewell to the Wild West and the myth of open borders. The heroes of *Butch Cassidy and the Sundance Kid* are likeable outlaws who run away from the American West to Bolivia because of advances in technology and the law, so that they can continue their existence as bandits there. The decline of the traditional Wild West lifestyle and its heroes' efforts to maintain it against all reason is one of Sam Peckinpah's recurring themes. He places a symbol of this at the end of *The Ballad of Cable Hogue* when the hero tries in vain to stop a runaway driverless car with his bare hands, losing his life in the process. Peckinpah's Western

einander konfrontiert. Während Billy the Kid beschließt, sein Dasein als Gesetzloser fortzusetzen, obwohl er weiß, daß er dies mit dem Leben bezahlen wird, erkauft sich Pat Garret Respektabilität und Wohlstand, indem er auf die Seite des Gesetzes wechselt und verachtet sich insgeheim dafür. Im Mittelpunkt von *The Wild Bunch* steht eine wüste Bande von Gesetzlosen, die angesichts des Vordringens einer neuen Zeit, in der Anstand, Fairneß und Kameradschaftsgeist ein Anachronismus sind, den Moralkodex des Westens längst hinter sich gelassen haben. Nach dem Raub einer Ladung Gewehre fliehen sie nach Mexiko, um die Gewehre an den Chef marodierender Armeeeinheiten zu verkaufen, obwohl sie wissen, daß dieser sie gegen rebellierende Bauern einsetzen wird, mit denen sie sympathisieren. Als der mexikanische Bandenchef einen von ihnen foltert und tötet, besinnen sie sich auf die alten Werte des Westens und beschließen spontan eine selbstmörderische Racheaktion, bei der es ihnen zwar gelingt, den größten Teil ihrer Widersacher zu töten, sie aber selber allesamt umkommen. Wie bei den Antihelden der fünfziger Jahre liegt hier gerade im Scheitern der Helden ihr moralischer Sieg über eine Welt, die als korrupt und verdorben empfunden wird.

Die Auseinandersetzung mit der Gültigkeit des Moralkodexes des Westens bildet auch ein zentrales Element des Subgenres der Rodeofilme, deren Helden versuchen, die traditionellen Werte in die heutige Zeit zu retten. In Sam Peckinpahs *Junior Bonner* (1972) schlägt der Titelheld eine gesicherte Stellung aus und entscheidet sich bewußt für das unsichere und unstete Leben als Rodeoreiter, obwohl er am Beispiel seines Vaters sieht, daß er dabei ständig am Rande des finanziellen Ruins steht, seine Gesundheit zugrunde richtet, auf eine feste Bindung und ein Familienleben verzichten muß und ihm im Alter ein Leben in Armut und Abhängigkeit bevorsteht. *The Electric Horseman* (1979) von Sydney Pollack handelt von einem bekannten Rodeoreiter, der angewidert von der Kommerzialisierung der alten Ideale des Westens durch Westernshows, Medien und Werbung ein teures Rennpferd stiehlt, um ihm die Freiheit zu schenken, und damit einen Akt der Selbstbefreiung vollzieht. Eine ähnlich kritische Haltung gegenüber den von den Medien geprägten Westernklischees vermittelt James Bridges' *Urban Cowboy* (1979), eine Liebesgeschichte vor dem Hintergrund des Milieus texanischer Ölarbeiter, die ihre Freizeit in einem riesigen Country- und Western-Saloon verbringen. Der junge Held richtet sein Verhalten am verfälschten Bild des Cowboys als Idealbild des »echten« Mannes aus und erregt damit die Bewunderung eines ebenso unreifen Mädchens. Die beiden verlieben sich und heiraten, müssen jedoch feststellen, daß das falsche Männlichkeitsideal untauglich zur Bewältigung des Alltags ist.

Eine allgemeine Tendenz des Western der Zeit ist die Demontage der Westernromantik. Neben dem neuen Realismus bei der Darstellung des Westens äußerte sich dies unter anderem in der graphischen Darstellung von Gewaltszenen, für die Peckinpah berühmt war. Er inszenierte das Finale von *The Wild Bunch* als eine Art Todesballett, bei dem er den Zuschauer minutenlang mit Bildern unbeschönigter Gewalt bombardiert, deren Plastizität durch Zeitlupensequenzen noch zusätzlich gesteigert wird. Der Showdown wird zu einem Amoklauf, den er ähnlich auch in anderen Filmen in Szene setzt. Daneben stellt er das klassische Ritual der Revolverduelle und des fairen Kampfes unter Männern in Frage, wenn in *The Wild Bunch* der Chef der Bande kaltblütig einen verwundeten Kumpanen erschießt, um sich auf der Flucht nicht mit ihm zu belasten, oder Pat Garrett den arglosen Billy the Kid durch einen Schuß in den Rücken tötet. In *Jeremiah Johnson*, einer Ballade über einen ehemaligen Soldaten, der zur Zeit der Indianerkämpfe in die Wildnis zieht, um dort als Trapper zu leben, konzentriert Sydney Pollack den Blick auf die anfängliche Unbeholfenheit des Helden sowie auf die Entbehrungen und Härten, die das Überleben in den Wäldern fordert. Dem stellt er die Legende entgegen. Ein hartes, nüchternes Bild des Lebens im Westen, das nichts mit dem glorifizierenden Mythen des klassischen Western gemeinsam hat, zeichnet auch Robert Benton in seiner ersten Regiearbeit *Bad Company* (1972, *In schlechter Gesellschaft*), der Geschichte eines jungen Mannes aus gutbürgerlichem Hause, der während des amerikanischen Bürgerkriegs vor der Zwangsrekrutierung flieht und sich einer Bande von Jugendlichen anschließt, die sich durch das Kriegsgebiet schlagen und schließlich in einer Welt jenseits jeder Zivilisation ankommen. Daneben bemüht sich eine Reihe von Filmen um eine Entromantisierung der Legende der klassischen Gesetzlosen des Westens. Ein früher Vorläufer ist Arthur Penns erster Kinofilm *The Left-Handed Gun* (1958, *Billy the Kid*), eine Variation der legendären Gestalt von Billy the Kid, in der Billy als ein unverstandener, rebellischer Jugendlicher porträtiert wird, den eine repressive, inhumane Gesellschaft zerstört, während Stan Dragoti in *Dirty Little Billy* (1972, *Dreckiger kleiner Billy*) die Legende von Billy the Kid mit der sozialen Realität konfrontiert. *The Great Northfield Minnesota Raid* (1972, *Der große Minnesota-Überfall*) von Philip Kaufman beschäftigt sich auf realistische

23. Jeff Bridges (Jake Rumsey) in *In schlechter Gesellschaft* von Robert Benton, 1972.
24. Robert Redford (Norman »Sonny« Steele) in *Der elektrische Reiter* von Sydney Pollack, 1979.
25. Paul Newman (William F. »Buffalo Bill« Cody) in *Buffalo Bill und die Indianer* von Robert Altman, 1975.

23. Jeff Bridges (Jake Rumsey) in *Bad Company* by Robert Benton, 1972.
24. Robert Redford (Norman »Sonny« Steele) in *The Electric Horseman* by Sydney Pollack, 1979.
25. Paul Newman (William F. »Buffalo Bill« Cody) in *Buffalo Bill and the Indians* by Robert Altman, 1975.

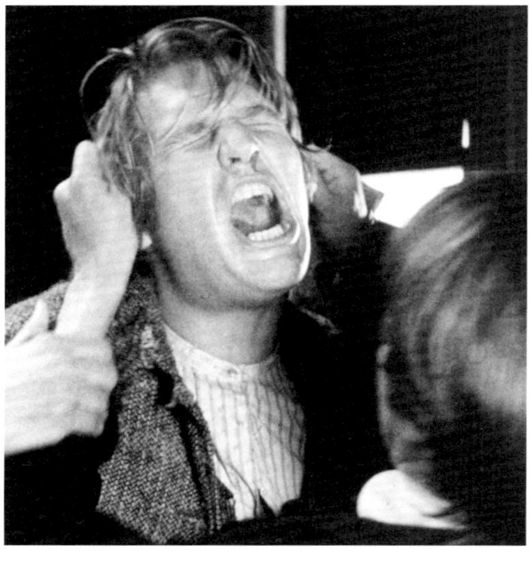

heroes are faced with the dilemma of sacrificing their ideal of freedom to dubious social progress, or being destroyed by it. He confronts these two attitudes in *Pat Garret and Billy the Kid*. Billy the Kid decides to continue his lawless existence, even though he knows that he will pay for this with his life, but Pat Garret buys himself respectability and prosperity by switching to the side of the law, while despising himself for this inwardly. At the centre of *The Wild Bunch* is a wild gang of outlaws who have long since left the moral code of the West behind in the face of the advance of a new age in which decency, fairness and a spirit of camaraderie are anachronistic. After stealing a consignment of guns they flee to Mexico to sell them to the boss of some looting army units even though they know they will be turned against rebellious peasants with whom they sympathize. When the boss of the Mexican gang tortures and kills one of their number they think back to the old Western values and decide spontaneously on a suicidal act of revenge in which they do succeed in killing some of their opponents, but all lose their own lives. As in the case of the fifties anti-heroes, it is precisely the heroes' failure that signals their moral victory over a world that is seen to be corrupt and spoiled, and thus a confirmation of the old ideals.

Examining the validity of the Western moral code also forms a central element in the subgenre of the rodeo film, whose heroes attempt to save traditional values and bring them over to the present day. In Sam Peckinpah's *Junior Bonner* (1972) the eponymous hero rejects a secure job and deliberately opts for an insecure and uncertain life as a rodeo rider, even though his father's example shows him that he will constantly be on the brink of financial ruin. He will ruin his health and will have to forego roots and family life, with a dependent and impoverished life to face in old age. *The Electric Horseman* (1979) by Sydney Pollack deals with a famous rodeo rider who is repelled by the commercialization of the old Western ideals by Western shows, the media and advertising. He steals a valuable racehorse to set it free, and by so doing performs an act of self-liberation. James Bridges's *Urban Cowboy* (1979) conveys a similarly critical attitude to Western clichés as purveyed by the media. This is a love story set in the milieu of Texan oil-workers who spend their leisure time in a gigantic Country and Western saloon. The young hero models his behaviour on the false image of the cowboy as the ideal of the »real« man, thus attracting the admiration of an equally immature girl. The two fall in love and marry, but have to acknowledge that this false idea of masculinity is not compatible with handling everyday life.

A general tendency of the Westerns of this period is that they dismantle the romanticism of the genre. Alongside the new realism in presenting the West this is expressed in the graphically violent scenes that Peckinpah was famous for. He staged the finale of *The Wild Bunch* as a kind of ballet of death in which he bombarded the spectator with images of relentless violence for minutes on end, their sculptural quality further enhanced by slow motion sequences. This showdown is the kind of crazed rampage that he used in other films as well. He also questions the classic ritual of revolver duels and fair fights among men when in *The Wild Bunch* a gangland boss shoots a wounded buddy in cold blood so that he will not be hampered by him in the getaway, or when Pat Garrett kills the unsuspecting Billy the Kid with a shot in the back. In *Jeremiah Johnson*, a ballad about a former soldier who goes out into the wilderness at the time of the Indian conflict to live as a trapper there, Sydney Pollack focuses on the hero's initial awkwardness, and on the privations and rigour of survival in the woods, and confronts these with the legend. Robert Benton also paints a hard, sober picture of life in the West that has nothing in common with the glorifying myths of the classic Western in his directorial début *Bad Company* (1972), the story of a young man from a good middle-class home who runs away from conscription in the American Civil War. He joins a gang of young people who fight their way through the war zone and finally end up in a world beyond any civilization. As well as this, a number of films try to de-romanticize the legend of the classical lawlessness of the West. An early forerunner is Arthur Penn's first cinema film *The Left-Handed Gun* (1958), a variation on the legendary figure of Billy the Kid, in which Billy is portrayed as a misunderstood, rebellious youth destroyed by a repressive, inhuman society, while in *Dirty Little Billy* (1972), Stan Dragoti confronts the legend of Billy the Kid with social reality. *The Great Northfield Minnesota Raid* (1972) by Philip Kaufman addresses a famous bank raid by Jesse James' gang in a realistic way. Robert Altman's *Buffalo Bill and the Indians* (1976) shows an ageing Buffalo Bill who runs a Wild West show in which he cultivates the idealized image of himself propagated by an ingenious writer of dime novels, and finally comes to believe in it himself.

26. Faye Dunaway (Bonnie Parker) und Warren Beatty (Clyde Barrow) in *Bonnie und Clyde* von Arthur Penn, 1967.
27. Paul Newman (Butch Cassidy) und Robert Redford (Sundance Kid) in *Zwei Banditen* von George Roy Hill, 1969.
28. Keith Carradine (Bowie) und Shelley Duvall (Keechie Mobley) in *Diebe wie wir* von Robert Altman, 1974.
29. Sean Connery (John Anderson) und Christopher Walken (The Kid) in *Der Anderson Clan* von Sidney Lumet, 1971.
30. Paul Newman (Henry Gondorff) und Robert Redford (Johnny Hooker) in *Der Clou* von George Roy Hill, 1973.
31. Goldie Hawn (Lou Jean Poplin), William Atherton (Clovis Michael Poplin) und Michael Sacks (Patrolman Maxwell Slide) in *The Sugarland Express* von Steven Spielberg, 1974.

26. Faye Dunaway (Bonnie Parker) and Warren Beatty (Clyde Barrow) in *Bonnie and Clyde* by Arthur Penn, 1967.
27. Paul Newman (Butch Cassidy) and Robert Redford (Sundance Kid) in *Butch Cassidy and the Sundance Kid* by George Roy Hill, 1969.
28. Keith Carradine (Bowie) and Shelley Duvall (Keechie Mobley) in *Thieves Like Us* by Robert Altman, 1974.
29. Sean Connery (John Anderson) and Christopher Walken (The Kid) in *The Anderson Tapes* by Sidney Lumet, 1971.
30. Paul Newman (Henry Gondorff) and Robert Redford (Johnny Hooker) in *The Sting* by George Roy Hill, 1973.
31. Goldie Hawn (Lou Jean Poplin), William Atherton (Clovis Michael Poplin) and Michael Sacks (Patrolman Maxwell Slide) in *The Sugarland Express* by Steven Spielberg, 1974.

Weise mit einem berühmten Bankraub der Bande von Jesse James. Robert Altmans *Buffalo Bill and the Indians* (1976, *Buffalo Bill und die Indianer*) zeigt einen gealterten Buffalo Bill, der in seiner Wildwest-Show das idealisierte Bild kultiviert, das ein findiger Schreiber von Groschenromanen von ihm verbreitet, und schließlich selbst daran glaubt.

Gangsterfilme – romantische Outlaws und soziale Verlierer

Im Gangsterfilm gab es verschiedene Variationen. Die klassische Formel des Genres lebt von der Faszination des Bösen, indem sie den Aufstieg und Fall einer oftmals charismatischen Gangsterfigur beschreibt, durch deren Untergang Gesetz und Ordnung wiederhergestellt und der bestehende Moralkodex bestätigt werden. Dem stellte das neue Hollywood die Stilisierung des Gangsters zum Sozialrebellen nach dem Vorbild von *Bonnie and Clyde* entgegen. Das Handlungsmuster dieser Filme steht in der Tradition des ländlichen Gangsterfilms, der bis dahin hauptsächlich in B-Filmen entwickelt wurde, und ist eng verwandt mit modernen Western, wie *The Electric Horseman* und *Butch Cassidy and The Sundance Kid*. Die Helden repräsentieren das Ideal einer unbegrenzten Freiheit aus der Zeit der offenen Grenzen, das sich in Anbetracht einer feindseligen und korrupten Gesellschaft scheinbar nur noch durch den Verstoß gegen die Gesetze verwirklichen läßt. Sie wehren sich gegen ein ödes Leben in Armut, wie in *Bonnie and Clyde* und *Thunderbolt and Lightfoot* (1974, *Die Letzten beißen die Hunde*) von Michael Cimino, gegen die Zwangsadoption ihres Kindes, wie in *The Sugarland Express* (1974) von Steven Spielberg, oder den Mangel an anderen Lebensperspektiven, wie in Robert Altmans *Thieves Like Us* (1974, *Diebe wie wir*), und werden so zu Sympathieträgern, zumal sie nie mit einem starken Gegenspieler konfrontiert werden. Ein wichtiges Element ist die Legendenbildung um die Helden, durch die sie schon zu Lebzeiten zu Volksidolen werden. Prototypen des sympathischen Gesetzlosen verkörpern Faye Dunaway und Warren Beatty in *Bonnie and Clyde* sowie Robert Redford und Paul Newman in *Butch Cassidy and the Sundance Kid*. In beiden Filmen werden die Abenteuerlust, die Verwegenheit und der Gerechtigkeitssinn der Protagonisten herausgestellt, die gepaart sind mit Selbstironie und Witz. Der zentrale Konflikt liegt zwischen Gesetz und Ordnung und einem anarchistischen Freiheitsideal, das dem der traditionellen Westernhelden entspricht. Während dieses im klassischen Western jedoch der Durchsetzung zivilisatorischer Werte, also der Integration in die Gesellschaft diente und sich ihr unterordnete, richtet es sich hier gegen die soziale Ordnung und wird zum Mittel der gesellschaftlichen Desintegration. Durch ihr Scheitern erlangen die Helden den Status von Märtyrern. Ihre Wertvorstellungen werden ausdrücklich bestätigt, während gleichzeitig der Zu-

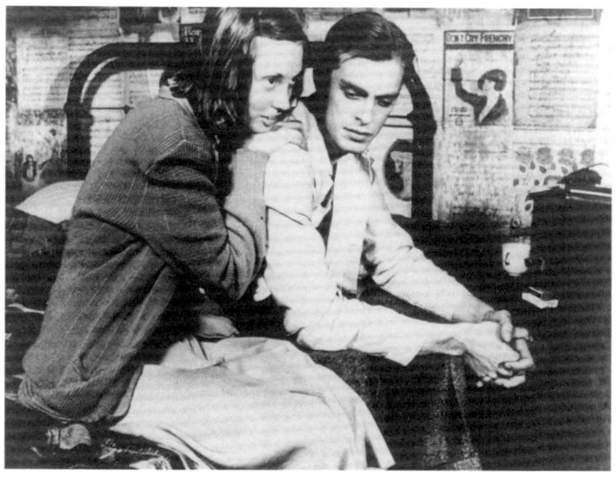

Gangster films – romantic outlaws and social losers

A range of variations appear in the gangster film. The classic formula for the genre draws on the fascination of evil by describing the rise and fall of an often charismatic gangster figure through whose demise law and order are restored and the existing moral code is confirmed. New Hollywood countered this by introducing stylized gangsters as social rebels, following the model of *Bonnie and Clyde*. The plot pattern of these films is in the tradition of the rural gangster film that had been mainly developed in B movies until that time and is closely related to modern Westerns like *The Electric Horseman* and *Butch Cassidy and the Sundance Kid*. The heroes represent the ideal of unlimited freedom from the time of the open frontiers, an ideal that can apparently be realized only by breaking the law, given a hostile and corrupt society. These gangsters resist a dreary life of poverty, as in *Bonnie and Clyde* and *Thunderbolt and Lightfoot* (1974) by Michael Cimino, the compulsory adoption of their child, as in Steven Spielberg's *The Sugarland Express* (1974) or the lack of other views of life as in Robert Altman's *Thieves Like Us* (1974) and thus attract sympathy, especially as they never meet a powerful opponent with opposing views. One important element is the way in which a legend is built up around the heroes, so that they become popular idols even in their own lifetimes. Prototypes of the attractive outlaw are embodied by Faye Dunaway and Warren Beatty in *Bonnie and Clyde* and by Robert Redford and Paul Newman in *Butch Cassidy and the Sundance Kid*. Both these films emphasize the protagonists' adventurousness, audacity and sense of justice, coupled with self-mockery and wit. The central conflict is between law and order and an anarchistic ideal of freedom corresponding with that of the traditional Western hero. In the classic Western this aimed to establish the values of civilization, in other words integration into society, and subordinated itself to that society, but here it is directed against the social order and becomes a device for demolishing society. Failure gives the heroes the status of martyrs. Their values are expressly confirmed, while at the same time the audience can leave the cinema with the comforting feeling that law and order have been re-established.

One variation on the theme of the attractive outlaw uses swindler heroes and other rogues in films like *The Anderson Tapes* (1971) by Sidney Lumet, *The Sting* (1973) by George Roy Hill, *Paper Moon* (1973) by Peter Bogdanovich or *The Brink's Job* (1978) by William Friedkin, in which small-time crooks defeat an apparently all-powerful system through ingenuity and courage. *The Anderson Tapes* combines the elements of the rogues' comedy with a satire on the surveillance and bugging business. A group of break-in specialists are preparing a major coup and are bugged for different reasons by a number of state institutions, but their suspicions are never aroused because of their bureaucratic mentality and lack of coordination. In

schauer das Kino mit dem beruhigenden Gefühl verlassen kann, daß Gesetz und Ordnung wiederhergestellt worden sind.

Eine Variante des sympathischen Outlaws bilden die Helden der Gaunerkomödien aus Filmen, wie *The Anderson Tapes* (1971, *Der Anderson Clan*) von Sidney Lumet, *The Sting* (1973, *Der Clou*) von George Roy Hill, *Paper Moon* (1973) von Peter Bogdanovich oder *The Brink's Job* (1978, *Das große Dings bei Brinks*) von William Friedkin, in denen kleine Ganoven mit Findigkeit und Mut ein scheinbar mächtiges System besiegen. *The Anderson Tapes* verbindet die Elemente der Gaunerkomödie mit einer Persiflage auf die Überwachungs- und Abhörgesellschaft. Eine Gruppe von Einbruchsspezialisten bereitet einen großen Coup vor und wird dabei aus unterschiedlichen Gründen von verschiedenen staatlichen Stellen abgehört, die aufgrund ihrer Bürokratenmentalität und mangelnder Koordination jedoch keinerlei Verdacht schöpfen. In *The Sting* verkörpern Robert Redford und Paul Newman zwei kleine Gauner, welche im Chicago der dreißiger Jahre den Tod eines Freundes rächen, indem sie mit einem ausgeklügelten Betrugsmanöver einen Gangsterboß um eine größere Geldsumme erleichtern. *Paper Moon* spielt ebenfalls in der Depressionszeit und handelt von den Abenteuern eines kleinen Betrügers und dessen unehelicher Tochter, die sich ihm nach dem Tode ihrer Mutter gegen seinen Willen anschließt. Gemeinsam schlagen sie sich notdürftig durch das Leben und wachsen zu einem gut eingespielten Duo zusammen. Die Story von *The Brink's Job* basiert auf einem berühmten Raubüberfall aus dem Jahr 1950, bei dem eine Bande kleiner Ganoven in Boston einen vermeintlich hochgradig gesicherten Geldtransport überfällt und dabei eine Million Dollar erbeutet.

Der Typ des Gangsters als Sozialrebell verfestigte sich schnell zu einem neuen Mythos, dem Terrence Malick mit *Badlands* (1973, *Badlands – Zerschossene Träume*) und Robert Altman mit *Thieves Like Us* Filme entgegenstellten, die zwar auf demselben Grundmuster basieren, jedoch die neuen Konventionen untergruben, indem sie die Helden als soziale Verlierer entlarven, deren Haltung auf einem oberflächlichen, falschen Romantizismus beruht. Sie haben Ähnlichkeit mit den Protagonisten der urbanen Gangsterfilme, den sozialen Underdogs, die sich mit Kleinkriminalität durchschlagen, aus John Schlesingers *Midnight Cowboy,* und Martin Scorseses *Mean Streets* (1973, *Hexenkessel*), oder den zerrissenen, verstörten Charakteren am Rande der Gesellschaft, wie die Bankräuber aus Sydney Lumets *Dog Day Afternoon* (1975, *Hundstage*), welche sich in ihrer Realitätsferne in eine Situation begeben, der sie nicht gewachsen sind. Zu dieser Kategorie gehören auch Travis Bickle aus Martin Scorseses *Taxidriver* (1976), der sich dazu berufen fühlt, eine minderjährige Prostituierte zu retten, und dabei ein Blutbad anrichtet, oder der Held in John Cassavetes' *The Killing of a Chinese Bookie* (1976), ein Nachtklubbesitzer, welcher aufgrund seiner Spielschulden von Gangstern dazu erpreßt wird, einen Mord zu begehen. Diese Helden sind, wie der klassische Gangster, ein Produkt der modernen Großstadt, in deren Schattenseiten sie sich bewegen. Doch während jener die soziale Korruption zu seinem Vorteil auszunutzen versteht, sind sie Opfer der Gesellschaft. Bei diesen Gangsterfilmen handelt es sich mehr als alles andere um Milieu- und Charakterstudien, welche die Zerstörung der Persönlichkeit durch die urbane Massengesellschaft anklagen. Der Grundkonflikt liegt zwischen dem individuellen Kampf um das materielle und ideelle Überleben und einer sozialen Ordnung, die dieses nicht zuläßt, ein Konflikt, der als unlösbar dargestellt wird. Daher erscheint es belanglos, ob die Helden zum Schluß an einem konkreten Problem scheitern oder es bewältigen, denn sie sind soziale Verlierer und werden es bleiben.

Die einzigen Gangsterfilme von New Hollywood, die sich der klassischen Handlungsformel näherten, waren *The Godfather* (1972) und *The Godfather: Part II* (1974) von Francis Ford Coppola. Entsprechend der klassischen Vorbilder zeigt *The Godfather I*, wie Vito Corleone in den zwanziger und dreißiger Jahren die traditionellen amerikanischen Tugenden, also Durchsetzungsvermögen, Initiative, Loyalität, Einfallsreichtum und Familiensinn, für den Aufbau eines kriminellen Imperiums nutzt. In *The Godfather II* erbt der Sohn Michael mit der Rolle seines Vaters den Traum vom Vorstoß in die Höhen der politischen Macht und in ein respektables Leben. Seine Aktivitäten konzentriert er auf legale und halblegale Geschäftszweige und verleiht sich das Image eines seriösen Geschäftsmannes. Wie in früheren Zeiten stützt sich sein Einfluß jedoch auf die Bestechung von korrupten Politikern und Polizisten. Damit repräsentiert er den typischen Vertreter des Establishments, wie das neue Hollywood ihn sah, einen rücksichtslosen Machtmenschen, der nicht davor zurückschreckt, zu illegalen Mitteln und Gewalt zu greifen, wenn seine Interessen es verlangen. Anders als in den klassischen Gangsterfilmen steht am Ende die Ausweitung der Macht des Paten und dessen Anerkennung als achtbarer Geschäftsmann, die einhergeht mit dem Zerfall der Familie, wodurch die soziale Ordnung und deren Grundwerte ernsthaft in Frage gestellt werden.

32. Ryan O'Neal (Moses Pray) und Tatum O'Neal (Addie Loggins) in *Paper Moon* von Peter Bogdanovich, 1973.
33. Sissy Spacek (Holly Sargis) und Martin Sheen (Kit Carruthers) in *Badlands – Zerschossene Träume* von Terrence Malick, 1973.
34. Dustin Hoffman (Rico »Ratso« Rizzo) und Jon Voight (Joe Buck) in *Asphalt-Cowboy* von John Schlesinger, 1969.
35. Ben Gazzara (Cosmo Vitelli) in *Der Tod eines chinesischen Buchmachers* von John Cassavetes, 1976.
36. Marlon Brando (Don Vito Corleone) und Robert Duvall (Tom Hagen) in *Der Pate* von Francis Ford Coppola, 1972.
37. Al Pacino (Michael Corleone) und John Cazale (Fredo Corleone) in *Der Pate: Teil II* von Francis Ford Coppola, 1974.

32. Ryan O'Neal (Moses Pray) and Tatum O'Neal (Addie Loggins) in *Paper Moon* by Peter Bogdanovich, 1973.
33. Sissy Spacek (Holly Sargis) and Martin Sheen (Kit Carruthers) in *Badlands* by Terrence Malick, 1973.
34. Dustin Hoffman (Rico »Ratso« Rizzo) and Jon Voight (Joe Buck) in *Midnight Cowboy* by John Schlesinger, 1969.
35. Ben Gazzara (Cosmo Vitelli) in *The Killing of a Chinese Bookie* by John Cassavetes, 1976.
36. Marlon Brando (Don Vito Corleone) und Robert Duvall (Tom Hagen) in *The Godfather* by Francis Ford Coppola, 1972.
37. Al Pacino (Michael Corleone) and John Cazale (Fredo Corleone) in *The Godfather: Part II* by Francis Ford Coppola, 1974.

The Sting, Robert Redford and Paul Newman play two small-time crooks who avenge the death of a friend in thirties Chicago by relieving a gangster boss of a large sum of money with an ingenious piece of deception. *Paper Moon* is also set in the depression and deals with the adventure of a small-time swindler and his illegitimate daughter who attaches herself to him against his will after the death of her mother. They struggle through a makeshift life together, and grow to be a well-established duo. The story of *The Brink's Job* is based on a famous robbery in 1950, in which a gang of small-time crooks in Boston ambushed a supposedly heavily protected consignment of money and got away with a million dollars.

The type of the gangster as a social rebel rapidly established itself as a new myth. This was countered by Terrence Malick with *Badlands* (1973) and Robert Altman with *Thieves Like Us* (1974), films that are based on the same basic pattern but undermined the new conventions by unmasking the heroes as social losers whose attitude derives from a superficial, false romanticism. They are similar to the protagonists of urban gangster films, the social underdogs who make their way through life as petty criminals in films like John Schlesinger's *Midnight Cowboy* (1969) and Martin Scorsese's *Mean Streets* (1973), or the broken, distraught characters on the fringes of society like the bank robbers from Sidney Lumet's *Dog Day Afternoon* (1975), who are so far removed from reality that they get entangled in a situation that they are unable to cope with. Travis Bickle from Martin Scorsese's *Taxi Driver* (1976) is another character of this type; he feels it incumbent on him to rescue a child prostitute, thus causing a blood-bath, or the hero of John Cassavetes' *The Killing of a Chinese Bookie* (1976), a night-club owner who is blackmailed by gangsters into committing a murder because of his gambling debts. These heroes, like the classic gangsters, are products of the modern cities on whose shady sides they eke out their existence. But while the classic gangster knows how to exploit social corruption to his own advantage, they are the victims of society. These gangster films are more than anything else milieu and character studies accusing urban mass society of destroying personalities. The basic conflict is about the individual fight for material and intellectual survival and a social order that does not permit this, a conflict that is presented as insoluble. For this reason it does not seem important whether the heroes are destroyed by the actual problem or come to terms with it: they are social losers, and will remain so.

The only New Hollywood gangster films that came close to the classic action formula were *The Godfather* (1972) and *The Godfather: Part II* (1974) by Francis Ford Coppola. Like its classic predecessors, *The Godfather I* shows how Vito Corleone uses the traditional American virtues in the twenties and thirties, in other words ability to assert oneself, initiative, loyalty, a wealth of ideas and a sense of family, to build up a criminal empire. In *The Godfather II*, Corleone's son

38. Peter Fonda (Wyatt »Captain America« Earp) und Dennis Hopper (Billy) in *Easy Rider* von Dennis Hopper, 1969.
39. Jack Nicholson (Billy Budduskey), Otis Young (Mulhall) und Randy Quaid (Seaman Meadows) in *Das letzte Kommando* von Hal Ashby, 1973.
40. Art Carney (Harry) in *Harry und Tonto* von Paul Mazursky, 1974.
41. Shirley Knight (Natalie Ravenna) in *Liebe niemals einen Fremden* von Francis Ford Coppola, 1969.

38. Peter Fonda (Wyatt »Captain America« Earp) and Dennis Hopper (Billy) in *Easy Rider* by Dennis Hopper, 1969.
39. Jack Nicholson (Billy Budduskey), Otis Young (Mulhall) and Randy Quaid (Seaman Meadows) in *The Last Detail* by Hal Ashby, 1973.
40. Art Carney (Harry) in *Harry and Tonto* by Paul Mazursky, 1974.
41. Shirley Knight (Natalie Ravenna) in *Rain People* by Francis Ford Coppola, 1969.

Road-Movies – Ausbruch, Flucht und Suche

Mit dem Erfolg von *Easy Rider* und *Bonnie and Clyde* etablierten sich die Road-Movies. Bis Mitte der siebziger Jahre folgte ihnen eine ganze Welle von Filmen, die deren Merkmale variierten und die Konventionen eines neuen Genres bestimmten. Dabei fließen in der Regel Elemente anderer Genres ein, wie die des Western, des Gangsterfilms, des Dramas oder der Komödie, welche sich allerdings einem durchgängigen, charakteristischen Muster unterordnen. Das Grundmerkmal des Road-Movies ist das Motiv der Reise, das inhaltlich mit der Entwurzelung der Helden verbunden ist. Die Stationen und episodenhaften Begegnungen auf dieser Reise spiegeln die Befindlichkeiten des »American Way of Life« wider und dienen einer kritischen Auseinandersetzung mit dem Lebensstil, den Verhaltensweisen und Wertvorstellungen der Amerikaner. Road-Movies zeigen Seiten der amerikanischen Gesellschaft, die in dem Bild von Amerika, das klassische Hollywoodfilme verbreiten, selten auftauchen. Die häufigsten Schauplätze sind verlassene Landstraßen, schäbige Schnellrestaurants und Motels oder verschlafene Kleinstädte des Westens, gelegentlich aber auch Großstädte, wie in *The Last Detail* (1973, *Das letzte Kommando*) von Hal Ashby, wo zwei ältere, dienstmüde Soldaten beschließen, einem jungen, schüchternen Matrosen, den sie zum Antritt einer mehrjährigen Haftstrafe in ein Militärgefängnis überführen sollen, einige Dinge über das Leben beizubringen, und mit ihm unterwegs durch Bars, Coffeeshops und billige Hotels ziehen, in eine Party in East Village geraten, ihrem Schützling in einem Bordell sein erstes sexuelles Erlebnis verschaffen und schließlich an einem Lagerfeuer in einem verschneiten Park landen, bevor sie ihn im Gefängnis abliefern.

Die Reise ist sowohl Ausbruch und Flucht als auch die Suche nach einer anderen Art zu leben, welche in *Easy Rider* in die Metapher der Suche nach Amerika gekleidet ist. In *Rain People* (1969, *Liebe niemals einen Fremden*) von Francis Ford Coppola und *Alice Doesn't Live Here Anymore* (1974, *Alice lebt hier nicht mehr*) von Martin Scorsese geht es um Frauen, die aufbrechen, um eine Alternative zu ihrem Dasein als Ehefrau und Mutter zu finden, angesichts ihrer Erlebnisse jedoch zu dem Schluß kommen, daß Ehe und Familie trotz aller Schwächen nach wie vor die beste Option darstellen. Paul Mazursky schildert in *Harry and Tonto* (1974) die Erlebnisse eines pensionierten Lehrers, der nach dem Tod seiner Frau und dem Verlust seiner Wohnung mit seiner Katze eine Reise von New York über Chicago und Las Vegas nach Kalifornien unternimmt, seine erwachsenen Kinder und alte Freunde besucht, neue Bekanntschaften schließt und dabei seinen Lebensmut wiederfindet.

In diesen Filmen werden die Möglichkeiten und Beschränkungen von Durchschnittsmenschen innerhalb der bestehenden Verhältnisse ausgelotet, mit denen sich die Protagonisten irgendwie arrangieren. Die typischen Helden des Road-Movies sind allerdings Menschen, denen

Michael inherits the dream of thrusting up into the heights of political power and into a respectable life, along with his father's role. He focuses his activities on legal and semi-legal business areas and acquires the image of a serious businessman. But as in earlier days his influence is built on bribing corrupt politicians and policemen. Thus he is a typical establishment figure as New Hollywood saw them, a ruthless power figure who is not afraid to resort to illegal methods and violence if his interests require it. Differently from classic gangster films, this one ends with the godfather extending his power and being acknowledged as a respectable businessman; this goes hand in hand with the breakdown of the family, which seriously questions the social order and its fundamental values.

Road movies – escape, flight and search

Easy Rider and *Bonnie and Clyde* established the success of road movies. A whole flood of films followed them until the mid seventies, varying their features and defining the conventions of a new genre. Here elements of other genres become involved as a rule, for example Westerns, gangster films, dramas or comedies, though they are all subject to a universal, characteristic pattern. The essential characteristic of the road movie is the journey, which is linked in terms of content with the uprooting of the hero, standing for both his lack of a place to live and of an emotional and intellectual home. The stations and episodic encounters on this journey reflect the »American Way of Life«, and permit critical analysis of American life-styles, behaviour and values. Road movies show aspects of American society that are seldom part of the image of America disseminated by classical Hollywood movies. The most frequent locations are lonely country roads, shabby fast-food restaurants and motels or sleepy western towns, though cities do sometimes occur, as in *The Last Detail* (1973) by Hal Ashby, in which two old friends, service-weary soldiers, decide to teach a shy young sailor, whom they are supposed to be taking to a military prison to serve a lengthy sentence, a thing or two about life. They take him to numerous bars, coffee-shops and cheap hotels en route, find themselves at a party in East Village, fix up their protégé's first sexual experience in a brothel and finally end up at a camp-fire in a snowy park before they deliver him to prison.

The journey is both an escape and a flight, and also a search for another way of life, which in *Easy Rider* is also dressed up as a metaphor of a search for America. In *Rain People* (1969) by Francis Ford Coppola and *Alice Doesn't Live Here Anymore* (1974) by Martin Scorsese the theme is women who escape to find an alternative to their lives as wives and mothers, but in the light of their experiences come to the conclusion that marriage and family are still the best option despite all their drawbacks. In *Harry and Tonto* (1974), Paul Mazursky presents the experiences of a retired teacher who, after the death of his wife and the loss of his home, sets off on a journey with his cat to California from New York via Chicago and Las Vegas, visits his grown-up children and old friends, makes new acquaintances and finds the courage to go on living.

These films explore the possibilities and limitations applicable to ordinary people in existing conditions and how they manage to come to terms with them in some way. In fact the typical heroes of road movies are people who seem to find life within normal society impossible, romantic outlaws on the run, following the pattern of *Bonnie and Clyde*, *The Sugarland Express* and *Thunderbolt and Lightfoot*, or voluntary drop-outs as in *Easy Rider*, Arthur Penn's hippie ballad *Alice's Restaurant* (1969) or *Two-Lane Blacktop* (1971) by Monte Hellman. Their attitude derives from frustration with a monotonous, obsessive world that no longer admits individuality, creativity, adventures, dreams and ideals, muzzles instinct, emotion and spontaneity, and they rebel against it by placing themselves outside society. The external movement of the journey is equated with the feeling of freedom. Outsider heroes consequently refuse to settle down, as in *Easy Rider*, where the protagonists refuse an offer to become part of a hippie commune. Here they frequently combine radical opportunism with an idealistic sense of community. The so-called buddy movies are a typical expression of this. They are centred around a male duo and are focused emotionally on a male friendship, usually idealized. As well as *Easy Rider* and *Thunderbolt and Lightfoot*, these include Jerry Schatzberg's *Scarecrow* (1973), a film about a young sailor and an ex-convict, each of whom has arrived at a low point in his life. They meet on a country road, each hoping to realize a dream. They become friends and learn how to cope with life's disappointments from each other.

The heroes react to the point of view of marriage, family and an ordered life within the hated establishment by escaping, like Robert Dupea, the main character in Bob Rafelson's *Five Easy*

ein Leben innerhalb der etablierten Gesellschaft unmöglich erscheint, romantische Outlaws auf der Flucht nach dem Muster von *Bonnie and Clyde*, *The Sugarland Express* und *Thunderbolt and Lightfoot* oder freiwillige Aussteiger, wie in *Easy Rider*, Arthur Penns Hippieballade *Alice's Restaurant* (1969) oder *Two-Lane Blacktop* (1971) von Monte Hellman. Ihre Haltung ist geprägt von Frustration, bewirkt durch eine monotone, zwanghafte Welt, die keine Individualität, Kreativität, Abenteuer, Träume und Ideale mehr zuläßt und Instinkt, Gefühl und Spontaneität knebelt und gegen die sie rebellieren, indem sie sich außerhalb der Gesellschaft stellen. Die äußere Bewegung der Reise wird gleichgesetzt mit dem Gefühl der Freiheit. Entsprechend weigern sich die Außenseiterhelden, seßhaft zu werden, wie in *Easy Rider*, wo die Protagonisten das Angebot, sich einer Hippie-Kommune anzuschließen, ablehnen. Dabei verbinden sie häufig einen radikalen Individualismus mit einem idealistischen Gemeinschaftssinn. Einen typischen Ausdruck davon bilden die sogenannten Buddy-Filme, in denen ein männliches Duo im Mittelpunkt steht und eine in der Regel idealisierte Männerfreundschaft das emotionale Zentrum bildet. Darunter fallen neben *Easy Rider* und *Thunderbolt and Lightfoot* unter anderem *Scarecrow* (1973, *Asphalt-Blüten*) von Jerry Schatzberg, ein Film, der von einem jungen Seemann und einem Exhäftling handelt, die beide an einem Tiefpunkt ihres Lebens angekommen sind. Sie treffen sich auf der Landstraße, beide unterwegs mit der Hoffnung, einen Traum zu verwirklichen, freunden sich an und lernen voneinander, die Enttäuschungen des Lebens zu bewältigen.

Auf die Perspektive von Ehe, Familie und einem geregelten Leben innerhalb des verhaßten Establishment reagieren die Helden mit Flucht wie Robert Dupea, der Protagonist aus Bob Rafelsons *Five Easy Pieces* (1971, *Ein Mann sucht sich selbst*), der nach jahrelangem Herumziehen als Arbeiter auf einem Ölfeld in Texas landet, jedoch weder in dem urwüchsigen Arbeitermilieu noch in der kultivierten Eintönigkeit der angesehenen Musikerfamilie, der er entstammt, eine erstrebenswerte Lebensperspektive entdecken kann. Am Ende läßt er alles zurück, was ihn mit seinem bisherigen Leben verbindet, und steigt in einen Lastwagen, der ihn auf eine Reise ins Ungewisse mitnehmen wird. *Two-Lane Blacktop* geht einen Schritt weiter. Hier werden Charaktere ohne Namen, ohne Vergangenheit und ohne Zukunft, also ohne Identität gezeigt: zwei junge Männer, genannt der Fahrer und der Mechaniker, die mit einem hochgezüchteten Chevrolet durch den Südwesten der USA fahren und ihr Geld mit Autorennen auf einsamen Landstraßen verdienen. Die Menschen, denen sie unterwegs begegnen, bleiben ebenso anonym wie sie selbst. Schließlich treffen sie auf GTO, so genannt nach seinem Wagen, der ähnlich wie sie auf dem Weg nach Nirgendwo ist, und verabreden ein Rennen von New Mexico zur Ostküste der USA. Doch im Mittelpunkt steht nicht die Spannung des privaten Rennens – es scheint unwichtig, wer verliert oder gewinnt, und schließlich wird keiner von ihnen an die Ostküste fahren und den Wettpreis abholen –, sondern die Leere und Bedeutungslosigkeit des Daseins, das Aufgeben der Suche nach neuen Idealen, das Fehlen jeglicher Illusion. Sie befinden sich in ständiger Bewegung ohne Ziel. Der Weg ist ihr Ziel, denn die Helden all dieser Filme wissen von vornherein, das ihre Suche vergeblich ist, weil das, was sie suchen, nicht existiert, und das verleiht ihnen einen grundsätzlichen Zug von Melancholie.

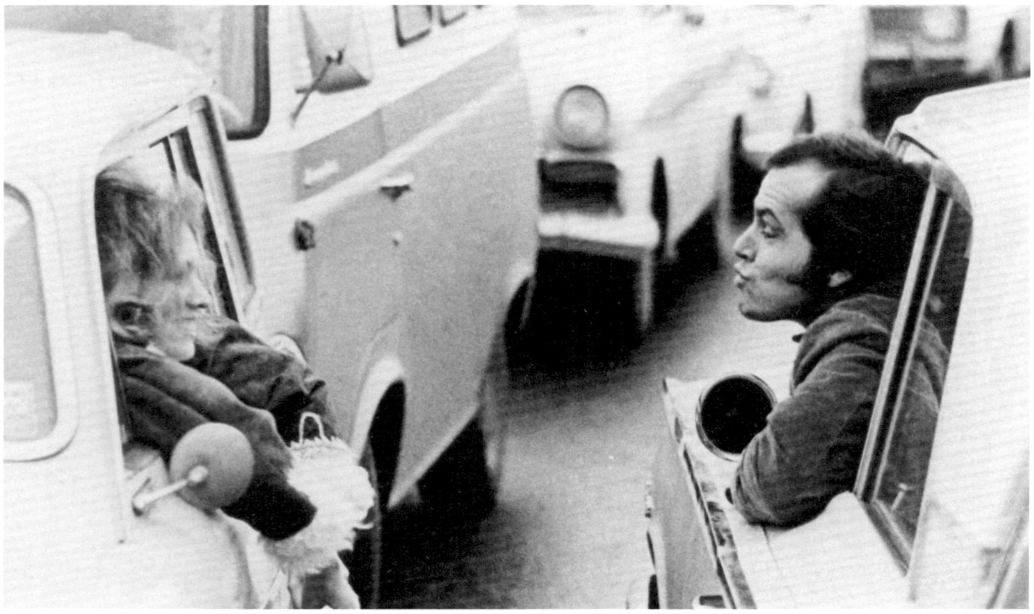

42. Jack Nicholson (Robert Eroica Dupea) in *Ein Mann sucht sich selbst* von Bob Rafelson, 1971.
43. *Fluchtpunkt San Franzisko* von Richard C. Sarafian, 1971.
44. Gene Hackman (Max) und Al Pacino (Lion) in *Asphalt-Blüten* von Jerry Schatzberg, 1973.
45. Arlo Guthrie (Arlo) in *Alice's Restaurant* von Arthur Penn, 1969.
46. Mark Frechette (Mark) in *Zabriskie Point* von Michelangelo Antonioni, 1970.

42. Jack Nicholson (Robert Eroica Dupea) in *Five Easy Pieces* by Bob Rafelson, 1971.
43. *Vanishing Point* by Richard C. Sarafian, 1971.
44. Gene Hackman (Max) and Al Pacino (Lion) in *Scarecrow* by Jerry Schatzberg, 1973.
45. Arlo Guthrie (Arlo) in *Alice's Restaurant* by Arthur Penn, 1969.
46. Mark Frechette (Mark) in *Zabriskie Point* by Michelangelo Antonioni, 1970.

Pieces (1971) who ends up as a worker in a Texas oilfield after wandering around for years, but is unable to find a view of life worth striving for either in the earthy workers' milieu or in the cultivated monotony of the family of musicians from which he comes. Finally he leaves everything connecting him with his previous life behind and gets into a lorry that will take him on a journey into the unknown. *Two-Lane Blacktop* takes things a step further. Here characters are shown without names, without a past and without a future, in other words without an identity: two young men, called the driver and the mechanic, who are driving a thoroughbred Chevrolet through the south-west USA and earning their living by racing cars on lonely country roads. The people they meet on the way remain as anonymous as they are. Finally they meet GTO, called this because of his car, who like them is on the way to nowhere, and agree on a race from Mexico to the east coast of the USA. But the movie is not centred on the tensions of the private race – it doesn't seem to matter who wins or loses, and ultimately neither of them will drive to the east coast and collect the prize – but on the emptiness and loneliness of existence, the meaningless search for new ideals, the lack of any illusions. They find themselves constantly on the move, without any aim. The journey is their destination: the heroes of all these films know from the outset that their search is in vain, because what they are looking for does not exist, and this gives them a fundamental trait of melancholy.

Frequently, as in *Easy Rider*, the journey ends in death. In *Zabriskie Point* (1970), by Michelangelo Antonioni, a young man comes under suspicion of having shot a policeman at a demonstration and escapes to the desert in a light plane. When he decides to come back, he is shot by the police on the airfield. The hero of *Vanishing Point* (1971) by Richard C. Sarafian, triggers hot pursuit from the police on a private motor race from Denver to San Francisco, but he is able to outwit them again and again with the assistance of a coloured disc-jockey who declares him to be the »last American hero«. But when there is no longer any means of escape, he deliberately drives to his death. Sam Pekinpah's *Convoy* (1978) works to a similar pattern. Here a group of truckers get themselves involved with the police in a wild chase, and again the hero brings about his own death by a suicidal effort to escape, though Peckinpah defies the new conventions by adding on a happy ending. The central conflict in all these films is between the individual's aspiration towards freedom and self-determination and the social compulsions working against this. The solution is at best a compromise, and at worst the character's downfall, but in any case leads to the insight that modern society sets tight limits on the free development of personalities.

Häufig steht, wie in *Easy Rider*, am Ende der Reise der Tod. In *Zabriskie Point* (1970) von Michelangelo Antonioni gerät ein junger Mann in den Verdacht, bei einer Demonstration einen Polizisten erschossen zu haben. Mit einem Kleinflugzeug flieht er in die Wüste. Als er sich entschließt zurückzukehren, wird er auf dem Flugfeld von der Polizei erschossen. Der Held aus *Vanishing Point* (1971, *Fluchtpunkt San Franzisko*) von Richard C. Sarafian löst bei einem privaten Autorennen von Denver nach San Franzisko eine wilde Verfolgungsjagd mit der Polizei aus, kann sie jedoch mit Hilfe eines farbigen Discjockeys, der ihn zum »letzten Helden Amerikas« erklärt, immer wieder überlisten. Als es für ihn kein Entkommen mehr gibt, fährt er bewußt in den Tod. Nach ähnlichem Muster funktioniert Sam Peckinpahs *Convoy* (1978). Hier liefert sich eine Gruppe von Truckern eine wilde Verfolgungsjagd mit der Polizei, an deren Ende der Held ebenfalls bei einem selbstmörderischen Fluchtversuch seinen Tod provoziert, wobei Peckinpah allerdings den neuen Konventionen trotzt, indem er ein Happy-End anhängt. Der zentrale Konflikt all dieser Filme entsteht aus dem Streben des Individuums nach Freiheit und Selbstbestimmung und den sozialen Zwängen, die dem entgegenstehen. Die Lösung ist bestenfalls ein Kompromiß, schlimmstenfalls der Untergang, führt jedoch in jedem Fall zu der Erkenntnis, daß der freien Entfaltung der Persönlichkeit in der modernen Gesellschaft enge Grenzen gesetzt sind.

47. Jack Nicholson (Jake Gittes) und Faye Dunaway (Evelyn Cross Mulwray) in *Chinatown* von Roman Polanski, 1974.
48. Gene Hackman (Harry Caul) in *Der Dialog* von Francis Ford Coppola, 1974.
49. Gene Hackman (Harry Moseby), Melanie Griffith (Delly Grastner) und Jennifer Warren (Paula) in *Heiße Spur* von Arthur Penn, 1975.

47. Jack Nicholson (Jake Gittes) and Faye Dunaway (Evelyn Cross Mulwray) in *Chinatown* by Roman Polanski, 1974.
48. Gene Hackman (Harry Caul) in *The Conversation* by Francis Ford Coppola, 1974.
49. Gene Hackman (Harry Moseby), Melanie Griffith (Delly Grastner) and Jennifer Warren (Paula) in *Night Moves* by Arthur Penn, 1975.

Detektivfilme – Einblick in die dunklen Seiten der Gesellschaft

Der klassische Detektivfilm war die historische und thematische Erweiterung und Ergänzung des Gangsterfilms.Typischer Held dieser Filme ist der Privatdetektiv. Er arbeitet für Geld und gerät durch seine Fälle in ein mysteriöses und bedrohliches Umfeld. Im Gegensatz zum klassischen Gangster bewegt er sich sowohl in der Unterschicht als auch in der Oberschicht, deren Vertreter sich in der Regel als korrupter erweisen als die typischen Kriminellen. Seine Einsicht in die dunklen Seiten des urbanen Amerika hat ihn zu einem Zyniker gemacht, der nach einem eigenen Wertesystem handelt, weil er dem Gesetz mißtraut. Sein Verhalten ist geprägt von Frustration und Resignation. Er legt die kulturellen Konflikte seines Milieus offen, löst die unmittelbaren, ohne jedoch das Milieu zu ändern. Eine häufig auftauchende Figur ist die Femme fatale des Genres, eine mysteriöse, sinnliche, verführerische, aber auch berechnende Frau, die beide Seiten betrügt. Die besonderen Eigenschaften des Helden machen ihn zu einem Mann zwischen den Fronten, der weder auf der Seite der sozialen Ordnung noch auf der der Kriminellen steht. Das Genre eignete sich somit von jeher dazu, einen kritischen Blick hinter die Kulissen der Gesellschaft zu werfen, was dem gesellschaftskritischen Ansatz des neuen Hollywood entgegenkam und zu einer Vorliebe für diese Filmgattung führte, die aktualisiert und an die Weltsicht der siebziger Jahre angepaßt wurde.

Wie ihre klassischen Vorbilder tauchen die Kriminalfilme von New Hollywood in eine Welt aus Kriminalität und Verderbtheit ein: Die Helden kämpfen als Einzelgänger gegen ein zunächst undurchdringliches Dickicht aus Korruption, schaffen es aber dennoch irgendwie, die Wahrheit ans Licht zu bringen und in den meisten Fällen auch zu überleben. Ein Unterschied besteht darin, daß sie häufig einem übermächtigen Gegner gegenüberstehen, dem sie hoffnungslos unterlegen sind und der letztlich den Sieg davonträgt, wie in *Chinatown* (1974) von Roman Polanski, *The Conversation* (1974, *Der Dialog*) von Francis Ford Coppola oder *Night Moves* (1975, *Heiße Spur*) von Arthur Penn, Filme, die dem klassischen Muster folgen und es zu einem Kommentar über die Desintegration der amerikanischen Gesellschaft benutzen. Die Helden entsprechen dem Typ des zynischen, von der Welt enttäuschten Detektivs, der über einen scheinbaren Routineauftrag auf ein Verbrechen stößt, dem er machtlos gegenübersteht. In *Chinatown* gerät der Privatdetektiv Jack Gittes durch Nachforschungen über die angebliche Untreue eines Ehemanns in ein Netz von Manipulationen, Inzucht, Verkommenheit und Korruption, das ihm keine Chance läßt. Am Ende sieht er hilflos mit an, wie seine Geliebte ermordet wird und ihre Tochter dem verbrecherischen, perversen Großvater überlassen bleibt. *The Conversation* konzentriert den Blick auf die existentielle Unsicherheit und Entfremdung des Helden, eines Abhörspezialisten, den das Wissen um die Möglichkeit, in die Privatsphäre eines jeden Menschen einzudringen, zu einem kauzigen Einzelgänger gemacht hat, dessen Mißtrauen an Paranoia grenzt. Weil er ein heimlich mitgeschnittenes Gespräch falsch interpretiert, kann unter seinen Augen ein Mord geschehen, und er wird selbst Opfer einer elektronischen Überwachung. Der Detektiv aus *Night Moves* bewegt sich in einer Welt, in der ihm alles zu entgleiten droht. Er erhält den Auftrag, eine junge Ausreißerin nach Hause zurückzubringen, und sieht sich von Verrat umgeben: Seine Auftraggeberin benutzt ihn, sein Liebesabenteuer mit einer attraktiven Frau entpuppt sich

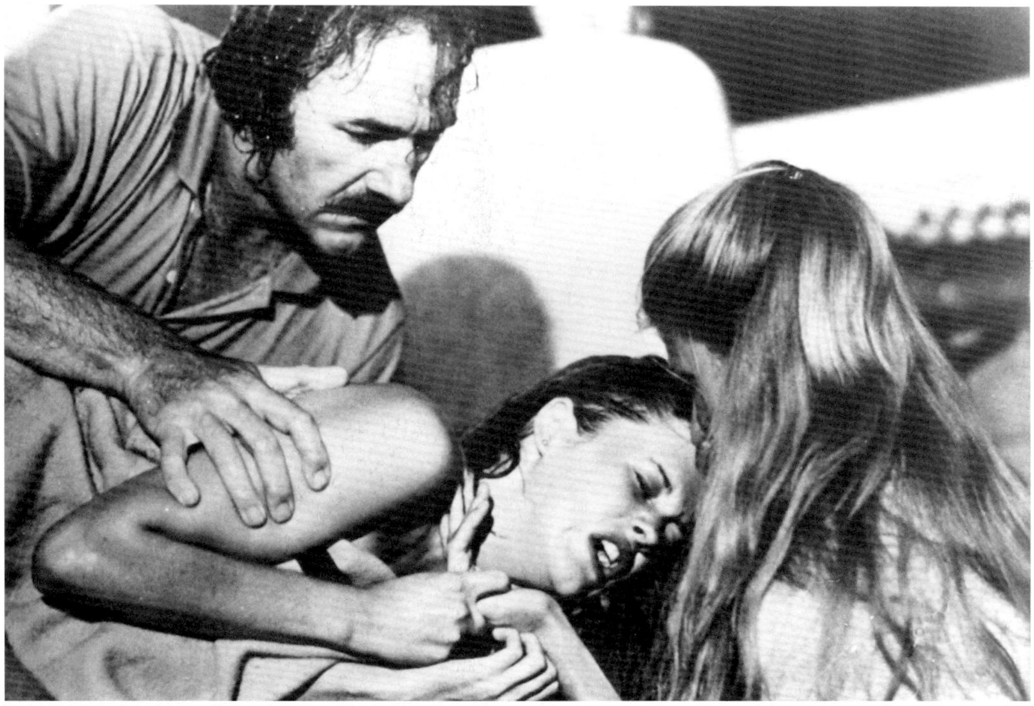

Detective films – a view of the dark side of society

The classic detective film was the historic and thematic extension of and complement to the gangster movie. The typical hero of these films is the private detective. He works for money, and his cases take him into a mysterious and threatening environment. Unlike the classical gangster, he moves among both the lower and upper classes, with the latter's representatives usually turning out to be more corrupt than the typical criminal. His insights into the darker side of urban America have made him into a cynic who works to his own system of values because he mistrusts the law. His attitude derives from frustration and resignation. He reveals the culture conflicts of his milieu and solves the immediate ones without changing that milieu. A character who frequently appears is the femme fatale of the genre, a mysterious, sensual, seductive but also calculating woman who betrays both sides. The hero's special qualities make him a man between two fronts who is neither on the side of social order nor that of the criminal. This meant that the genre was always suitable for casting a critical look behind the scenes of society. This fitted in with New Hollywood's socio-critical approach and led to a preference for this kind of film, which was brought up to date and adapted to the world view of the seventies.

Like the classical models, the New Hollywood thriller plunge into a world of criminality and corruption: the heroes are loners fighting against what at first seems to be an impenetrable thicket of depravity, but somehow manage to bring the truth to light, and also to survive in most cases. One difference lies in the fact that they are often facing an all-powerful opponent to whom they are hopelessly inferior and who ultimately wins, as in *Chinatown* (1974) by Roman Polanski, *The Conversation* (1974) by Francis Ford Coppola or *Night Moves* (1975) by Arthur Penn. These are all films following the classical pattern, using it to comment on the disintegration of American society. The heroes are all of the cynical detective type, disenchanted with the world, and brought up against a crime that he is powerless to resist by a routine commission. In *Chinatown*, private detective Jack Gittes's investigations into a husband's alleged infidelity entangle him in a net of manipulation, inbreeding and corruption that defeat him completely. Ultimately he watches helplessly as his girlfriend is murdered and her daughter handed over to the criminal and perverse grandfather. *The Conversation* concentrates on the hero's existential uncertainty and alienation. He is a bugging specialist whose awareness that it is possible to penetrate the private life of any individual has made him into a quirky loner whose suspiciousness borders on paranoia. Because he misinterprets a conversation that he has recorded, he is forced to witness a murder and he is subjected to electronic surveillance himself. The detective in *Night Moves* operates in a world in which everything seems to be slipping away from him. He is commissioned to bring a young runaway girl home, and sees himself surrounded by treachery: his client uses him, his affair with an attractive woman turns out to be a ploy, the girl

50. Dustin Hoffman (Carl Bernstein, Reporter der *Washington Post*) und Robert Redford (Bob Woodward, Reporter der *Washington Post*) in *Die Unbestechlichen* von Alan J. Pakula, 1976.
51. Warren Beatty (Joseph Frady) in *Zeuge einer Verschwörung* von Alan J. Pakula, 1974.
52. Jane Fonda (Kimberly Wells) und Michael Douglas (Richard Adams) in *Das China-Syndrom* von James Bridges, 1979.
53. Robert Redford (Joe Turner), Faye Dunaway (Kathy Hale) und Cliff Robertson (Higgins) in *Die drei Tage des Condors* von Sydney Pollack, 1975.

50. Dustin Hoffman (Carl Bernstein, reporter of the *Washington Post*) and Robert Redford (Bob Woodward, reporter of the *Washington Post*) in *All the President's Men* by Alan J. Pakula, 1976.
51. Warren Beatty (Joseph Frady) in *The Parallax View* by Alan J. Pakula, 1974.
52. Jane Fonda (Kimberly Wells) and Michael Douglas (Richard Adams) in *The China Syndrome* by James Bridges, 1979.
53. Robert Redford (Joe Turner), Faye Dunaway (Kathy Hale) and Cliff Robertson (Higgins) in *The Three Days of the Condor* by Sydney Pollack, 1975.

als Täuschungsmanöver, das Mädchen, das er zurückbringt, wird kurz darauf ermordet, seine Frau verläßt ihn, und sein Freund erweist sich als Mörder. Wenn er am Schluß verletzt und hilflos in einem Boot auf dem Meer treibt, wird dies zu einer Metapher für die Unsicherheit der Existenz.

Die wichtigste Veränderung des Genres liegt in den verschiedenen Modifikationen des Helden und deren Gegenspielern. Eine Variante ist der Held wider Willen, der sich unversehens in kriminelle Machenschaften verwickelt sieht und ihnen gegenüber reagieren muß. Dabei handelt es sich gelegentlich um Journalisten, wie in *The Parallax View* (1974, *Zeuge einer Verschwörung*) und *All the President's Men* (1976, *Die Unbestechlichen*) von Alan J. Pakula oder *The China Syndrome* (1979) von James Bridges, manchmal auch um harmlose Intellektuelle oder Wissenschaftler, wie in *The Day of the Dolphin* (1973, *Der Tag des Delphins*) von Mike Nichols, *Three Days of the Condor* (1975, *Die drei Tage des Condors*) von Sydney Pollack und *Marathon Man* (1976) von John Schlesinger. Ihre Weltsicht ist grundlegend anders als die des klassischen Detektivs. In der Regel sind sie sozial integrierte Bürger ohne ausgeprägtes kritisches Bewußtsein, mehr Opfer der Umstände als Helden. Ihr Handeln entspringt neben professionellem Interesse ihrem Sinn für Gerechtigkeit und Fairneß oder ist die Reaktion auf eine konkrete Bedrohung. Dabei stehen sie Verschwörungen obskurer offizieller und halboffizieller Institutionen oder mächtiger Konzerne gegenüber, denen sie hoffnungslos unterlegen sind und deren Charakter sie meist nie ganz durchschauen. Der Film, der den moralischen Verfall und den Machtmißbrauch von Politikern am deutlichsten benennt und seinerzeit wegen seines realen Hintergrunds eine besondere Sprengkraft hatte, ist *All the President's Men*, in dem Robert Redford und Dustin Hoffman die beiden Reporter der *Washington Post* spielen, die den Watergate-Skandal aufdeckten. *The Day of the Dolphin*, ein etwas naiver und teilweise unlogischer Thriller, handelt vom einem Wissenschaftler, der mit sprechenden Delphinen experimentiert und von ominösen Regierungsagenten in ein Komplott zur Ermordung des US-Präsidenten verwickelt wird. In *Three Days of the Condor* gerät ein Literaturwissenschaftler, der in einer Unterabteilung der CIA arbeitet, in den Brennpunkt eines Verschleierungsmanövers des Geheimdienstes und muß um sein Leben kämpfen. Ein ähnliches Motiv findet sich in *Marathon Man*, wo ein unbeteiligter Student von einem ehemaligen KZ-Arzt gejagt wird, dessen Gewalttaten ein undurchsichtiger Geheimdienst der Regierung im Tausch von Informationen unterstützt. In *The Parallax View* kommt ein Journalist einer mysteriösen Gesellschaft auf die Spur, die mit Hilfe von psychologischen Tests Auftragsmörder für politische Morde rekrutiert und diese durch eine Gehirnwäsche für ihre Aufgabe vorbereitet, und wird schließlich deren Opfer. *The China Syndrome* handelt von einer Journalistin, die mit Hilfe eines leitenden Ingenieurs einen Beinahe-GAU in einem Atomkraftwerk aufdeckt, den die Manager des Unternehmens mit kriminellen Methoden zu verschleiern suchen.

he brings back is murdered shortly afterwards, his wife leaves him and his friend turns out to be a murderer. At the end he is left drifting in a boat at sea, a metaphor for the uncertainty of existence.

The most important change in the genre lies in the various modifications undergone by the hero and his opponents. One variant is the reluctant hero who is unexpectedly dragged into criminal wheeling and dealing and has to respond to it. Here journalists are often involved, as in *The Parallax View* (1974) and *All the President's Men* (1976) by Alan J. Pakula or *The China Syndrome* (1979) by James Bridges, and sometimes also harmless intellectuals or scientists as in *The Day of the Dolphin* (1973) by Mike Nichols, *Three Days of the Condor* (1975) by Sydney Pollack and *Marathon Man* (1976) by John Schlesinger. Their world view is fundamentally different from that of the classical detective. As a rule they are socially integrated citizens without any marked critical awareness, more victims of circumstance than heroes. Apart from professional interest, their actions arise from their sense of justice and fairness, or is a reaction to a concrete threat. They are faced with conspiracies in public or semi-public institutions or powerful commercial groups to which they are hopelessly inferior and whose character they usually do not fully understand. The film that most clearly identifies politicians' moral decay and abuse of power, and which was particularly explosive in its day because of its real background, is *All the President's Men*, in which Robert Redford and Dustin Hoffman play the two *Washington Post* reporters who uncovered the Watergate scandal. *The Day of the Dolphin,* a somewhat more naïve and rather illogical thriller, deals with a scientist who is experimenting with talking dolphins and is drawn into a plot to murder the American president by sinister government agents. In *Three Days of the Condor*, a literary academic who works in a sub-department of the CIA is dragged into the middle of a secret service cover-up and has to fight for his life. There is a similar theme in *Marathon Man*, where an innocent student is being pursued by a former concentration camp doctor whose violence is supported by an opaque secret service in exchange for information. In *The Parallax View*, a journalist gets on the trail of a mysterious group who are recruiting hitmen for political assassinations by using psychological tests, finally falling victim to them. *The China Syndrome* deals with a journalist who with the help of a leading engineer discovers a near MCA in an atomic power station that the company managers try to cover up by criminal means.

In these films, the central conflict arises from the contradiction that the heroes believe in the existing system of values, while corrupt social institutions trample it underfoot. Even when the heroes win through, as in *All the President's Men* or *The China Syndrome*, these experiences do erode their faith in the social order, a breach with the prevailing circumstances that viewers understand as well. This conflict situation is evidence of a profound mistrust of the opaque mechanisms of economics, politics and science that the individual can no longer control. There

In diesen Filmen entsteht der zentrale Konflikt durch den Widerspruch, daß die Helden an das bestehende Wertesystem glauben, während korrupte gesellschaftliche Institutionen es mit Füßen treten. Auch wenn die Helden sich durchsetzen, wie in *All the President's Men* oder *The China Syndrome*, bewirken diese Erlebnisse doch eine Erschütterung ihres Vertrauens in die soziale Ordnung, einen Bruch mit dem Bestehenden, den auch die Zuschauer nachvollziehen. Diese Konfliktkonstellation zeugt von einem tiefen Mißtrauen gegenüber den undurchsichtigen Mechanismen von Wirtschaft, Politik und Wissenschaft, die das Individuum nicht mehr kontrollieren kann. Es gibt keinen starken individuellen Gegenspieler mehr, denn der Feind ist nicht eindeutig auszumachen. Darin kommt eine typische Haltung der linken Gegenkultur zum Ausdruck, die das Establishment als komplex, undurchschaubar und feindselig empfand.

Mit dem Wertverlust und der Suche nach brauchbaren moralischen Prinzipien befassen sich *Klute* (1971) von Alan J. Pakula, *The Yakuza* (1975) von Sydney Pollack und *The Late Show* (1977, *Die Katze kennt den Mörder*) von Robert Benton. In *The Yakuza* reist ein amerikanischer Privatdetektiv nach Japan, um die Tochter eines Amerikaners aus den Händen der Yakuza zu befreien. Er wird von seinem Auftraggeber verraten, gerät in ein Komplott, das an die Wunden seiner Vergangenheit rührt, und entdeckt schließlich in dem strengen traditionellen Ehrenkodex Japans ein überlegenes Wertesystem. Die Helden aus *Klute* und *The Late Show* sind Detektive, die ein altmodisches Ehrgefühl repräsentieren, das mit einem typischen Phänomen der siebziger Jahre konfrontiert wird: der moralischen Verunsicherung und emotionalen Labilität. Pakula benutzt in *Klute* den scheinbar konventionellen Plot einer Mörderjagd zu einer Milieu- und Charakterstudie, in deren Zentrum das Callgirl Bree steht. Dokumentiert durch ihre Sitzungen bei einer Psychiaterin, zeigt der Film ihre Ängste und ihre Sehnsucht nach Stabilität, die im Widerspruch stehen zu der sexuellen Freizügigkeit der großstädtischen Subkultur, in der sie sich bewegt. Mit dem lakonischen Kleinstadtmenschen Klute begegnet ihr das erste Mal ein moralisch integerer Mann, dessen Unerschütterlichkeit sich auf Werte wie Anstand, Verläßlichkeit und Verantwortungsbewußtsein stützt. Eine ähnliche Konstellation liegt *The Late Show* zugrunde, wo ein alternder Privatdetektiv aus Los Angeles sich daran macht, den Mord an seinem Expartner aufzuklären und dabei von einer jungen Möchte-Gern-Schauspielerin unterstützt wird, die sich mit allen möglichen Jobs, einschließlich des gelegentlichen Verkaufs von Drogen, über Wasser hält. Eine weitere Abweichung von den klassischen Vorbildern besteht hier in der Figur des Detektivs. Er ist ein alter Mann, schwerhörig, mit einem schmerzenden Bein und einem Magengeschwür, der nichts gemeinsam hat mit dem Idealbild des coolen Privatdetektivs à la Humphrey Bogart. Das gleiche gilt für Elliott Gould als Detektiv Philip Marlowe in Altmans parodistischem Remake des Klassikers *The Long Goodbye* (1973), wo ein Teil der Komik darauf beruht, daß der Protagonist vergeblich versucht, das Filmideal zu kopieren. Eine weitere Variante des klassischen Film Noir ist *Gloria* (1980, *Gloria – die Gangsterbraut*) von John Cassavetes. Hier wandelt sich die klassische Femme fatale zur positiven Heldin, die angesichts der Bedrohung eines Kindes den Kampf gegen die Mafia aufnimmt und sich und ihm buchstäblich den Weg ins Leben freischießt.

Actionfilme – der einsame Held im Kampf gegen das Böse

Eine wichtige, äußerst folgenreiche Entwicklung war die Verschmelzung von Elementen des klassischen Abenteuerfilms und des Detektivfilms mit den Mythen des Westerns zum Actionfilm. Am deutlichsten zeigt sich diese Verbindung bei Sam Peckinpah, der in all seinen Filmen die Möglichkeit der Selbstbehauptung in der modernen Welt durch den Rückgriff auf die Werte des alten Westens untersucht. *Bring Me the Head of Alfredo García* (1973, *Bring mir den Kopf von Alfredo Garcia*) verlagert die Thematik von *The Wild Bunch* in die moderne Zeit. Der Protagonist, ein heruntergekommener Barpianist, reagiert wie Peckinpahs Westernhelden auf den Verlust seiner Ideale mit Verbitterung und Zynismus. Er ist ein Trinker, Lügner und Opportunist ohne Moral, der nichts dabei findet, seine Freundin Elita zu mißhandeln und ein Grab zu öffnen, um den Kopf einer Leiche zu stehlen. Doch als Elita wegen des Kopfes von Gangstern ermordet wird, macht er eine Wandlung durch und unternimmt einen irrwitzigen Rachefeldzug. Zum Schluß stirbt er selbst im Kugelhagel seiner Verfolger, doch er hat durch die Rückbesinnung auf die Verhaltensweisen des Westens für Gerechtigkeit gesorgt und seine Würde zurückerobert.

Auch das Handlungsmuster von *Straw Dogs* (1971, *Wer Gewalt sät*), *The Getaway* (1972), *The Killer Elite* (1975), *Convoy* (1978) und *The Osterman Weekend* (1983) basiert auf den typischen Konstellationen des Western. Die Protagonisten sehen sich unversehens in einen Kampf

54. Donald Sutherland (John Klute) und Jane Fonda (Bree Daniel) in *Klute* von Alan J. Pakula, 1971.
55. Art Carney (Ira Wells) und Lily Tomlin (Margo Sperling) in *Die Katze kennt den Mörder* von Robert Benton, 1977.
56. Elliot Gould (Philip Marlowe) und Steve Coit (Detective Farmer) in *Der Tod kennt keine Wiederkehr* von Robert Altman, 1973.

54. Donald Sutherland (John Klute) and Jane Fonda (Bree Daniel) in *Klute* by Alan J. Pakula, 1971.
55. Art Carney (Ira Wells) and Lily Tomlin (Margo Sperling) in *The Late Show* by Robert Benton, 1977.
56. Elliot Gould (Philip Marlowe) and Steve Coit (detective Farmer) in *The Long Goodbye* by Robert Altman, 1973.

isn't a strong individual opponent any more, as the enemy can no longer be discerned with any precision. This expresses a typical left-wing alternative culture attitude, which sees the establishment as complex, opaque and hostile.

Klute (1971) by Alan J. Pakula, *The Yakuza* (1975) by Sydney Pollack and *The Late Show* (1977) by Robert Benton deal with the loss of values and the search for viable moral principles. In *The Yakuza* an American private detective travels to Japan to rescue an American man's daughter from the Yakuza. He is betrayed by his client, drawn into a plot that opens up wounds from his past and finally discovers a superior system of values in Japan's severe traditional moral code. The heroes from *Klute* and *The Late Show* are detectives who represent an old-fashioned code of honour that is confronted with a typical seventies phenomenon; moral insecurity and emotional instability. In *Klute*, Pakula uses an apparently conventional murder hunt plot for a milieu and character study based around a callgirl known as Bree. The film shows her fear and longing for stability, documented via her sessions with a psychiatrist; these are in conflict with the sexual liberality of the metropolitan culture in which she lives. Klute is a laconic small-town guy, the first man of moral integrity she has met, whose equanimity derives from values like decency, reliability and a sense of responsibility. *The Late Show* is based on a similar set of circumstances: an ageing private detective in Los Angeles sets about clearing up his ex-partner's murder, supported by a young would-be actress who keeps her head above water with all sorts of jobs, including the occasional sale of drugs. He is an old man, hard of hearing, with pains in one leg and a stomach ulcer. He has nothing in common with the ideal image of a cool detective à la Humphrey Bogart. The same applies to Elliott Gould as the detective Philip Marlowe in Altman's parody remake of the classic *The Long Goodbye*, where some of the comedy lies in the fact that the protagonist tries his hardest to mimic the cinematic ideal. Another variant on the classic film noir is *Gloria* (1980), by John Cassavetes. Here the classic femme fatale is transformed into a positive heroine who takes up the struggle with the Mafia when faced with threats to a child, and literally shoots herself a pathway into life for the pair of them.

Action films – the lonely hero fighting evil

One important and very far-reaching development was the fusing of the elements of the classic adventure film and the detective film with the Western myths to produce the action film. This connection is most obvious in the work of Sam Peckinpah, who examines the possibility of making one's way in the modern world by going back to the values of the old West in all his

mit einem skrupellosen Gegenspieler verstrickt, dem sie nur mit brutaler Gewalt beikommen können. Wie der typische Westernheld, der sich nur widerwillig in einen Konflikt hineinziehen läßt, versuchen die Protagonisten zunächst, einer Konfrontation auszuweichen, sehen sich jedoch aufgrund einer unmittelbaren Bedrohung, fast immer verbunden mit dem Motiv von Verrat und Rache, zum Handeln gezwungen. Der Konflikt ist zugespitzt auf die Konfrontation Mann gegen Mann und endet unweigerlich in einem großen gewaltsamen Finale, das eine Variation des Showdowns im Western darstellt.

Typisch für die Zeit, hat bei Peckinpah die Seite des Bösen die Gestalt von obskuren Geheimdienstagenten (*The Killer Elite*, *The Osterman Weekend*), gewissenlosen Regierungsbeamten und Politikern (Convoy) oder mächtigen Gangstern, deren Einfluß bis in die obersten Sphären von Politik und Wirtschaft reicht (*The Getaway*, *Bring Me the Head of Alfredo García*). Als wahren Feind macht er die moderne Gesellschaft aus, deren allgegenwärtige Korruption und Gewalt nicht nur den individuellen Lebensstil und die persönliche Freiheit bedrohen, sondern auch eine Konfliktlösung mit zivilisierten Mitteln unmöglich erscheinen lassen. Eine Studie über das Entstehen von Gewalt ist *Straw Dogs*, die Geschichte eines friedfertigen amerikanischen Mathematikprofessors, der sich den Anfeindungen einer Gruppe englischer Dorfbewohner ausgesetzt sieht und zunächst versucht, den Konflikt friedlich beizulegen. Doch schließlich geraten er und seine Frau in eine Situation äußerster Gefahr, die ihn zwingt, seine Vorstellungen von zivilisiertem Verhalten aufzugeben und die Angreifer in einer Orgie von Gewalt unschädlich zu machen. Auch bei den anderen Helden Peckinpahs handelt es sich um Opfer von Gewalt, die mit Gegengewalt reagieren. In *The Getaway* läßt sich ein kleiner Bankräuber mit einem mächtigen Gangsterboß ein, um einer Gefängnisstrafe zu entgehen, und gerät daraufhin in den Mittelpunkt eines Komplotts, dem er nur entkommen kann, indem er sich und seiner Frau den Weg nach Mexiko freikämpft. Die Rebellion der Fernfahrer aus *Convoy* wird von den Schikanen eines Sheriffs provoziert und durch die willkürliche Verhaftung eines Kollegen angeheizt. *The Osterman Weekend* handelt von der Konfrontation eines liberalen Fernsehmoderators mit einem traumatisierten CIA-Agenten, der seinen Vorgesetzten den Mord an seiner Frau anlastet und den Journalisten für einen Rachefeldzug mißbraucht. Der Held von *The Killer Elite* ist der Ex-Agent einer obskuren, halboffiziellen Geheimdienstorganisation, der eine letzte gefährliche Mission übernimmt, um Rache an einem verräterischen Kollegen zu üben, welcher ihn zum Krüppel geschossen hat. Nachdem er seinen Gegenspieler in einem abschließenden Duell töten konnte, stellt er fest, daß sie beide nur Werkzeuge eines korrupten Systems waren, dessen Machtinteressen sie durch ihren Einsatz gedient haben, und setzt sich mit ungewissem Ziel ab. Dieses Schlußbild, das Assoziationen zu dem einsamen Westernhelden weckt, der allein in den Sonnenuntergang reitet, wiederholt sich in *Straw Dogs*, *The Getaway* und *Convoy*. Desillusio-

57. Warren Oates (Bennie) in *Bringt mir den Kopf von Alfredo García* von Sam Peckinpah, 1973.
58. Ali MacGraw (Carol Ainsley McCoy) und Steve McQueen (Carter »Doc« McCoy) in *The Getaway von* Sam Peckinpah, 1972.
59. Dustin Hoffman (David Sumner) in *Wer Gewalt sät* von Sam Peckinpah, 1971.

57. Warren Oates (Bennie) in *Bring me the Head of Alfredo García* by Sam Peckinpah, 1973.
58. Ali MacGraw (Carol Ainsley McCoy) and Steve McQueen (Carter »Doc« McCoy) in *The Getaway* by Sam Peckinpah, 1972.
59. Dustin Hoffman (David Sumner) in *Straw Dogs* by Sam Peckinpah, 1971.

films. *Bring me the Head of Alfredo Garcia* (1973) shifts the subject-matter of *The Wild Bunch* into the modern era. The leading character, a down-and-out bar pianist, reacts like Peckinpah's Western heroes to the loss of his ideals, with bitterness and cynicism. He is a drinker, a liar and an opportunist without any morals who thinks nothing of ill-treating his girl-friend Elita and opening a grave to steal a corpse's head. But when Elita is murdered by gangsters because of the head he undergoes a transformation and mounts a crazy revenge campaign. Finally he dies himself in a hail of bullets from his pursuers, but going back to the behaviour of the West brought justice, and restored his dignity.

The plots of *Straw Dogs* (1971), *The Getaway* (1972), *The Killer Elite* (1975), *Convoy* (1978) and *The Osterman Weekend* (1983) are also based on typical Western sets of ideas. The leading men are unexpectedly drawn into fights with an unscrupulous opponent who can only be tackled with violence. Like the typical Western hero, who allows himself to be drawn into conflicts only reluctantly, these heroes first try to avoid a confrontation, but are then forced to act because of a direct threat, almost always linked with the theme of treachery and revenge. The conflict intensifies into a man-to-man confrontation and inevitably ends in a major, violent finale, a variation on the showdown in the Western.

Typically for the period, Peckinpah's villains take the form of obscure secret service agents (*The Killer Elite*, *The Osterman Weekend*), unscrupulous government officials and politicians (*Convoy*) or powerful gangsters whose influence whose influence extends to the highest levels of politics and business (*The Getaway*, *Bring me the Head of Alfredo Garcia*). He identifies modern society as the true enemy: its omnipresent corruption and violence are a threat not just to individual lifestyles and personal freedom, but also makes it impossible to resolve conflicts by civilized means. *Straw Dogs* is a study about the emergence of violence. It tells the story of a peaceable American mathematics professor who is exposed to the hostility of a group of English villagers and tries at first to deal with the conflict peacefully. But finally he and his wife find themselves in an extremely dangerous situation that compels him to abandon his ideas of civilized behaviour and get his attackers out of the way in an orgy of violence. Peckinpah's other heroes are also victims of violence who respond with violence. In *The Getaway* a petty bank-robber takes on a powerful gangster boss in order to avoid a jail sentence. This puts him at the centre of a plot that he can escape from only by fighting his way to Mexico and freedom with his wife. The long-distance lorry-drivers in *Convoy* rebel because they are harassed by a sheriff and fired up by the arbitrary arrest of a colleague. *The Osterman Weekend* deals with a confrontation between a liberal television presenter and a traumatized CIA agent who accuses

niert steigen die Helden aus der etablierten Gesellschaft aus. Und wie in Peckinpahs Western heißt das gelobte Land häufig Mexiko, wo man hofft, noch einen letzten Rest des ursprünglichen Freiheitsideals des Westens zu finden.

Der klassische Grundkonflikt des Western Zivilisation versus Wildnis, der sich in den Gegensätzen soziale Ordnung, Vernunft, Ausgleich versus Anarchie, Barbarei, Gewalt fortsetzt, steht auch im Mittelpunkt von *Deliverance* (1972, *Beim Sterben ist jeder der Erste*). Darin verbindet John Boorman das Grundmuster des Abenteuerfilms mit Elementen des Psychothrillers. Vier Geschäftsleute werden auf einem Kanuausflug von zwei primitiven Hillbillys terrorisiert, und der Traum von Freiheit und Abenteuer verwandelt sich immer mehr in einen Alptraum, bei dem schließlich die Grenzen zwischen realer und eingebildeter Bedrohung verschwimmen. Am Ende ist einer von ihnen tot, die anderen können sich retten, doch ihr Selbstbild ist für immer beschädigt, und sie werden fortan mit ihren Ängsten und Schuldgefühlen weiterleben müssen.

Daneben entstand eine Variante des Actionfilms, die wesentlich stärker auf den Konventionen des klassischen Kriminalfilms aufbaut, eine Art von urbanem Western in der Nachfolge von *Bullitt* (1968), wo bereits dessen typische Elemente geprägt werden: ein Polizist, der sich trotz Drohungen und Bestechungsversuchen nicht beirren läßt, ein dubioser Politiker und ein karrierebewußter Vorgesetzter, die ihn unter Druck setzen, dunkle Großstadtstraßen und schäbige Hotelzimmer, spektakuläre Verfolgungsjagden und ein großer Showdown, bei dem der Verbrecher zur Strecke gebracht wird. Einem ähnlichen Muster folgen (1969, *Coogan's großer Bluff*), die *Dirty-Harry*-Filme *Dirty Harry* (1971), *Magnum Force* (1973, *Callahan, Dirty Harry II*) und *The Enforcer* (1976, *Der Unerbittliche*) oder William Friedkins *French Connection* (1971, *Brennpunkt Brooklyn*), wobei allerdings das gesellschaftskritische Element stärker betont ist. Die Helden sind ebenfalls Polizisten, doch obwohl sie das Gesetz vertreten, mißtrauen sie ihm gleichzeitig, denn sie halten die gesellschaftlichen Institutionen für korrupt und unfähig, die Bürger vor Gesetzesbrechern zu schützen. Diese Auffassung wird bestätigt, wenn Gerichte offensichtlich Schuldige freisprechen, Vorgesetzte den Tatendrang der Helden bremsen oder sich als bestechlich erweisen. Sowohl Doyle in *French Connection* als auch Callahan in *Calahan* (*Dirty Harry II*) lösen den Fall auf eigene Faust und gegen den Widerstand der Polizeiführung. Das macht sie zu Rebellen gegen das System und, trotz ihrer formalen Integration, zu gesellschaftlichen Außenseitern. Wie der Detektiv des Film Noir sind sie zynische Einzelgänger ohne engere persönliche Bindungen, die den Verlust an Emotionalität und Menschlichkeit verkörpern, den die moderne Gesellschaft mit sich bringt. Sie vertrauen vor allem auf ihre Intuition, um zwischen Gut und Böse zu unterscheiden und verstoßen bedenkenlos gegen bestehende Gesetze, wenn es ihrem Gerechtigkeitssinn entspricht. Wie der klassische Westernheld, der eingreift, weil sich die Gemeinschaft als zu schwach erweist, um die Regeln der Zivilisation durchzusetzen, sind Helden wie Callahan oder Doyle Besessene am Rande der Gesellschaft, die sich auf einen überlegenen, scheinbar naturgegebenen Moralkodex stützen und deren Vorgehen nach klassischem Muster durch den Sieg über das Böse gerechtfertigt wird.

60. James Caan (Mike Locken) in *Die Killer-Elite* von Sam Peckinpah, 1975.
61. Nick Nolte (Ray Hicks) und Richard Masur (Danskin) in *Dreckige Hunde* von Karel Reisz, 1978.
62. Jon Voight (Ed Gentry), Ronny Cox (Drew Ballinger), Bill McKinney (Mountain Man) und Burt Reynolds (Lewis Medlock) in *Beim Sterben ist jeder der Erste* von John Boorman, 1972.
63. Gene Hackman (Jimmy »Popeye« Doyle) in *Brennpunkt Brooklyn* von William Friedkin, 1971.
64. *Convoy* von Sam Peckinpah, 1978.

60. James Caan (Mike Locken) in *The Killer Elite* by Sam Peckinpah, 1975.
61. Nick Nolte (Ray Hicks) and Richard Masur (Danskin) in *Who'll Stop the Rain* by Karel Reisz, 1978.
62. Jon Voight (Ed Gentry), Ronny Cox (Drew Ballinger), Bill McKinney (Mountain Man) and Burt Reynolds (Lewis Medlock) in *Deliverance* by John Boorman, 1972.
63. Gene Hackman (Jimmy »Popeye« Doyle) in *French Connection* by William Friedkin, 1971.
64. *Convoy* by Sam Peckinpah, 1978.

his superiors of murdering his wife and uses the journalist to mount a revenge campaign. The hero of *The Killer Elite* is a former agent from an obscure, semi-official secret service organization who takes on a final dangerous mission for the sake of revenge on a treacherous colleague who crippled him with gunshot wounds. After killing his opponent in a final duel, he realizes that they were both pawns in a corrupt system whose power interests they served by becoming involved and gets away with no definite destination in mind. This final image, which suggests associations with the lonely Western hero riding off into the sunset is repeated in *Straw Dogs*, *The Getaway* and *Convoy*. The disillusioned heroes detach themselves from established society. And as in Peckinpah's Western, the promised land is often Mexico, where people hope to find a final remnant of the West's original ideals of freedom.

The classic basic conflict of Western civilization versus the wilderness, continued in the contrast between social order, reason and balance versus anarchy, barbarism and violence is also central to *Deliverance* (1972). Here John Boorman links the basic pattern of the adventure film with elements of the psychological thriller. Four businessmen on a canoeing trip are terrorized by two primitive hillbillies, and the dream of freedom and adventure increasingly turns into a nightmare in which the borders between real and imaginary threats are blurred. At the end one of them is dead, the others are able to get away, but their self-image is permanently damaged, and they will have to live with their fears and feelings of guilt from then on.

Alongside this a variant on the action film emerged that builds much more strongly on the conventions of the classical thriller, a kind of urban Western following *Bullitt* (1968), where the typical elements are already established: a policeman who does not allow himself to be deterred by threats and attempted bribery, a dubious politician and a career-conscious superior who put pressure on him, dark city streets and shabby hotel rooms, spectacular chases and a major showdown in which the criminal is hunted down. A similar pattern is followed by *Coogan's Bluff* (1969), the *Dirty Harry* films *Dirty Harry* (1971), *Magnum Force* (1973) and *The Enforcer* (1976), or William Friedkin's *French Connection* (1971), in which admittedly the social element is more heavily emphasized. The heroes are policemen again, but although they represent the law, they mistrust it, as they feel that social institutions are corrupt and unable to protect the public from lawbreakers. This view is confirmed when courts clear people who are clearly guilty, superiors hold back the hero's will to actor turn out to be open to bribery. Both Doyle in *The French Connection* and Callahan in *Magnum Force* solve the case themselves, despite resistance from their police superiors. This makes them into rebels against the system, social outcasts despite their formal integration. Like detectives in films noirs, they are cynical loners without any close personal ties. They embody the loss of emotional quality and humanity that modern society entails. They trust their intuition above all when they need to distinguish between good and evil, and unhesitatingly infringe existing laws if this is consistent with their sense of justice. Like the classic Western hero, who intervenes because society turns out to be too weak to maintain the rules of civilization, heroes like Callahan or Doyle are obsessives on

Variationen des Actionhelden sind traumatisierte, aber kampfgestählte Vietamveteranen, die als Rächer gegen das Establishment auftreten, beispielsweise in *Who'll Stop the Rain* (1978, *Dreckige Hunde*) von Karel Reisz, *Cutter's Way* (1981, *Cutter's Way – Keine Gnade*) von Ivan Passer und dem ersten Rambo-Film *First Blood* (1982, *Rambo*) von Ted Kotcheff. Ebenso dazu gehören die Helden der Blaxploitation-Filme, die ihre Nachfolge in den *Shaft*- und *Cleopatra-Jones*-Filmen fanden, welche Anfang der siebziger Jahre von MGM und Warner produziert wurden. Eine interessante Variante des Genres liefert Steven Spielberg in *Duel* (1971), wo er bereits mit Spannungselementen experimentiert, die er später in *Jaws* (1975) meisterhaft weiterentwickelt. Der Film handelt von einem Geschäftsmann, der zu einem Termin aufbricht und auf der Landstraße von einem Lastwagen verfolgt wird, welcher sich zusehends in ein bedrohliches Monstrum zu verwandeln scheint und ihn in ein Duell auf Leben und Tod zwingt.

Kriegsfilme – die offene Wunde Vietnam

Ein Genre, das angesichts der negativen Auswirkungen des Vietnamkriegs von New Hollywood vollkommen ignoriert wurde, war der klassische Kriegsfilm, bei dem es letztlich immer um die Bestätigung und Idealisierung der Überlegenheit des amerikanischen Wertesystems ging. *Castle Keep* (1969, *Ein Schloß in den Ardennen*) von Sydney Pollack, der einzige ernsthafte Kriegsfilm des neuen Hollywood aus der Zeit des Vietnamkrieges, klagt die Sinnlosigkeit des Krieges an. Der Film erzählt von einer Gruppe kriegsmüder Soldaten, die sich gegen Ende des Zweiten Weltkriegs in einem alten Schloß in den französischen Ardennen einquartiert und auf Befehl ihres Offiziers eine unsinnige Schlacht gegen eine Truppe von versprengten Deutschen entfesselt. Die wenigen anderen Kriegsfilme, wie Robert Altmans *M.A.S.H.* (1970), Mike Nichols' *Catch-22* (1970) oder Steven Spielbergs *1941* (1979), behandeln das Thema dagegen in Form von Satiren oder Slapstick-Komödien, die sich über den Militarismus der Amerikaner und die Gepflogenheiten der Armee lustig machen und damit das amerikanische Selbstwertgefühl ernsthaft in Frage stellen. In *M.A.S.H.* versteckt Robert Altman die Kritik hinter der Parodie, indem er den Krieg aus der Warte einer Gruppe von Ärzten eines Militärlazaretts im Koreakrieg zeigt. Sie machen keinen Hehl daraus, daß sie nicht aus patriotischen Gefühlen, sondern wegen eines Einberufungsbefehls am Krieg teilnehmen und fest entschlossen sind, das Beste aus der Situation zu machen, indem sie sich die Zeit mit infantilen Streichen, makabren Scherzen und Golfspielen vertreiben oder ein Football-Match organisieren, um bei den Wetten abzukassieren. *Catch-22* ist eine dunkle, bittere Satire über die Absurditäten des Krieges. Der Film spielt auf einem Stützpunkt der amerikanischen Luftwaffe in Italien zur Zeit des Zweiten Welt-

65. Elliot Gould (Capt. John Francis Xavier »Trapper John« McIntyre) und Donald Sutherland (Capt. Benjamin Franklin »Hawkeye« Pierce, MD) in *M.A.S.H.* von Robert Altman, 1970.
66. Paula Prentiss (Nurse Duckett) und Collin Wilcox Paxton (Nurse Cramer) in *Catch-22* von Mike Nichols, 1970.

65. Elliot Gould (Capt. John Francis Xavier »Trapper John« McIntyre) and Donald Sutherland (Capt. Benjamin Franklin »Hawkeye« Pierce, MD) in *M.A.S.H.* by Robert Altman, 1970.
66. Paula Prentiss (Nurse Duckett) and Collin Wilcox Paxton (Nurse Cramer) in *Catch-22* by Mike Nichols, 1970.

the fringe of society who operate according to a superior, apparently naturally acquired moral code, and whose approach is justified by victory over evil, on the classical pattern.

Variations on the action hero are traumatized but battle-tried Vietnam veterans who act as avengers against the establishment, as in *Who'll Stop the Rain* (1978) by Karel Reisz, *Cutter's Way* (1981) by Ivan Passer, the first Rambo-Film *First Blood* (1982) by Ted Kotcheff and the heroes of the blaxploitation films, which were succeeded by the *Shaft* and *Cleopatra Jones* films produced by MGM and Warner in the early seventies, also fall into this category. Steven Spielberg delivers an interesting variant on this genre in *Duel* (1971), where he is already experimenting with the elements of tension that he developed in *Jaws* (1975) in a masterly fashion. The film deals with a businessman who is on his way to keep an appointment when he is followed on the road by a lorry that seems increasingly to turn into a threatening monster and forces him into a life and death duel.

War films – Vietnam as an open wound

One genre that was completely ignored by New Hollywood in view of the negative effects of the Vietnam War was the classical war film, which was ultimately always about confirming and idealizing the superiority of the American system of values. *Castle Keep* (1969), by Sydney Pollack, the only serious New Hollywood war film from the time of the Vietnam War, attacks the senselessness of war. It tells the story of a group of war-weary soldiers who billet themselves in a old chateau in the French Ardennes towards the end of the Second World War, and then get involved in a senseless battle on the orders of an officer with a troop of German soldiers who have lost touch with their units. The small number of other war films like Robert Altman's *M.A.S.H.* (1970), Mike Nichols's *Catch-22* (1970) or Steven Spielberg's *1941* (1979) treat the theme satirically or as slapstick comedy, making fun of American militarism and army customs and thus seriously questioning the American sense of self-worth. In *M.A.S.H.* Robert Altman hides his criticism behind parody by showing the war from the point of view of a group of doctors in a military hospital in the Korean War. They make no bones about the fact that they are involved in the war because they were called up, not because of any sense of patriotism, and are fiercely determined to make the best of the situation by killing time with infantile tricks, macabre jokes and games of golf, or by organizing a football match so that they can cash in on the betting. *Catch-22* is a dark and bitter satire on the absurdity of war. It is set in an American base in Italy at the time of the Second World War, where the bomber pilot Yossarian sees himself faced with corruption, arbitrariness and chaos. Ultimately he manages to get sent home by blackmail, but thinks better of it at the last minute and escapes across the sea in a rubber dinghy. This gives the phrase *Catch-22*, which indicates a choice between two impossible alternatives, a meaning that applies not just to the war but to the whole of American society.

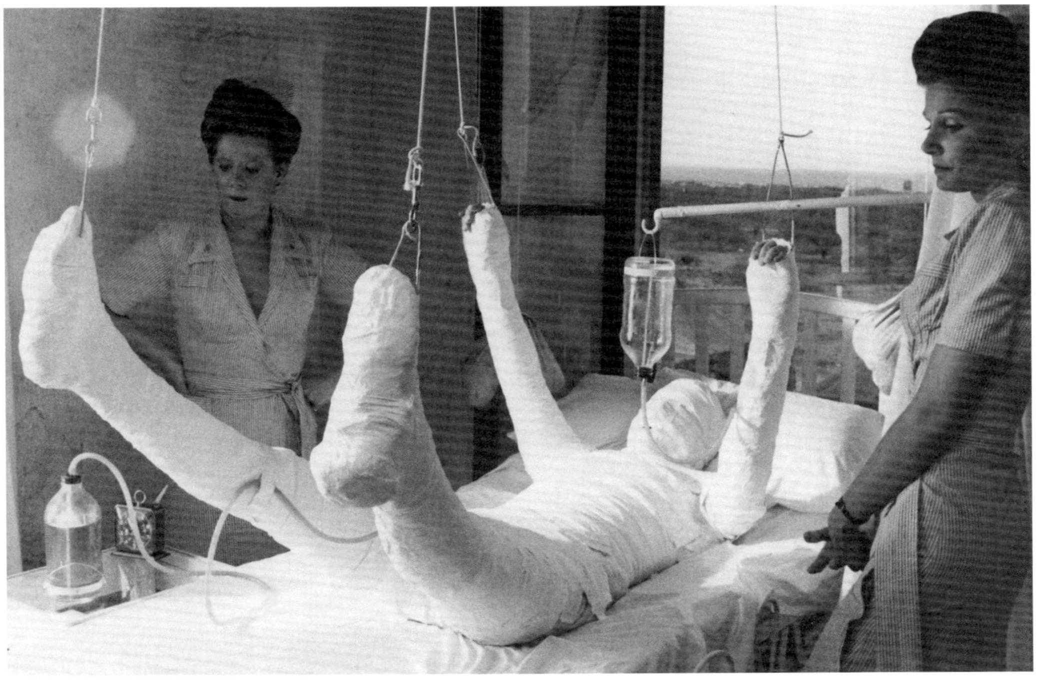

67. *Apocalypse Now* von Francis Ford Coppola, 1979.
68. Robert De Niro (Michael) und John Savage (Steven) in *Die durch die Hölle gehen* von Michael Cimino, 1978.
69. Jane Fonda (Sally Hyde) und Jon Voight (Luke Martin) in *Coming home – Sie kehren heim* von Hal Ashby, 1977.

67. *Apocalypse Now* von Francis Ford Coppola, 1979.
68. Robert De Niro (Michael) and John Savage (Steven) in *The Deer Hunter* by Michael Cimino, 1978.
69. Jane Fonda (Sally Hyde) and Jon Voight (Luke Martin) in *Coming Home* by Hal Ashby, 1977.

kriegs, wo sich der Bomberpilot Yossarian mit Korruption, Willkür und Chaos konfrontiert sieht. Am Ende erreicht er durch Erpressung seine vorzeitige Rückkehr in die Heimat, überlegt es sich jedoch im letzten Moment anders und flüchtet in einem Schlauchboot hinaus auf das Meer. Damit erhält das Kürzel *Catch-22*, das für die Wahl zwischen zwei unmöglichen Alternativen steht, eine Bedeutung, die nicht nur auf den Krieg, sondern auf die ganze amerikanische Gesellschaft verweist.

Erst Ende der siebziger Jahre begannen die Filmemacher von New Hollywood mit einer Aufarbeitung des Traumas Vietnam. Die drei herausragenden Filme über das Thema, *Apocalypse Now* (1979) von Francis Ford Coppola, *The Deer Hunter* (1978, *Die durch die Hölle gehen*) von Michael Cimino und *Coming Home* (1978, *Coming home – Sie kehren heim*) von Hal Ashby, stützen sich auf die Konventionen des Dramas und haben mit dem klassischen Kriegsfilm kaum etwas gemeinsam. *Apocalypse Now*, der einzige Film jener Zeit, der ganz in Vietnam spielt, setzt sich mit dem moralischen Verfall und der Entmenschlichung durch den Krieg auseinander. Williard, ein Spezialagent der Armee, erhält den Auftrag, den ehemaligen Colonel Kurtz zu töten, der mit einer Gruppe von Deserteuren im Dschungel über ein Imperium von Eingeborenen herrscht. Die Reise den Fluß hinunter zeigt die Brutalität und Absurdität des Krieges und wird gleichzeitig für Williard zu einer Konfrontation mit den eigenen dunklen Seiten seiner Persönlichkeit. Die Beschäftigung mit Kurtz zieht ihn immer mehr in einen Sog des Bösen hinein, das ihn fasziniert und gleichzeitig mit Selbstekel erfüllt. Kurtz, der sich vor den Grauen des Krieges in den Wahnsinn geflüchtet hat, ist sein Double, die Steigerung dessen, was ihn quält, Ausdruck der Abgründe seiner Seele. Wenn er ihn am Ende tötet, wird dies zu einem rituellen Akt der Befreiung, die gleichzeitig eine Selbstbefreiung ist. *The Deer Hunter* befaßt sich in einer ähnlich komplexen Metaphorik mit den Wunden, die der Krieg bei denen schlug, die an ihn glaubten. Im Mittelpunkt stehen die drei Stahlarbeiter Michael, Steven und Nick aus einer Kleinstadt in Pennsylvania, die sich als Freiwillige zum Kriegsdienst melden, weil sie es für ihre patriotische Pflicht halten und sie sich davon ein aufregendes Abenteuer versprechen. Doch in Vietnam zerbröckeln die Männlichkeitsideale im Angesicht des Todes. Alle drei überleben dank der Nervenstärke und Kaltblütigkeit, die sich Michael durch seine Passion für die Jagd angeeignet hat, aber sie sind für immer gezeichnet. Wenn Michael sich in dem Versuch, sein früheres Leben zurückzuholen, unmittelbar nach seiner Rückkehr auf die Jagd begibt und dabei einem Hirsch, den er bereits im Visier hat, das Leben schenkt, wird dies zum Sinnbild dafür, daß die Dinge nie wieder so sein werden wie zuvor. *Coming Home* konzentriert sich auf die Situation der Veteranen und deren Schwierigkeiten, mit den traumatischen Erlebnissen des Krieges weiterzuleben. Während frühere Filme, wie *Dog Day Afternoon* und *Taxi Driver*, die Kriegsheimkehrer als verstörte, manische Charaktere zeigen, die sich auf dem schmalen Grat zwischen Wahnsinn und Normalität bewegen und eine Gefahr für die Zivilisation darstellen, werden die Veteranen hier vor allem als Opfer eines unmenschlichen Krieges betrachtet. Der Film schildert

It was not until the late seventies that film-makers started to address the trauma of Vietnam. The three outstanding films on this theme, *Apocalypse Now* (1979) by Francis Ford Coppola, *The Deer Hunter* (1978) by Michael Cimino and *Coming Home* (1978) by Hal Ashby used the conventions of the drama and have very little in common with the classic war film. *Apocalypse Now*, the only film from that period set entirely in Vietnam, examines moral decay and dehumanization by war. Williard, an army special agent, is commissioned to kill the former Colonel Kurtz, who is ruling over an empire of natives in the jungle with a group of deserters. The journey down the river shows the brutality and absurdity of war, and at the same time causes Williard to confront his own darker nature. His encounter with Kurtz draws him further and further into an undertow of evil, which fascinates him and at the same time fills him with revulsion. Kurtz, who has taken refuge in madness because of the war, is his double, an intensification of everything that torments him, an expression of the dark depths of his soul. When he finally kills him, this becomes a ritual act of liberation that is a self-liberation. *The Deer Hunter* uses a similarly complex set of metaphors to analyse the wounds the war inflicts on those who believed in it. The film is built around three steelworkers from a small town in Pennsylvania, Michael, Steven and Nick. They volunteer for the war because they consider it to be their patriotic duty, and think that it will be an exciting adventure. But in Vietnam their manly ideals crumble when faced with death. All three of them survive because of the strength of nerve and cold-blooded qualities that Michael has acquired because of his passion for hunting, but they are marked for life. When Michael goes hunting immediately after his return in an attempt to get his former life back and allows a deer that he already has in his sights to live, this becomes a symbol of the fact that things will never be the same again. *Coming Home* concentrates on the situation of the veterans and the difficulties they have in living with the traumatic effects of the war. Earlier films like *Dog Day Afternoon* and *Taxi Driver* portrayed men coming back from the war as manic characters who had been destroyed, on a knife-edge between madness and normality and representing a danger to civilization, the veterans here are seen above all as victims of an inhuman war. The film uses a triangular story involving the invalid veteran Luke Martin, Sally, an officer's wife and her husband Bob to show various possibilities for dealing with the trauma of the Vietnam War. Luke is profoundly embittered about the neglectful way the veterans are treated by the state, but finds a new zest for life in his relationship with Sally, and she moves from being a conformist soldier's wife into political maturity. Bob, however, cannot get over the trauma on his return. He went to Vietnam in the expectation of returning as a feted hero, but instead of this became involved in the hell of a dirty, senseless war that was not supported by the majority of Americans, and so his world has collapsed around him.

A constant feature of these very different films is a clear rejection of militarism and war, which was a typical new Hollywood attitude.

anhand einer Dreiecksgeschichte zwischen dem invaliden Veteranen Luke Martin, der Offiziersgattin Sally und deren Mann Bob verschiedene Möglichkeiten, mit dem Trauma des Vietnamkriegs umzugehen. Während Luke, der zutiefst verbittert über die Nachlässigkeit ist, mit der die Veteranen vom Staat behandelt werden, durch seine Beziehung zu Sally neuen Lebensmut findet, und diese durch ihn von der konformistischen Soldatenfrau zu einem politisch bewußten Menschen heranreift, kann Bob nach seiner Rückkehr sein Trauma nicht überwinden. Denn für ihn, der in der Erwartung nach Vietnam ging, als gefeierter Held zurückzukehren, statt dessen jedoch in die Hölle eines schmutzigen, sinnlosen Krieges geraten ist, der von der Mehrheit der Amerikaner nicht unterstützt wird, bricht eine Welt zusammen.

Ein durchgängiges Merkmal dieser sehr unterschiedlichen Filme ist eine eindeutige Ablehnung von Militarismus und Krieg, die eine typische Haltung von New Hollywood war.

Science-fiction-Filme – Zivilisationskritik und Endzeitstimmung

Der Science-fiction-Film, traditionell ein Genre, das die geheimen Ängste vor der Unberechenbarkeit der modernen Technik oder der Bedrohung durch eine fremde Macht ritualisierte, wurde von New Hollywood als geeignetes Mittel zur Verarbeitung der zeitgenössischen Zivilisationskritik betrachtet. Das allgemeine Mißtrauen gegen das Establishment schlug sich in Filmen nieder, welche den Mißbrauch der modernen Technik anprangern. Einer der ersten war Robert Altmans Science-fiction-Film *Countdown* (1968, *Countdown: Start zum Mond*), der schildert, wie die amerikanische Raumfahrtbehörde im Wettlauf mit den Russen um die erste bemannte Mondlandung darauf verfällt, einen Astronauten auf den Mond zu schicken, obwohl keine technische Möglichkeit zur Rückkehr besteht, damit er dort in einer Versorgungsstation ausharrt, bis die Technik soweit entwickelt ist, um ihn zurückzuholen.

Ein Ausdruck des neu entstandenen ökologischen Bewußtseins ist die große Zahl der Science-fiction-Filme, die sich mit der Zerstörung der zivilisierten Welt durch eine außer Kontrolle geratene Technik und die bedenkenlose Ausbeutung der natürlichen Ressourcen befassen. Die wesentliche Abweichung von den klassischen Konventionen besteht darin, daß die Fähigkeit der Menschheit zur Bewältigung der Probleme, die aus einer technisierten Umwelt erwachsen, bestritten wird, während in den klassischen Vertretern des Genres die Gefahr gewöhnlich durch die überlegene amerikanische Technik oder einen Zufall abgewendet wird.

Ein typisches Motiv der Science-fiction-Filme der siebziger Jahre sind apokalyptische Szenarien, durch die das Ende der menschlichen Zivilisation heraufbeschworen wird. Ein Vorläufer ist Franklin J. Schaffners *Planet of The Apes* (1968, *Der Planet der Affen*), der in einer Gesellschaft spielt, in der Affen die überlegenen, intelligenten Wesen sind, während die Menschen sich auf der primitiven Stufe der Affen befinden. Am Schluß macht der Held die Entdeckung, daß es

70. *Countdown: Start zum Mond* von Robert Altman, 1968.
71. *2001 – Odyssee im Weltraum* von Stanley Kubrick, 1968.

70. *Countdown by* Robert Altman, 1968.
71. *2001 – A Space Odyssey* by Stanley Kubrick, 1968.

Science-fiction films – criticism of civilization and a mood of apocalypse

New Hollywood saw the science-fiction film, traditionally a genre that ritualized secret anxieties about the unpredictablity of modern technology or threats from an alien power, as a suitable device for conveying a modern critique of civilization. General mistrust of the establishment manifested itself in films attacking the abuse of modern technology. One of the first was Robert Altman's science-fiction film *Countdown* (1968), which showed the American space authority in competition with the Russians over the first manned moon landing hitting on the idea of sending an astronaut to the moon even though there was no possibility of bringing him back; he was to wait in a supply station until such technology was developed.

The large number of films dealing with the destruction of the civilized world by technology that has got out of control and the mindless exploitation of natural resources expressed the new ecological awareness. The principal departure from classical conventions is that man's ability to tackle the problems arising from a technical environment is challenged, while in classical examples of the genre the danger is usually averted by superior American technology or by chance.

Apocalyptic scenarios evoking the end of human civilization are a typical motif in seventies science-fiction films. One forerunner is Franklin J. Schaffner's *The Planet of the Apes* (1968), which is set in a society where apes are the superior, intelligent beings, while man is at a more primitive stage. At the end the hero discovers that this is a future civilization on earth: evolution has been reversed after civilization has been destroyed by a nuclear war. The idea of a more highly developed species dominating mankind also forms the basis for *Phase IV* (1973) by Saul Bass, an independently produced low budget film that has now acquired cult status. It uses the style of a research report to show ants that have acquired superior intelligence from nuclear experiments come to dominate humanity because of their more highly developed sense of community. Stanley Kubrick's masterpiece *2001 – A Space Odyssey* (1968), which set new standards for the genre both aesthetically and also because of its complexity, addresses the dawn of civilization, man's survival in a technology-dominated existence, and the mysteries that lie hidden in unknown areas of time and space. *Silent Running* (1971) by Douglas Trumbell shows a society in which the land has been concreted over and plants and animals exterminated. A group of men are commissioned to preserve the very last of the flora and fauna artificially in space stations. When they are instructed to blow the complex up, one of their number resists. He leaves a space capsule containing a wood behind in a distant region of the universe, in the care of a robot, and blows himself up with the mother ship in a simulated accident. Robert Altman's *Quintet* (1979) is set in an apocalyptic society of the future in which the earth is covered with ice and animals and plants have largely been eliminated. The final remains of civilization are to be found in a few settlements where packs of stray dogs feed on the corpses that are thrown into the streets; a warming fire has become a luxury as there is no more fuel. The women are infertile, and humanity is dying out. Life has lost its value in the face of the inevitable end, and only a bizarre game called quintet, in which the players have to kill each other, offers the possibility of any sense of elation.

72. Fernando Rey (Grigor) und Paul Newman (Essex) in *Quintett* von Robert Altman, 1979.
73. Helen Horton (Mildred Eldridge) und Alan Gifford (Mr. Eldridge) in *Phase IV* von Saul Bass, 1973.
74. Donald Sutherland (Matthew Bennell) und Brooke Adams (Elizabeth Driscoll) in *Die Invasion der Körperfresser* von Philip Kaufman, 1978.
75. *Begegnungen der dritten Art* von Steven Spielberg, 1977.

72. Fernando Rey (Grigor) and Paul Newman (Essex) in *Quintet* by Robert Altman, 1979.
73. Helen Horton (Mildred Eldridge) and Alan Gifford (Mr. Eldridge) in *Phase IV* by Saul Bass, 1973.
74. Donald Sutherland (Matthew Bennell) and Brooke Adams (Elizabeth Driscoll) in *The Invasion of the Body Snatchers* by Philip Kaufman, 1978.
75. *Close Encounters of the Third Kind* by Steven Spielberg, 1977.

sich um eine Zukunftsgesellschaft auf der Erde handelt, wo eine Umkehrung der Evolution stattgefunden hat, nachdem die Zivilisation durch einen Atomkrieg zerstört worden ist. Die Idee einer höher entwickelten Spezies, welche die Menschheit unter ihre Herrschaft bringt, liegt auch *Phase IV* (1973) von Saul Bass zugrunde, ein unabhängig produzierter Low-Budget-Film, der mittlerweile Kultstatus hat. Er schildert im Stil eines Forschungsberichts, wie ein Ameisenvolk, das unter dem Einfluß nuklearer Experimente eine überlegene Intelligenz erlangt hat, sich aufgrund seines ausgeprägteren Gemeinschaftsgeistes die Menschen unterwirft. Stanley Kubricks Meisterwerk *2001 – A Space Odyssey* (1968, *2001 – Odyssee im Weltraum*), das sowohl ästhetisch als auch durch seine Komplexität neue Maßstäbe für das Genre setzte, befaßt sich mit der Entstehung der Zivilisation, dem Überleben des Menschen in einer von der Technik dominierten Existenz und den Mysterien, die in unbekannten Gefilden von Zeit und Raum verborgen liegen. *Silent Running* (1971, *Lautlos im Weltraum*) von Douglas Trumbell schildert eine Gesellschaft, in der die Erde zubetoniert und die Pflanzen- und Tierwelt ausgerottet ist. Eine Gruppe von Männern hat den Auftrag, in Raumstationen einen letzten Rest der Flora und Fauna künstlich zu erhalten. Als sie die Anweisung bekommen, die Anlage zu sprengen, leistet einer von ihnen Widerstand. Er läßt eine Raumkapsel mit einem Wald unter der Obhut eines Roboters in einer entlegenen Region des Weltraums zurück und sprengt sich selbst mit dem Mutterschiff in die Luft, um einen Unfall vorzutäuschen. Robert Altmans *Quintet* (1979) spielt in einer Endzeitgesellschaft der Zukunft, in der die Erde von Eis bedeckt ist und Tiere und Pflanzen weitgehend ausgerottet sind. Der letzte Rest von Zivilisation findet sich in einigen wenigen Ansiedlungen, in denen sich Horden streunender Hunde von den Leichen ernähren, die auf die Straße geworfen werden, und ein wärmendes Feuer zum Luxus geworden ist, da es keinen Brennstoff mehr gibt. Die Frauen sind unfruchtbar, die Menschheit ist im Aussterben begriffen. Angesichts des unvermeidlichen Untergangs hat das Leben seinen Wert verloren, und einzig ein bizarres Spiel namens Quintett, bei dem die Spieler sich gegenseitig töten müssen, bietet die Möglichkeit, ihm ein Hochgefühl abzugewinnen.

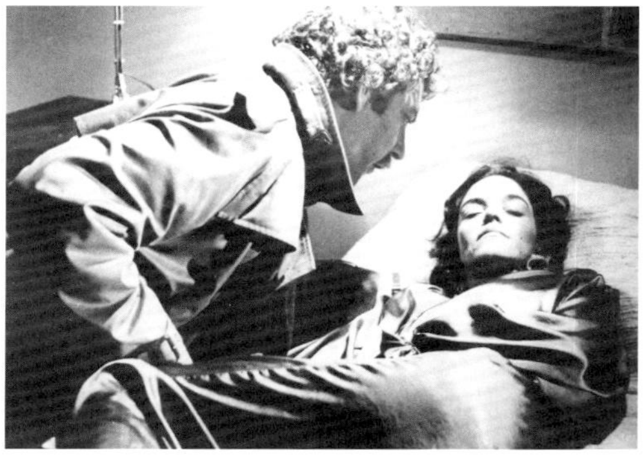

Das Motiv des gesichtslosen, hoch technisierten, alles beherrschenden Staates bestimmt die Gesellschaft, die George Lucas in *THX-1138* (1970) in Szene setzt. Da sich die Menschen in der Vergangenheit als unfähig erwiesen haben, verantwortlich mit ihrem Lebensraum umzugehen, und die Eroberfläche unbewohnbar geworden ist, leben sie in einer uniformen, unterirdischen Welt, wo sie unter ständiger Überwachung eines anonymen technischen Apparates stehen und die Entscheidungsgewalt über ihr eigenes Leben vollkommen verloren haben. Eine ähnliche Grundidee liegt Filmen wie *Logan's Run* (1976, *Flucht ins 21. Jahrhundert*) von Michael Anderson und Norman Jewisons *Rollerball* (1975) zugrunde. *The Invasion of the Body Snat-*

The idea of a faceless, high-tech, all-powerful state drives the society that George Lucas presents in *THX-1138* (1970). As mankind has shown itself incapable in the past of handling its environment responsibly, and the surface of the earth has become uninhabitable, they live in a uniform underground world in which they are constantly under surveillance by an anonymous technical apparatus and have lost the power of decision over their own lives. Films like *Logan's Run* (1976) by Michael Anderson and Norman Jewison's *Rollerball* (1975) are built around a similar idea. *The Invasion of the Body Snatchers* (1978) by Philip Kaufman, a remake of the film of the same name by Don Siegel in 1956, transfers the story of an invasion by beings from another solar system who take over human bodies and turn them into robots into the seventies, combining it with criticism of an anonymous mass society of homogenized people.

Another modification typical of films criticizing the establishment is to be found in Steven Spielberg's *Close Encounters of the Third Kind* (1977) and *E.T.– The Extra-Terrestrial* (1982), which reverse the classic formula according to which alien powers are fundamentally hostile and threatening to human civilization. In these films the aliens are friendly, intelligent creatures, and the representatives of the American state and the scientists present a threat.

Horror films – everyday life undermined by evil

Like science-fiction films, horror films also make their effect by playing with the viewers' subliminal anxiety, particularly fears of things that are different. According to the basic formula of the genre, normality is threatened by an alien, hostile being or phenomenon. Classical monsters of the genre are vampires, zombies and ghosts, deformed beings created by an abortive natural development like King Kong and Godzilla, or by the conscious or unconscious intervention of man, frequently in the form of a mad scientist, as in the case of Frankenstein. The figure of the werewolf is based on the idea of the split personality: a man changes into a wolf at full moon, or a double on the pattern of *Dr. Jekyll and Mr. Hyde* and the devil or other beings who take over human bodies.

In the fifties, horror films were made largely in the form of clichéd, rapidly produced B-movies, but in the sixties and especially in the seventies they were revalued. Given the painful sense of social degeneration and a feeling of powerlessness in the face of the evils of society, the genre clearly became more attractive as a device for living out secret fears harmlessly. The genre first entered the ranks of the blockbuster with *Rosemary's Baby* (1968) by Roman Polanski and the *The Exorcist* (1973) by William Friedkin, shaking off the stigma of cheap cinema.

chers (1978, *Die Invasion der Körperfresser*) von Philip Kaufman, ein Remake des gleichnamigen Films von Don Siegel aus dem Jahre 1956, überträgt die Geschichte der Invasion von Lebewesen aus einem anderen Sonnensystem, die sich die Körper der Menschen aneignen und sie in gefühllose Roboter verwandeln, auf die siebziger Jahre und verbindet sie mit der Kritik an einer anonymen Massengesellschaft gleichgeschalteter Menschen.

Eine weitere Modifikation, die charakteristisch für die Kritik am Establishment ist, findet sich in Steven Spielbergs *Close Encounters of the Third Kind* (1977, *Unheimliche Begegnung der dritten Art*) und *E.T.– The Extra-Terrestrial* (1982, *E.T. – Der Außerirdische*). In Umkehrung der klassischen Formel, nach der fremde Mächte grundsätzlich als feindselig und bedrohlich für die menschliche Zivilisation dargestellt wurden, sind bei ihm die Außerirdischen freundliche, intelligente Wesen, die Vertreter des amerikanischen Staates und die Wissenschaftler hingegen treten als Bedrohung auf.

Horrorfilme – die Unterwanderung des Alltags durch das Böse

Wie der Science-fiction-Film bezieht auch der Horrorfilm seine Wirkung aus dem Spiel mit den unterschwelligen Ängsten des Zuschauers, insbesondere der Angst vor dem Andersartigen. Gemäß der Grundformel des Genres wird die Normalität durch ein fremdes, feindseliges Wesen oder Phänomen bedroht. Klassische Monster des Genres sind Vampire, Zombies und Geister, deformierte Wesen, entstanden durch eine Fehlentwicklung der Natur, wie King Kong und Godzilla, oder durch die bewußte oder unbewußte Einwirkung des Menschen, die häufig mit der Gestalt des verrückten Wissenschaftlers verbunden ist, wie im Fall von Frankenstein. Auf der Idee der gespaltenen Persönlichkeit beruht die Gestalt des Werwolfs, der sich bei Vollmond vom Menschen in einen Wolf verwandelt, des Doppelgängers nach dem Muster von *Dr. Jekyll und Mr. Hyde* und des Teufels oder anderer Dämonen, die sich der Körper von Menschen bemächtigen.

Nachdem der Horrorfilm in den fünfziger Jahren überwiegend in Form von klischeehaften, schnell produzierten B-Filmen verbreitet war, erfuhr er im Laufe der sechziger Jahre, insbesondere aber in den siebziger Jahren eine Aufwertung. In Anbetracht der schmerzhaft empfundenen gesellschaftlichen Desintegration und des Gefühls der Machtlosigkeit gegenüber den Übeln der Gesellschaft wuchs offensichtlich der Reiz des Genres als Mittel für das folgenlose Ausleben geheimer Ängste. Mit *Rosemary's Baby* (1968) von Roman Polanski und *The Exorcist*

76. Mia Farrow (Rosemary Woodhouse) in *Rosemary's Baby* von Roman Polanski, 1968.
77. Roy Scheider (Martin Brody) und Lorraine Gary (Ellen Brody) in *Der weiße Hai*, Steven Spielberg, 1974.
78. Margot Kidder (Danielle Breton) in *Schwestern des Bösen* von Brian De Palma, 1973.
79. Max von Sydow (Father Merrin), Linda Blair (Regan MacNeil) und Jason Miller (Father Damien Karras) in *Der Exorzist* von William Friedkin, 1973.

76. Mia Farrow (Rosemary Woodhouse) in *Rosemary's Baby* by Roman Polanski, 1968.
77. Roy Scheider (Martin Brody) and Lorraine Gary (Ellen Brody) in *Jaws* by Steven Spielberg, 1974.
78. Margot Kidder (Danielle Breton) in *Sisters* by Brian De Palma, 1973.
79. Max von Sydow (Father Merrin), Linda Blair (Regan MacNeil) and Jason Miller (Father Damien Karras) in *The Exorcist* by William Friedkin, 1973.

Like *The Omen* (1976), another hit for the genre, both these films dealt with satanism, the reincarnation of the anti-Christ and possession by the devil, in which evil takes the form of innocent children. Later, Stanley Kubrick's *The Shining* (1980) was a masterfully staged, powerful symphony of horror about a father possessed by demons who tries to kill his wife and little son in a snowed-up, lonely country house. This expanded the characteristic features of the genre and gave them an artistic dimension. In Steven Spielberg's film *Jaws* (1975) the classical monster in the form of a bloodthirsty white shark breaks into a bathing-beach idyll and makes the holidaymakers panic. Another modification was the science-fiction horror of Philip Kaufman's *The Invasion of the Body Snatchers* and Ridley Scott's *Alien* (1979), dealing with threats to human existence from a hostile extra-terrestrial being. Evil penetrates normality unnoticed at first in all these films, then undermines and destroys it.

The sub-genre of the psycho-thriller emerged in succession to Hitchcock. This is based on characters whose psychological flaws like paranoia, memory loss, fetishism, oedipal relationships, split personality or voyeurism are essential to the plot. Brian De Palma in particular was concerned in films like *Sisters* (1973), *The Phantom of Paradise* (1974), *Obsession* (1976), *Carrie* (1976), *The Fury* (1978), *Dressed to Kill* (1980) and *Blow Out* (1981) to carry on the Hitchcock tradition. In *Sisters* and *Dressed to Kill* the basic pattern of a murder witnessed by chance and the subsequent search for the killer is combined with the split personality motif. For his film *Obsession*, De Palma uses the typical Hitchcock motif of the double and links it with the apparently random repetition of events in the life of an estate agent who meets a girl who looks astonishingly similar to his wife sixteen years after his wife and daughter were abducted and disappeared. In *The Phantom of Paradise* he shifts the plot of *The Phantom of the Opera* to the rock music scene, combining it with a sarcastic commentary about show business. His *Carrie*, 1976, is the first mainstream film linking the elements of the horror film with the high-school milieu. In it Sissy Spacek plays a young girl with supernatural powers who avenges herself cruelly for being humiliated by her fellow students when she runs amok at the school prom.

Subsequently to this, Hollywood discovered the youth horror thriller. Two independent, low-budget productions turned out to be particularly influential here: *The Texas Chain Saw Massacre* (1974) by Tobe Hooper, who later made *Poltergeist* (1982) with Spielberg's help, thus establishing himself in the mainstream, and *Halloween* (1978) by John Carpenter. Both rapidly became cult films and generated a chain of sequels. Despite the bloody events they tell of, these films derive their horror above all from the nerve-jangling cat-and-mouse game between

(1973) von William Friedkin drang das Genre erstmalig in den Bereich der Blockbuster vor und überwand das Stigma des Billigkinos. Wie *The Omen* (1976, *Das Omen*), einem weiteren Hit des Genres, beschäftigen sich beide Filme mit Satanismus, der Wiedergeburt des Antichrist und der Besessenheit vom Teufel, in der das Böse die Gestalt unschuldiger Kinder annimmt. Später drehte Stanley Kubrick mit *The Shining* (1980, *Shining*) eine meisterhaft inszenierte, suggestive Symphonie des Schreckens über einen von Dämonen besessenen Familienvater, der in einem eingeschneiten, einsamen Landschloß seine Frau und seinen kleinen Sohn umzubringen versucht. Hier wurden die Genremerkmale erweitert und ihnen eine künstlerische Dimension verliehen. In Steven Spielbergs Film *Jaws* (1975, *Der weiße Hai*) dringt das klassische Monster in Gestalt eines blutgierigen weißen Hais in die Idylle eines Badeorts ein und versetzt die Urlauber in Panik. Eine weitere Abwandlung war der Science-fiction-Horror von Philip Kaufmans *The Invasion of the Body Snatchers* und Ridley Scotts *Alien – Das unheimliche Wesen aus einer fremden Welt* (1979), die von der Bedrohung der menschlichen Existenz durch ein feindseliges außerirdisches Wesen handeln. In all diesen Filme dringt das Böse zunächst unerkannt in die Normalität ein, unterwandert und zerstört sie.

In der Nachfolge von Hitchcock entstand außerdem das Subgenre des Psychothrillers, der auf Charakteren beruht, deren psychische Deformierungen, wie Paranoia, Gedächtnisverlust, Fetischismus, ödipale Beziehungen, Persönlichkeitsspaltung oder Voyeurismus, wesentlich für die Entwicklung der Handlung sind. Besonders Brian De Palma bemühte sich in Filmen, wie *Sisters* (1973), *The Phantom of the Paradise* (1974, *Phantom im Paradies*), *Obsession* (1976, *Schwarzer Engel*), *Carrie* (1976, *Carrie – des Satans jüngste Tochter*), *The Fury* (1978, *Teufelskreis Alpha*), *Dressed to Kill* (1980) und *Blow Out* (1981, *Blow Out – Der Tod löscht alle Spuren*), um die Fortführung der Traditionen Hitchcocks. *Sisters* und *Dressed to Kill* kombinieren das Grundmuster eines zufällig beobachteten Mordes und der anschließenden Suche nach dem Mörder mit dem Motiv der gespaltenen Persönlichkeit. In *Obsession* verwendet De Palma das typische Hitchcock-Motiv des Doppelgängers und verknüpft es mit der scheinbar zufälligen Wiederholung von Ereignissen im Leben eines Immobilienmaklers, der sechzehn Jahre, nachdem seine Frau und seine Tochter Opfer einer Entführung geworden und verschwunden sind, einem Mädchen begegnet, das seiner Frau verblüffend ähnlich sieht, während er in *The Phantom of Paradise* das Handlungsmuster von *Das Phantom der Oper* in die Rockmusikszene verlagert und mit einem sarkastischen Kommentar über das Showbusiness verbindet. Mit *Carrie* schuf er 1976 den ersten Mainstream-Film, der Elemente des Horrorfilms mit dem Highschool-Milieu verbindet. Darin spielt Sissy Spacek ein junges Mädchen mit übersinnlichen Kräften, das angesichts der Demütigung durch ihre Mitschüler auf dem Schulabschlußball in einem wahren Amoklauf grausame Rache nimmt.

In der Folge entdeckte Hollywood den Jugend-Horror-Thriller. Als besonders einflußreich erwiesen sich hier allerdings zwei unabhängige Low-Budget-Produktionen, *The Texas Chain Saw Massacre* (1974, *Blutgericht in Texas*) von Tobe Hooper, der später mit Hilfe Spielbergs *Poltergeist* (1982) drehte und sich damit im Mainstream etablierte, und *Halloween* (1978) von John Carpenter. Beide entwickelten sich rasch zu Kultfilmen und zogen eine Reihe von Fortsetzungen nach sich. Trotz der blutigen Ereignisse, von denen sie erzählen, beziehen diese Filme ihren Gruseleffekt vor allem aus dem nervenaufreibenden Katz- und Mausspiel zwischen psychopathischem Mörder und Opfer und aus Andeutungen, die im Kopf des Zuschauers weitergesponnen werden. Ihre Gestaltung lehnt an die Distanzierungs- und Identifikationsmechanismen an, die Hitchcock entwickelte, den subjektive Blick beispielsweise, der sich oft auf Details richtet, die eine unheilschwangere Bedeutung erhalten, den Wechsel der Perspektive vom Protagonisten auf den Antagonisten, durch den Distanz geschaffen und dem Publikum gezeigt wird, was mit den Charakteren geschieht, und das beunruhigende Ende. Diese Stilelemente schaffen eine alptraumhafte Atmosphäre; in den siebziger Jahren prägen sie das Genre entscheidend.

Typisch für den Horrorfilm der Zeit ist, daß es im Gegensatz zum klassischen Handlungsmuster in den seltensten Fällen gelingt, die Gefahr endgültig zu beseitigen. In *Rosemary's Baby* und *The Omen* siegt der Antichrist, das Ende von *Sisters*, *Obsession*, *Carrie* und *Blow Out* ist zwiespältig, und in anderen Fällen, wie *Alien* und *Halloween,* können sich die Protagonistinnen zwar retten, die Bedrohung besteht jedoch weiter. Auf diese Art schlugen sich die Ängste vor den scheinbar vielfältigen, allgegenwärtigen und undefinierbaren Gefahren nieder, die ein wesentlicher Bestandteil der allgemeinen sozialen Verunsicherung waren. Andererseits kam es dem Interesse der Filmindustrie entgegen, erfolgreiche Formeln in Fortsetzungsfilmen maximal auszunutzen.

80. Sissy Spacek (Carrie White) in *Carrie – des Satans jüngste Tochter* von Brian De Palma, 1976.
81. Amy Irving (Gillian Bellaver) in *Teufelskreis Alpha* von Brian De Palma, 1978.
82. Jack Nicholson (Jack Torrance) in *Shining* von Stanley Kubrick, 1980.

80. Sissy Spacek (Carrie White) in *Carrie*by Brian De Palma, 1976.
81. Amy Irving (Gillian Bellaver) in *The Fury* by Brian De Palma, 1978.
82. Jack Nicholson (Jack Torrance) in *Shining* by Stanley Kubrick, 1980.

the psychopathic murderer and his victim and from allusions that continue to develop in the audience's mind. Their design draws on the distancing and identification mechanisms that Hitchcock developed, the subjective eye, for example, which is often directed at details that acquire ominous significance, the change of perspective from protagonist to antagonist, created by distance to show the audience what was happening with the characters, and the disturbing ending, all stylistic elements that create a nightmarish atmosphere and were the hallmark of the genre in the seventies.

It is typical of the horror films of the period that unlike the classic plot pattern they very seldom succeed in getting rid of the danger entirely. In *Rosemary's Baby* and *The Omen* the anti-Christ wins, the endings of *Sisters*, *Obsession*, *Carrie* and *Blow Out* are ambiguous, and in other cases like *Alien* and *Halloween* the leading characters save themselves, but the threat persists. This showed the effect of fears of the apparently multiple, omnipresent and indefinable dangers that were essential features of a general social anxiety. On the other hand, it was in the interest of the film industry to exploit successful formulae to the maximum in sequels.

Musical films – melancholy and popular culture

The film musical, which enjoyed another period of great success in the sixties, was of little interest to the New Hollywood film-makers. The stories of personal fulfilment conveyed through a symbiosis of romantic love, music and dance that determine the conventions of the genre were obviously unfitting at a time dominated by desperate world-weariness and a feeling of impotence. The few musicals made by New Hollywood also differed crucially from their classic predecessors because of their gloomy basic atmosphere. They do not present the world as a wonderfully romantic place, but are set against the background of increasing Nazi terror in thirties Berlin or celebrate death, like *Cabaret* (1972) and *All That Jazz* (1979) – both by Bob Fosse – or reverse the classic formula, like Martin Scorsese's *New York, New York* (1977). The world view in these films is much closer to melodrama than the classical musical. *Cabaret* tells the story of a love affair between an American night-club singer and an English writer in thirties Berlin, reflecting above all the decadence moral degeneracy of a dark period. *All That Jazz* shows the memories and thoughts of a famous Broadway director who is in a coma after a heart attack. Its associative, dream-like narrative method borrows from the classical conven-

Musicalfilme – Melancholie und Popkultur

Der Musicalfilm, der in den sechziger Jahren noch einmal eine große Zeit hatte, stieß bei den Filmemachern des neuen Hollywood auf nur wenig Interesse. Die Geschichten von persönlicher Erfüllung durch die Symbiose von romantischer Liebe, Musik und Tanz, welche die Konventionen des Genres bestimmten, paßte offensichtlich wenig in eine Zeit, die von verzweifeltem Weltschmerz und dem Gefühl der Ohnmacht geprägt war. Die spärlich gesäten Musicals des neuen Hollywood weichen denn auch durch ihre düstere Grundstimmung entscheidend von ihren klassischen Vorläufern ab. Sie präsentieren die Welt nicht als einen wunderbaren und romantischen Ort, sondern spielen vor dem Hintergrund des voranschreitenden Naziterrors im Berlin der dreißiger Jahre oder zelebrieren den Tod, wie *Cabaret* (1972) und *All That Jazz* (1979, *Hinter dem Rampenlicht*) – beide von Bob Fosse –, oder kehren die klassische Formel um, wie Martin Scorseses *New York, New York* (1977). Die Weltsicht dieser Filme kommt der des Melodramas weitaus näher als der des klassischen Musicals. *Cabaret* erzählt die Liebesaffäre zwischen einer amerikanischen Nachtklubsängerin und einem englischen Schriftsteller im Berlin der dreißiger Jahre und spiegelt vor allem die Dekadenz und den moralischen Verfall in einer finsteren Zeit wider. *All That Jazz* zeigt die Erinnerungen und Gedanken eines berühmten Broadway-Regisseurs, der nach einem Herzanfall im Koma liegt. In einer assoziativen, traumhaften

83. Liza Minelli (Sally Bowles) und Joel Grey (Master of Ceremonies) in *Cabaret* von Bob Fosse, 1972.
84. Liza Minnelli (Francine Evans) und Robert De Niro (Jimmy Doyle) in *New York, New York* von Martin Scorsese, 1977.
85. *The Band* von Martin Scorsese, 1978.

83. Liza Minelli (Sally Bowles) and Joel Grey (Master of Ceremonies) in *Cabaret* by Bob Fosse, 1972.
84. Liza Minnelli (Francine Evans) and Robert De Niro (Jimmy Doyle) in *New York, New York* by Martin Scorsese, 1977.
85. The Band in *The Last Waltz* by Martin Scorsese, 1978.

tions, but deviates from them in terms of content, producing an image of a personality in conflict. The narrative is framed by a conversation with a mysterious woman in white who turns out to be death at the end of the film, taking the director with her in a final dance number. The basis pattern of *New York, New York* follows classical models. At the centre of the film is a pair of lovers, he is a jazz musician, she a singer. They meet, fall in love and marry. But unlike the traditional musical, where all conflicts are overcome by a common passion for music and dance, it is only when the couple separate that they are able to realize their professional dreams.

At the same time, rock and pop culture gave important impetus to the broadening of the genre. Robert Lester's sixties Beatles films turned out to be particularly influential. They served as models for a series of similar films about American pop stars, including William Friedkin's cinema début *Good Times* (1967) about the duo Sonny & Cher and Bob Rafelson's first film

Erzählweise, die sich an klassische Konventionen anlehnt, jedoch inhaltlich vollkommen davon abweicht, entsteht das Bild einer zwiespältigen Persönlichkeit. Den Rahmen der Erzählung bildet eine Konversation mit einer mysteriösen Frau in Weiß, die sich am Ende des Films als der Tod entpuppt und den Mann in einer letzten Tanznummer mit sich nimmt. Die Grundkonstellation von *New York, New York* entspricht den klassischen Vorbildern. Im Mittelpunkt steht ein Liebespaar, er ist Jazzmusiker, sie Sängerin. Beide lernen sich kennen, verlieben sich ineinander und heiraten. Doch im Gegensatz zum traditionellen Musical, wo durch die gemeinsame Leidenschaft für Musik und Tanz alle Konflikte überwunden werden, macht hier erst die Trennung des Paares den Weg zur Verwirklichung ihrer beruflichen Träume frei.

Zugleich gab die Rock- und Popkultur wichtige Impulse für eine Ausweitung des Genres. Als überaus einflußreich erwiesen sich Robert Lesters Beatles-Filme der sechziger Jahre. Sie dienten als Vorbild für eine Reihe ähnlicher Produktionen über amerikanische Popstars, darunter William Friedkins Kinodebüt *Good Times* (1967) über das Duo Sonny & Cher und Bob Rafelsons erster Film *Head* (1968) über die von ihm kreierte Retortenband *The Monkees*. Besondere Popularität genossen Dokumentationen über Rockkonzerte, wie *Monterey Pop* (1969), *Woodstock* (1970), *Gimme Shelter* (1970), *Good To See You Again*, *Alice Cooper* (1974), oder Martin Scorseses *The Last Waltz* (1978, *The Band*) über das Abschiedskonzert der Begleitgruppe von Bob Dylan, *The Band*. Lester beeinflußte darüber hinaus die neue Ästhetik des Hollywood-Films insgesamt. Sein rasanter, surrealer Stil vereinte alle neuen formalen Elemente europäischer Filme: Cinema Verité, Jump Cuts, die Auflösung von Farben und Formen, Lichteffekte, ungewöhnliche, extreme Kamerawinkel, der Einsatz von Handkameras, Zeitlupe und Zeitraffer, schnelle Kamerafahrten, ein rasanter Montagerhythmus, die Aufhebung der Einheit von Bild und Ton und der Logik des Ortswechsels. Diese stilistischen Mittel griff das neue Hollywood auf und etablierte sie im amerikanischen Kino.

Typische Zeiterscheinungen waren außerdem Rockmusicals, in denen die Hippiekultur mit religiösen Themen verbunden ist, wie *Godspell* (1973) und *Jesus Christ Superstar* (1973) und auch die außerordentlich erfolgreichen Rockopern *The Rocky Horror Picture Show* und *Tommy*, die zwar beide 1975 in England entstanden, jedoch von Hollywood vermarktet wurden. Daneben gab es eine Reihe von Filmen, die in der Rock- und Popmusikszene oder im Country- und Western-Milieu spielen und Musikszenen mit Elementen anderer Genres verbinden, wie *Nashville* (1975) und *A Perfect Couple* (1979, *Ein perfektes Paar*) von Robert Altman, *Urban Cowboy* (1980) von James Bridges, *Cisco Pike* (1972) von Bill Norton oder Alan Rudolphs Rock'n Roll-Komödie *Roadie* (1979), in der Meat Loaf einen dicken, jungen Mann vom Lande verkörpert, der aus Liebe zu einem Groupie ein berühmter Roadmanager in der Rockszene wird.

86. *Woodstock* von Michael Wadleigh, 1969.
87. *Jesus Christ Superstar* von Norman Jewison, 1973.

86. *Woodstock* by Michael Wadleigh, 1969.
87. *Jesus Christ Superstar* by Norman Jewison, 1973.

Head (1968) about the test-tube band he had created, *The Monkees*. Documentaries about rock concerts enjoyed particular popularity, like *Monterey Pop* (1969), *Woodstock* (1970), *Gimme Shelter* (1970), *Good To See You Again, Alice Cooper* (1974) or Martin Scorsese's *The Last Waltz* (1978) about the farewell concert by Bob Dylan's backing group *The Band*. Lester also influenced the aesthetics of Hollywood films as a whole. His ultra-rapid, surreal style brought together all the new formal elements of European films: cinéma vérité, jump cuts, dissolving colours and forms, lighting effects, unusual, extreme camera angles, the use of hand-held cameras, slow motion and speeding up, rapid camera tracking, a rapid montage rhythm, removal of the unity of image and sound and the logic of changing locations. These stylistic devices were taken up by New Hollywood and established in the American cinema.

Rock musicals in which hippie culture was combined with religious themes were also the order of the day, like *Godspell* (1973) and *Jesus Christ Superstar* (1973), as well as the extraordinarily successful rock operas *The Rocky Horror Picture Show* and *Tommy*, both made in England in 1975, but marketed by Hollywood. As well as this there were a series of films set in the rock and pop music scene or the Country and Western milieu and combining musical scenes with elements of other genres like *Nashville* (1975) and *A Perfect Couple* (1979) by Robert Altman, *Urban Cowboy* (1980) by James Bridges, *Cisco Pike* (1972) by Bill Norton or Alan Rudolph's rock'n' roll comedy *Roadie* (1979), in which Meat Loaf played a fat young man from the country who becomes a famous road manager on the rock scene as a result of his love for a groupie.

Comedies – the paradoxes of the »American way of life«

Comedy underwent a number of variations. The commonest form in classical Hollywood was the screwball comedy, popularized by directors like Frank Capra, George Cukor and Howard Hawks. They set the conventions: the basic theme was the war of the sexes, which could be set in all sorts of social scenes and also contain socio-critical elements sometimes, but inevitably had a happy ending, though often it was more like a truce. The most famous examples are comedies starring Spencer Tracy and Katherine Hepburn. In the fifties and sixties these conventions were expanded by the emergence of the »sitcom« in the style of the Rock Hudson and Doris Day comedies.

Komödien – die Paradoxien des »American Way of Life«

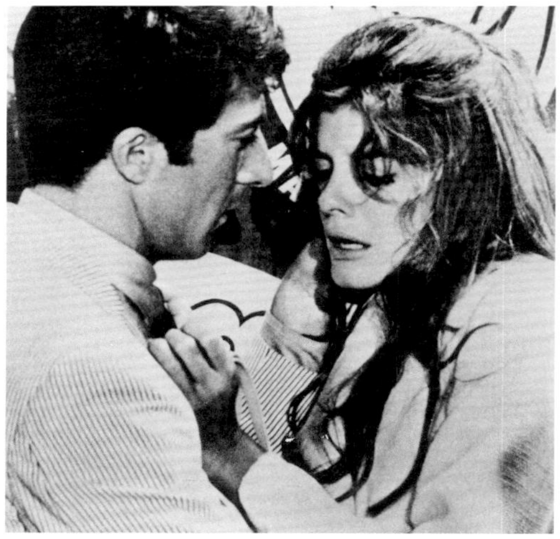

Die Komödie erfuhr eine Vielzahl von Variationen. Die im klassischen Hollywood am weitesten verbreitete Form war die Screwball-Komödie, die Regisseure, wie Frank Capra, George Cukor und Howard Hawks, populär machte. Sie bestimmte die Konventionen: Die Grundkonstellation bildete der Krieg der Geschlechter, der in den unterschiedlichsten sozialen Situationen angesiedelt sein konnte und mitunter sozialkritische Elemente enthielt, aber unweigerlich zu einem Happy-End führte, das allerdings oft eher wie ein Waffenstillstand wirkte. Komödien mit Spencer Tracy und Katherine Hepburn stellen die berühmtesten Beispiele dar. In den fünfziger und sechziger Jahren wurden diese Konventionen erweitert durch die Entstehung der »Sit-Com« im Stile der Komödien mit Rock Hudson und Doris Day.

Eine Reihe von Komödien des neuen Hollywood bauten auf den Konventionen der klassischen Screwball-Komödie auf und modernisierten sie durch die Einbeziehung zeitgenössischer Themen und Milieus. Dabei liegt der Grundkonflikt in der Regel in dem Zusammenstoß von konservativen, lustfeindlichen und liberalen, lustbetonten Lebensvorstellungen. In *What's Up Doc?* (1972, *Is' was, Doc*) von Peter Bogdanovich, einer Neufassung der klassischen Komödie *Bringing Up Baby* (1938, *Leoparden küßt man nicht*) von Howard Hawks, angelt sich eine extrovertierte junge Frau einen attraktiven, aber schüchternen Professor. John Cassavetes erzählt in *Minnie and Moskowitz* (1971), wie sich die kultivierte, aber einsame Museumsangestellte Minnie und der unkonventionelle, offenherzige Parkplatzwächter Moskowitz kennenlernen, sich ineinander verlieben und sich, trotz der kulturellen Unterschiede, zusammenraufen und heiraten. *A Perfect Couple* (1979) von Robert Altman schildert die schwierige Romanze zwischen der Sängerin einer Popgruppe und einem Liebhaber klassischer Musik, der unter der Fuchtel seiner konservativen griechischen Familie steht. Eine weitere, seinerzeit sehr erfolgreiche Komödie, die auf eine klassische Vorlage zurückgreift und diese mit zeitgenössischer Gesellschaftskritik anreichert, ist *Heaven Can Wait* (1978, *Der Himmel kann warten*), ein Remake von *Here Comes Mr. Jordan* (*Urlaub vom Himmel*) aus dem Jahre 1941, bei dem Warren Beatty Regie führte und die Hauptrolle spielte. Der Film handelt von einem Football-Spieler, der aufgrund eines Irrtums in der himmlischen Buchführung frühzeitig stirbt, im Körper eines Millionärs zurück auf die Erde geschickt wird und sich in eine britische Umweltaktivistin verliebt. Diese Konstellation dient der Kritik am oberflächlichen Lebensstil der Reichen, der Gewinnmaximierung um jeden Preis, und ist letztlich einetwas naives Plädoyer für eine menschenfreundliche und umweltverträgliche Wirtschaft.

Im übrigen war die häufigste Form des Genres im neuen Hollywood die Gesellschaftskomödie, in der typische soziale Erscheinungen Amerikas ironisiert oder karikiert wurden. Den Kulturschock, den der neue Lebensstil bei den Durchschnittsamerikanern hervorrief, thematisieren einige Filme, die um 1970 herum entstanden. Eine der wenigen Komödien über die Hippiekultur ist *Alice's Restaurant* (1969) von Arthur Penn. Eingerahmt von der Ballade *Alice's Restaurant* von Arlo Guthrie, schildert Penn episodenhaft die Entstehung der ersten authentischen Hippie-Kommune, Arlos Erscheinen vor der Musterungskommission, seinen unglücklichen Aufenthalt an einem College, wo er Musik studiert, seine Engagements in New Yorker Klubs oder seine Reisen per Anhalter durch die USA. Deutlich wird dabei die Kluft, die zwischen dem traditionellen Amerika und der jungen Aussteigergeneration besteht. Der erste amerikanische Film des Tschechen Milos Forman *Taking Off* (1971) handelt von den Eltern einer Fünfzehnjährigen, die sich im Hippiemilieu von Greenwich Village auf die Suche nach ihrer vermeintlich ausgerückten Tochter begeben und so das erste Mal in Kontakt mit dem Lebensstil der Gegenkultur geraten.

Neben *The Graduate* entstand eine Anzahl anderer Filme, die den Reifeprozeß und die sexuelle Initiation von jungen Männern zum Anlaß für eine Untersuchung des Generationenkonflikts und der satirischen Betrachtung der eingefahrenen Denk- und Verhaltensweisen des amerikanischen Mittelstands benutzten. Einer der ersten war Francis Ford Coppolas *You're a Big Boy Now* (1966, *Big Boy, jetzt wirst du ein Mann*), ein Film über einen Jugendlichen, der von seinem sich fortschrittlich gebärdenden Vater nach New York geschickt wird, damit er sich die Hörner abstößt und Erfahrungen sammelt, sich zunächst in einen männermordenden Vamp verliebt, in Schwierigkeiten gerät und schließlich von dem netten Mädchen von nebenan gerettet wird. Hal Ashby setzt sich in seinem Regiedebüt *The Landlord* (1970, *Der Hausbesitzer*) mit dem Reifeprozeß eines Millionärssohns auseinander, der ein marodes Haus in Brooklyn kauft, das er in ein psychedelisches Kunstwerk verwandeln will. Doch als die Hausbewohner, überwiegend Schwarze, sich dagegen wehren, ändert er seine Meinung und renoviert die Wohnungen, was das Unverständnis seiner exaltierten Eltern hervorruft. Ashbys *Harold and Maude* (1971) handelt

88. Barbra Streisand (Judy Maxwell) und Ryan O'Neal (Howard Bannister) in *Is' was, Doc?* von Peter Bogdanovich, 1972.
89. Paul Dooley (Alex Theodopoulos) und Marta Heflin (Sheila Shea) in *Ein perfektes Paar* von Robert Altman, 1979.
90. Dustin Hoffman (Benjamin Braddock) und Katharine Ross (Elaine Robinson) in *Die Reifeprüfung* von Mike Nichols, 1968.
91. Peter Kastner (Bernard Chanticleer) und Elizabeth Hartman (Barbara Darling) in *Big Boy, jetzt wirst Du ein Mann* von Francis Ford Coppola, 1966.
92. Buck Henry (Mr. Tyne) und Lynn Carlin (Lynn Tyne) in *Taking Off* von Milos Forman, 1971.

88. Barbra Streisand (Judy Maxwell) and Ryan O'Neal (Howard Bannister) in *What's Up Doc?* by Peter Bogdanovich, 1972.
89. Paul Dooley (Alex Theodopoulos) and Marta Heflin (Sheila Shea) in *A Perfect Couple* by Robert Altman, 1979.
90. Dustin Hoffman (Benjamin Braddock) and Katharine Ross (Elaine Robinson) in *The Graduate* by Mike Nichols, 1968.
91. Peter Kastner (Bernard Chanticleer) and Elizabeth Hartman (Barbara Darling) in *You're a Big Boy Now* by Francis Ford Coppola, 1966.
92. Buck Henry (Mr. Tyne) and Lynn Carlin (Lynn Tyne) in *Taking Off* by Milos Forman, 1971.

A number of New Hollywood comedies were based on the conventions of the classical screwball comedy, updating them by including contemporary themes and milieus. Here the basic conflict usually derived from a clash between conservative, killjoy ideas and liberal, hedonistic ones. In *What's Up Doc?* (1972) by Peter Bogdanovich, a new version of the classical comedy *Bringing Up Baby* (1938) by Howard Hawks, an extrovert young woman hooks an attractive but shy professor. In *Minnie and Moskowitz* (1971), John Cassevetes tells how a cultivated but lonely museum employee, Minnie and the unconventional, warm-hearted car park attendant get to know each other, fall in love, get together and marry despite the cultural differences. *A Perfect Couple* (1979) by Robert Altman depicts the difficult romance between a singer in a pop group and a classical music lover who is under the thumb of his conservative Greek family. Another comedy that was very successful in its day, based on a classical model and enriching it with contemporary social criticism is *Heaven Can Wait* (1978), a remake of *Here Comes Mr. Jordan* (1941), starring and directed by Warren Beatty. The film is about a footballer who dies early because of a celestial book-keeping error. He is sent back to earth in the body of a millionaire and falls in love with a British environmental activist. This pattern is used to criticize the superficial life-style of the rich, maximizing profit at any price and to make a somewhat naïve plea for an economy that is more people- and environment-friendly.

Otherwise the commonest form of the genre in New Hollywood was the social comedy, ironizing or caricaturing typical American social phenomena. The culture shock that the new life-style administered to the average American is addressed in some films made around 1970. One of the few comedies about hippie culture is *Alice's Restaurant* (1969) by Arthur Penn. Framed by Arlo Guthrie's ballad *Alice's Restaurant*, Penn's episodic film describes the emergence of the first authentic hippie commune, Arlo's appearance before the medical board, his unhappy period at a college where he studied music, his engagement in New York clubs and his hitch-hiking trips across the USA. This clearly shows the gulf between traditional America and the young drop-out generation. The first American film by the Czech director Milos Forman, *Taking Off* (1971) deals with the parents of a fifteen-year-old girl who go into the hippie milieu in Greenwich Village to look for their daughter, who they think has moved out and so come into contact with the alternative culture for the first time.

A number of films other than *The Graduate* use the process of reaching maturity and the sexual initiation of young men to examine the conflict between the generations and to take a satirical look at the deep-rooted patterns of thought and behaviour of the American middle class. One of the first was Francis Ford Coppola's *You're a Big Boy Now* (1966), a film about a youth who is sent to New York by his progressively minded father to sow his wild oats and accumulate experience. He falls in love with a man-eating vamp, gets into difficulties and is finally rescued by the nice girl from next door. In his directorial début *The Landlord* (1970), Hal Ashby

von der Freundschaft zwischen einem exzentrischen jungen Mann aus reichem Hause und einer lebenslustigen Neunundsiebzigjährigen. Ashby beschäftigt sich hier erneut mit den Paradoxien der Lebensauffassungen des Mittelstands, gegen die sich Harold mit einem bizarren Todeskult wehrt, bis er durch Maude lernt, sich über die starren gesellschaftlichen Regeln und Zwänge hinwegzusetzen und für ein selbstbestimmtes Leben, das Recht auf Kreativität und die freie Entfaltung der Persönlichkeit zu kämpfen. Das Milieu der Reichen und die damit verbundenen Deformierungen der Persönlichkeit, untersucht auch Bob Rafelson in *Stay Hungry* (1975, *Mister Universum*), einer Gesellschaftskomödie über einen jungen Millionär, der nichts mit sich und seinem Leben anzufangen weiß. Durch seine Liebesbeziehung mit der Empfangsdame eines Sportstudios und seine Freundschaft zu einem Bodybuilder erkennt er die Borniertheit, den Snobismus und den Standesdünkel hinter den Anstandsregeln der guten Gesellschaft und kann sich davon befreien. Robert Altmans *A Wedding* (1978, *Eine Hochzeit*) gibt einen Einblick in die Marotten, Vorurteile, eingefahrenen Denk- und Verhaltensweisen der amerikanischen Durchschnittsfamilie. Den Rahmen bildet eine Hochzeit zwischen den Kindern zweier Familien des gehobenen Mittelstands, darunter eine italienischer Abstammung, die von der anderen verdächtigt wird, Verbindungen zur Mafia zu haben.

Das Sexualverhalten der Amerikaner ironisiert Mike Nichols in *Carnal Knowledge* (1971, *Die Kunst zu lieben*). In einem langen Dialog, der beginnt, als sie gemeinsam das College besuchen, und über zwei Jahrzehnte hinweg fortgeführt wird, unterhalten sich zwei Freunde über ihr Sexualleben und ihr Verhältnis zu Frauen. Der eine entwickelt angesichts seiner sexuellen Bedürfnisse Schuldgefühle, der andere ist ein zynischer, draufgängerischer Macho, der Eroberungen wie Trophäen sammelt. Beide Verhaltensweisen werden als krankhafter Ausdruck einer verklemmten puritanischen Sexualmoral entlarvt. Mit den Auswirkungen der sexuellen Revolution beschäftigt sich *Shampoo* (1975) von Hal Ashby. Der Film spielt in Hollywood in den Tagen rund um die Präsidentenwahl von 1968, aus der Nixon siegreich hervorging. Warren Beatty verkörpert den Modefriseur George, der mit allen Frauen seines Umfelds, insbesondere seinen Kundinnen, schläft, wenn sich die Gelegenheit bietet. Während er von einem sexuellen Erlebnis zum anderen hetzt und sich dabei in immer größere Schwierigkeiten verstrickt, verliert er die einzige Frau, die er wirklich liebt, denn diese zieht es vor, einen Mann zu heiraten, der zwar kein so feuriger Liebhaber, dafür aber zuverlässig und verantwortungsbewußt ist.

In all diesen Filmen richtet sich die Kritik gegen die heuchlerische Doppelmoral, die Deformationen, die Vorurteile und sozialen Rituale des amerikanischen Mittelstands, die von der jüngeren Generation als lustfeindlich und beengend empfunden wurden. Dem setzte man als alternative Handlungsmaximen Spontaneität, Offenheit, Toleranz, das Vertrauen auf Gefühl und Intuition, kreatives Handeln und zwanglose Umgangsformen entgegen.

93. Ruth Gordon (Maude) und Bud Cort (Harold Chasen) in Harold und Maude von Hal Ashby, 1971.
94. Beau Bridges (Elgar Enders) und Walter Brooke (Mr. Enders) in *Der Hausbesitzer* von Hal Ashby, 1970.
95. Jack Nicholson (Jonathan Fuerst) in *Die Kunst zu lieben* von Mike Nichols, 1971.
96. Natalie Wood (Carol Sanders) in *Bob & Carol & Ted & Alice* von Paul Mazursky, 1969.
97. Warren Beatty (George Roundy), Julie Christie (Jackie Shawn) und Goldie Hawn (Jill) in *Shampoo* von Hal Ashby, 1975.

93. Ruth Gordon (Maude) and Bud Cort (Harold Chasen) in *Harold and Maude* by Hal Ashby, 1971.
94. Beau Bridges (Elgar Enders) and Walter Brooke (Mr. Enders) in *The Landlord* by Hal Ashby, 1970.
95. Jack Nicholson (Jonathan Fuerst) in *Carnal Knowledge* by Mike Nichols, 1971.
96. Natalie Wood (Carol Sanders) in *Bob & Carol & Ted & Alice* by Paul Mazursky, 1969.
97. Warren Beatty (George Roundy), Julie Christie (Jackie Shawn) and Goldie Hawn (Jill) in *Shampoo* by Hal Ashby, 1975.

examines the path to maturity of a millionaire's son who buys a tumble-down house in Brooklyn so that he can transform it into a psychedelic work of art. But when the residents, mainly black people, resist this, he changes his mind and renovates the apartments, which his exalted parents are completely unable to understand. Ashby's *Harold and Maude* (1971) deals with a friendship between an eccentric young man from a rich home and a seventy-nine-year-old woman who is full of the joys of life. Here Ashby again addresses the paradoxes of middle-class views of life, which Harold resists with a bizarre death cult, until he learns through Maude to rise above rigid social rules and constraints and to fight for a self-determined life, the right to be creative and the free development of the personality. Bob Rafelson also examines the rich milieu and the distortions of the personality associated with this in *Stay Hungry* (1975), a social comedy about a young millionaire who does not know what to do with himself or his life. Through his love for the receptionist in a gym and his friendship with a body-builder he comes to recognize the narrow-mindedness, snobbery and class arrogance behind the rules of decency in good society and is able to liberate himself from them. Robert Altman's *A Wedding* (1978) gives an insight into the fads, prejudices, deep-seated ways of thinking and behaving in the average American family. The framework is the marriage of two children from upper middle class families, one of which is Italian in origin and suspected by the other of having Mafia connections.

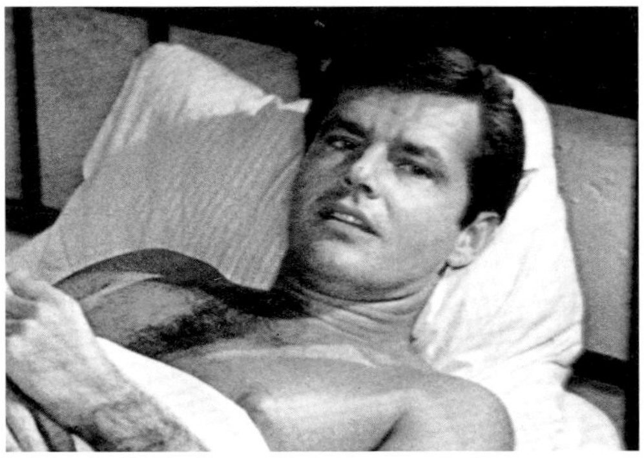

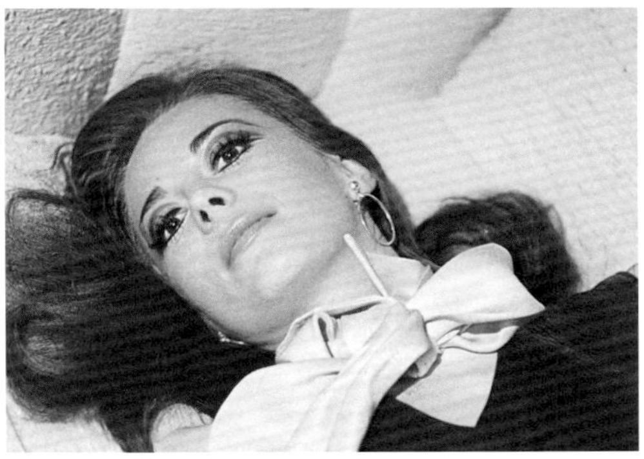

Mike Nichols takes an ironic look at American sexual behaviour in *Carnal Knowledge* (1971). Two friends talk about their sex lives and their relationships with women in a long dialogue that starts when they go to college together and continues over two decades. One starts to feel guilty because of his sexual needs, the other is a cynical, audacious macho man who collects conquests like trophies. Both attitudes are revealed as a sickly expression of inhibited, puritanical sexual morality. Hal Ashby's *Shampoo* (1975) deals with the effects of the sexual revolution. The film is set in Hollywood at the time of the 1968 presidential election, which was won by Nixon. Warren Beatty plays the fashionable hairdresser George, who sleeps with all the women around him, especially his clients, whenever the opportunity is offered. While he rushes from one sexual experience to the next and gets himself into ever-greater difficulties, he loses the only woman he really loves, as she prefers to marry a man who is not such a passionate lover, but is reliable and has a sense of responsibility.

All these films criticize hypocritical dual moral standards, the distortions, prejudices and social rituals of the American middle class, which the younger generation see as inimical to pleasure and restrictive. They oppose it with alternative maxims for action like spontaneity, frankness, tolerance, trust in emotions and intuition, creative actions and casual manners.

Paul Mazursky, einer der bedeutendsten Komödienregisseure der Zeit, erweiterte diese Thematik durch die ironische Betrachtung der Verunsicherung und Ängste, welche die Ideen der Gegenkultur in der liberalen, intellektuellen Mittelschicht hervorgerufen hatten. *Bob & Carol & Ted & Alice* (1969) beschäftigt sich mit den Bemühungen zweier junger Ehepaare, die neue sexuelle Freiheit, die Drogenkultur, den Anspruch einer offenen Beziehung und die absolute Ehrlichkeit beim Ausleben der eigenen Bedürfnisse in die Praxis umzusetzen, und offenbart ihre Unfähigkeit, mit dem neuen Lebensstil der sechziger Jahre umzugehen. Dieselben Themen fließen in *Blume in Love* (1973, *Heirat ausgeschlossen*) ein. Der Film handelt von einem Scheidungsanwalt, dessen Frau ihn verläßt, nachdem er eine Affäre hatte, und der daraufhin verzweifelt versucht, sie zurückzugewinnen, während in Rückblenden die Geschichte seiner Ehe Revue passiert. *Alex in Wonderworld* (1970, *Alex im Wunderland*) nimmt die Marotten der Traumfabrik Hollywood aufs Korn. In offener Anspielung auf den vorübergehenden Jugendkult der Filmindustrie, aber auch seine damalige eigene Situation, zeigt Mazursky einen jungen Regisseur, der nach einem ersten Erfolg als neuer Star gefeiert wird und unter dem Druck der Erwartungen an sich selbst und seiner familiären Probleme in eine Schaffenskrise gerät. Auch *Next Stop, Greenwich Village* (1976, *Ein Haar in der Suppe*) enthält offensichtlich autobiographische Elemente. Die Hauptfigur ist ein junger Schauspieler, der in den fünfziger Jahren sein bürgerliches Elternhaus verläßt und nach Greenwich Village zieht, wo er mit einer Gruppe exzentrischer Freunde lebt, die sich bemühen, dem bürgerlichen Spießertum ehrlichere und ungekünstelte Verhaltensweisen entgegenzustellen, sich dabei jedoch immer tiefer in Posen verstricken. Eine Art Fortsetzung dieses Film ist *Willie and Phil* (1980), in dem über ein Jahrzehnt hinweg die Erfahrungen zweier Freunde aus Greenwich Village verfolgt werden, die sich in dieselbe Frau verlieben, und versuchen, sich mit der Situation zu arrangieren. Gleichzeitig ist der Film eine feinsinnige Satire auf die kulturelle Entwicklung der siebziger Jahre, das Experimentieren mit neuen, unkonventionellen Lebensformen und die Suche nach Selbsterfahrung und einer neuen Identität, die verbreitete Phänomene der Zeit waren. In *Tempest* (1979, *Der Sturm*) verwandelt Mazursky Shakespeares *Der Sturm* in eine zeitgenössische Satire auf die Nöte eines gestreßten griechischstämmigen Star-Architekten aus New York, der in die Midlifecrisis gerät. Nachdem seine Frau sich aufgrund seiner Launenhaftigkeit von ihm getrennt hat, zieht er sich mit seiner halbwüchsigen Tochter und einer jungen Freundin auf eine griechische Insel zurück, um nach seinen Wurzeln zu suchen, geht jedoch seinen Begleiterinnen mit seinen spleenigen Ideen bald auf die Nerven. Mazurskys erfolgreichster Film der Siebziger, *An Unmarried Woman* (1978, *Eine entheiratete Frau*), durchleuchtet auf einfühlsame Art den Emanzipationsprozeß einer New Yorker Mittelstandsehefrau, die von ihrem Mann wegen einer anderen Frau verlassen wird und in eine tiefe Krise stürzt. Mit Hilfe ihrer Freundinnen und einer Psychiaterin gelingt es ihr, sich auf ihre eigenen Bedürfnisse und Interessen zu besinnen und sich ein selbstständiges Leben aufzubauen. Nach einiger Zeit findet sie einen neuen Partner. Als der sie drängt, ihn zu heiraten und mit ihm auf das Land zu ziehen, entscheidet sie sich schweren Herzens für ihre hart erkämpfte Unabhängigkeit. Wenn sie sich in der Schlußszene mit dem Abschiedsgeschenk ihres Freundes, einem überdimensionalen Gemälde, durch den New Yorker Verkehr quält, symbolisiert dies ihre Entschlossenheit, die Situation irgendwie zu bewältigen. Wie in all seinen Filmen behandelt Mazursky das an sich ernsthafte Thema mit einer verständnisvollen Ironie. Seine Figuren strampeln sich ab, bemühen sich, ihre Glücksvorstellungen zu verwirklichen, und stoßen an Grenzen. Das führt mitunter zu ergreifenden Momenten, hinter denen jedoch stets das Paradoxe der Situation hindurchscheint, das schließlich auch den Protagonisten selbst nicht entgeht. Am Ende steht die Einsicht in die beschränkten Möglichkeiten einer radikalen Veränderung, aber auch die Hoffnung, daß es trotzdem auf irgendeine Weise besser wird.

Dasselbe Element enthalten die nachdenklicheren Filme von Woody Allen, wie *Play it Again, Sam* (1972), die Verfilmung seines gleichnamigen Theaterstücks unter der Regie von Herbert Ross, *Annie Hall* (1977, *Der Stadtneurotiker*) und *Manhattan* (1979). Die Helden dieser Filme sind neurotische, desorientierte, lebensuntüchtige Großstadtmenschen, die gegen die Tücken der Realität ankämpfen und irgendwie versuchen zu überleben, oder, wie es in Manhattan heißt, »Leute, die sich selbst ständig solche neurotischen Probleme schaffen, die sie davon abhalten, sich mit unlösbareren, erschreckenderen Problemen des Universums auseinanderzusetzen«. Die Beziehungskomödien dieser beiden Regisseure enthalten Elemente der traditionellen Screwball-Komödie, unterscheiden sich von dieser jedoch grundsätzlich durch den häufig tragikomischen Charakter ihrer Protagonisten und den Verzicht auf ein klassisches Happyend.

Daneben entstand eine Reihe von Gesellschaftssatiren, die ihren Blick auf andere soziale Phänomene richten. Vor dem Hintergrund der erstarkenden Frauenbewegung produzierte

98. Ellen Greene (Sarah) und Lenny Baker (Larry Lapinsky) in *Ein Haar in der Suppe* von Paul Mazursky, 1976.
99. Jill Clayburgh (Erica Benton) und Penelope Russianoff (Tanya) in *Eine entheiratete Frau* von Paul Mazursky, 1978.
100. Woody Allen (Isaac Davis) und Mariel Hemingway (Tracy) in *Manhattan* von Woody Allen, 1979.
101. Woody Allen (Allan) in *Mach's noch einmal, Sam* von Herbert Ross, 1972.
102. Woody Allen (Alvy Singer), Diane Keaton (Annie Hall) und Tony Roberts (Rob) in *Der Stadtneurotiker*, von Woody Allen, 1977.

98. Ellen Greene (Sarah) and Lenny Baker (Larry Lapinsky) in *Next Stop, Greenwich Village* by Paul Mazursky, 1976.
99. Jill Clayburgh (Erica Benton) and Penelope Russianoff (Tanya) in *An Unmarried Woman* by Paul Mazursky, 1978.
100. Woody Allen (Isaac Davis) and Mariel Hemingway (Tracy) in *Manhattan* by Woody Allen, 1979.
101. Woody Allen (Allan) in *Play it Again, Sam* by Herbert Ross, 1972.
102. Woody Allen (Alvy Singer), Diane Keaton (Annie Hall) and Tony Roberts (Rob) in *Annie Hall* by Woody Allen, 1977.

Paul Mazursky, one of the most important comedy directors of the day, extended this theme by an ironic view of the sense of insecurity and fears that the ideas of the alternative culture aroused in the liberal, intellectual middle classes. *Bob & Carol & Ted & Alice* (1969) deals with the efforts of two young married couples to put into practice the new sexual freedom, drug culture, the right to have open relationships and absolute honesty in addressing one's own needs, revealing their own inability to handle the new sixties lifestyle. The same themes occur in *Blume in Love* (1973). The film is about a divorce lawyer whose wife leaves him after he has an affair and who then tries desperately to win her back, while his marriage is reviewed in a series of flashbacks. *Alex in Wonderland* (1970) attacks the quirks of the Hollywood dream factory. In an open allusion to the passing youth cult in the film industry, but also to his own situation, Mazursky shows a young director who is celebrated as a new star after his first success and gets into a creative crisis under the pressure of his own expectations and family problems. *Next Stop Greenwich Village* (1976) also contains autobiographical elements. The main character is a young actor who leaves his middle-class home in the fifties and moves to Greenwich Village, where he lives with a group of eccentric friends who try to set a more honest, natural way of life against middle-class morality, but find themselves increasingly striking poses. *Willie and Phil* (1980) is a kind of continuation of this film. It follows the experiences of two friends from Greenwich Village over a decade; they fall in love with the same woman and try to come to terms with the situation. At the same time the film is a subtle satire on the cultural developments of the seventies, experiments with new and unconventional ways of life and the search for self-experience and a new identity that were widespread phenomena of the day. In *Tempest* (1979), Mazursky transforms Shakespeare's *The Tempest* into a contemporary satire on the difficulties of a stressed New York star architect of Greek origin who gets into a mid-life crisis. After his wife leaves him because of his moodiness, he moves to a Greek island with his teenage daughter and a young friend to search for his origins, but soon gets on his young companions' nerves with his splenetic ideas. Mazursky's most successful film in the seventies, *An Unmarried Woman* (1978) casts empathetic light on the emancipation process undergone by a middle-class New York wife who is left by her husband for another woman and falls into a major crisis. With the help of her friends and a psychiatrist she manages to address her own needs and interests and to build up an independent life for herself. After a time she finds a new partner. When he presses her to marry him and move to the country with him she decides in favour of her hard-fought independence, with a heavy heart. In the final scene she makes her tortuous way through the New York traffic with a her friend's farewell present, an outsize painting, all of which symbolizes her determination to come to terms with the situation in some way. As in all his films, Mazursky treats this essentially serious subject with sympathetic irony. His characters

Jane Fonda mit ihrer Produktionsgesellschaft IPC Films unter der Regie von Colin Higgins *Nine to Five* (1980, *Warum eigentlich bringen wir den Chef nicht um*), eine überdrehte Komödie, welche den Zusammenhalt von Frauen in einer von Männern beherrschten Berufswelt zum Thema hat. Der Film handelt von drei Sekretärinnen in einem Großraumbüro, die aufgrund einer Reihe von Verwechslungen und Mißverständnissen beschließen, ihren Chef zu entführen. Seine Abwesenheit nutzen sie, um die Leitung der Abteilung in ihre Hände zu nehmen und in seinem Namen grundlegende Verbesserungen für die weiblichen Angestellten einzuführen. Die Möglichkeit von Frauen, sich durch eine berufliche Karriere zu emanzipieren, untersucht Sidney Lumet in *Just Tell Me What You Want* (1980, *Sag mir was du willst*), einer Komödie über eine Journalistin, die sich privat und beruflich aus dem Schatten ihres Partners, eines skrupellosen, erfolgreichen Geschäftsmannes lösen will, im beruflichen Erfolg jedoch keine Erfüllung findet und schließlich zu ihm zurückkehrt. Mit der veränderten Rolle der Geschlechter befaßt sich Alan J. Pakula in der Komödie *Starting Over* (1979, *Auf ein Neues*), in der Burt Reynolds einen Mann spielt, der nach der Trennung von seiner von feministischen Ideen beeinflußten Frau versucht, sein Leben neu einzurichten.

Ein weiteres wichtiges Thema war die Kritik an der Manipulation durch die modernen Massenmedien und das Showbusiness. Der Film, der die Medienkritik am deutlichsten formulierte und das gängige Bild des modernen Fernsehens in Hollywoodfilmen für die Zukunft entscheidend prägte, war *Network* (1976) von Sidney Lumet, eine Satire auf die Methoden des Kommerzfernsehens, das ungeachtet der journalistischen Ethik skrupellos alles vermarktet, was Quoten und Marktergebnisse verbessert. Selbst die Unzufriedenheit und der Protest der Menschen werden kommerzialisiert und in inhaltslose Phrasen und Gesten verpackt, welche jede reale Veränderung vereiteln. Die durch die Sensationslust der Medien beeinflußte Umwandlung des Sports in eine reine Kommerzshow thematisiert die Satire *Slap Shot* (1977, *Schlappschuß*) von George Roy Hill. Im Mittelpunkt des Films steht eine erfolglose Eishockeymannschaft, die Angst vor ihrer Auflösung hat. Als der Manager drei neue Spieler engagiert, welche sich durch Brutalität auszeichnen und jedes Match in eine Schlägerei verwandeln, wendet sich das Blatt. Die Mannschaft wird von Presse und Fans bejubelt und gewinnt schließlich sogar die Meisterschaft. Man löst sie aber dennoch auf, weil eine Verlustabschreibung für die Besitzerin finanziell vorteilhafter ist.

Die Erkenntnis über die Macht der Medien bei der Imagebildung, die sich durch die in den sechziger Jahren eingeführten Fernsehdebatten von Politikern gebildet hatte, stärkte das Bewußtsein der unheiligen Allianz von Medien und Politik, ein Thema, mit dem sich *Being There* (1979, *Willkommen Mr. Chance*) von Hal Ashby und *H.E.A.L.T.H.* (1979, *Der Gesundheits-Kongreß*) von Robert Altman beschäftigen. *Being There* erzählt die Geschichte von Mr. Chance, einem älteren Mann, der sein Leben lang als Gärtner in einem reichen Haus gearbeitet hat. Als sein Arbeitgeber stirbt, kommt er das erste Mal in seinem Leben mit der Außenwelt in Kontakt und findet durch einen Unfall Anschluß an ein reiches Ehepaar, das ihn in die gute Gesellschaft einführt. Obwohl er weder lesen noch schreiben kann und seine Weltsicht ausgesprochen simpel und beschränkt ist, legt man ihm seine Angewohnheit, jedes Thema auf die Begriffe der Gartenarbeit zu bringen, dem einzigen Metier, von dem er etwas versteht, als Weisheit aus. Aufgrund seiner Fähigkeit, komplexe Zusammenhänge auf Allgemeinplätze zu reduzieren, wird er schließlich zum Berater des amerikanischen Präsidenten ernannt. *H.E.A.L.T.H.* ist eine Polit-Satire rund um die Vorstandswahlen einer Gesundheitsorganisation gleichen Namens, in der die Kandidatinnen als heuchlerische, karrieresüchtige Intrigantinnen und der Wahlkampf als inhaltsloser Medienrummel entlarvt werden. Das Hohle der Welt des Showbusiness und der Politik enthüllt Robert Altman in *Nashville* (1975). In einer kaleidoskopartigen, tragikomischen Geschichte über 24 Personen, deren Lebensweg sich über fünf Tage kreuzt, zeigt er, wie Prominente und Fußvolk alles nur Erdenkliche tun, um in der glamourösen, von den Massenmedien beherrschten Hochburg der Country- und Western-Musik zu überleben, und vermittelt, in welcher Weise die Herrschaft des Kommerzes im Showgeschäft und die Oberflächlichkeit der Politik eine sinnentleerte Scheinwelt produzieren, die dann als amerikanischer Traum verkauft wird.

Wie die meisten Filme Altmans haben auch *H.E.A.L.T.H.* und *Nashville* durch ihre episodische Form die Qualität von Milieustudien, in denen ein ironischer Kommentar mit bissiger Gesellschaftskritik verbunden wird. Altmans Protagonisten sind merkwürdige Sonderlinge oder gesellschaftliche Außenseiter, wie die Titelfigur von *Brewster McCloud* (1970), ein junger Mann, der im Aerodrom von Houston mit einem Flugapparat experimentiert und dabei alle ermordet, die seinen Plänen im Wege stehen, oder die beiden Spieler aus *California Split* (1974), die in den Spielhallen und Kasinos von San Franzisko und Reno dem großen Gewinn hinterherjagen. Das Verhalten dieser Antihelden ist durch Realitätsverlust und Entfremdung geprägt, was durch die

103. Paul Newman (Reggie Dunlop) und Lindsay Crouse (Lily Braden) in *Schlappschuß* von George Roy Hill, 1977.
104. Peter Sellers (Chance Gardener) und Melvyn Douglas (Benjamin Rand) in *Willkommen, Mr. Chance* von Hal Ashby, 1979.
105. Dolly Parton (Doralee Rhodes), Jane Fonda (Judy Bernly) und Lily Tomlin (Violet Newstead) in *Warum eigentlich bringen wir den Chef nicht um* von Colin Higgins, 1980.
106. Faye Dunaway (Diana Christensen) in *Network* von Sidney Lumet, 1975.
107. Barbara Baxley (Lady Pearl) und Henry Gibson (Haven Hamilton) in *Nashville* von Robert Altman, 1974.

103. Paul Newman (Reggie Dunlop) and Lindsay Crouse (Lily Braden) in *Slap Shot* by George Roy Hill, 1977.
104. Peter Sellers (Chance Gardener) and Melvyn Douglas (Benjamin Rand) in *Being There* by Hal Ashby, 1979.
105. Dolly Parton (Doralee Rhodes), Jane Fonda (Judy Bernly) and Lily Tomlin (Violet Newstead) in *9 to 5* by Colin Higgins, 1980.
106. Faye Dunaway (Diana Christensen) in *Network* by Sidney Lumet, 1975.
107. Barbara Baxley (Lady Pearl) and Henry Gibson (Haven Hamilton) in *Nashville* by Robert Altman, 1974.

slave away, make an effort to realize their ideas of happiness and come up against limits. This leads to some moving moments, but the paradoxical nature of the situation shines out behind them and even the people involved are bound to be aware of it. Finally comes an insight into the limited possibilities for radical change, but also the hope that things will nevertheless improve in some way.

The same element is contained in Woody Allen's rather more reflective films like *Play it Again, Sam* (1972), a film version of his play of the same name directed by Herbert Ross, *Annie Hall* (1977) and *Manhattan* (1979). The heroes of these films are neurotic, disoriented people who are unable to cope with life, struggling with the perversities of reality and somehow trying to survive, or as it is put in Manhattan, »people who constantly create neurotic problems for themselves that stop them coming to terms with the insoluble, horrifying problems of the universe«. These two directors' comedies about relationships contain elements of the traditional screwball comedy, but differ from it fundamentally because of the frequently tragi-comic character of the leading figures and their refusal to accept a classical happy ending.

As well as this, a number of social satires looking at other social phenomena were produced. Against the background of the increasingly powerful women's movement, Jane Fonda and her production company IPC Films produced *9 to 5* (1980), directed by Colin Higgins, a crazy comedy addressing women's cohesion in a male-dominated professional world. The film is about three secretaries in an open-plan office who decide to abduct their boss as a result of a series of mix-ups and misunderstandings. They use his absence to take over the department and introduce fundamental improvements for the female employees in his name. Sidney Lumet examines women's opportunities to emancipate themselves through a professional career in *Just Tell Me What You Want* (1980), a comedy about a journalist he wants to remove herself privately and professionally from the shadow of her partner, an unscrupulous and successful businessman. She does not find professional success fulfilling, however, and goes back to him. Alan J. Pakula addresses the changed role of the sexes in the comedy *Starting Over* (1979), in which Burt Reynolds plays a man who tries to rearrange his life after separation from his wife, who is influenced by feminist ideas.

Another important theme was criticism of manipulation by the modern mass media and show-business. The film that formulated criticism of the media most clearly and went a long way to shape the accepted image for modern television for Hollywood films in the future was *Network* (1976) by Sidney Lumet. This is a satire on the methods used by commercial television, which unscrupulously markets anything that improves ratings and sales results, regard-

108. Rene Auberjonois (The Teacher) in *Nur Fliegen ist schöner* von Robert Altman, 1970.
109. Robert Redford (Bill McKay) in *Bill McKay – Der Kandidat* von Michael Ritchie, 1972.
110. Woody Allen (Fielding Mellish) und Louise Lasser (Nancy) in *Bananas* von Woody Allen, 1971.
111. Burt Reynolds (Billy Clyde Puckett) und Kris Kristofferson (Marvin »Shake« Tiller) in *Zwei ausgebuffte Profis* von Michael Ritchie, 1978.

108. Rene Auberjonois (The Teacher) in *Brewster McCloud* by Robert Altman, 1970.
109. Robert Redford (Bill McKay) in *The Candidate* by Michael Ritchie, 1972.
110. Woody Allen (Fielding Mellish) and Louise Lasser (Nancy) in *Bananas* by Woody Allen, 1971.
111. Burt Reynolds (Billy Clyde Puckett) and Kris Kristofferson (Marvin »Shake« Tiller) in *Semi-Tough* by Michael Ritchie, 1978.

distanzierte Sichtweise des unbeteiligten Beobachters unterstrichen wird. Stilmerkmale, wie sich überschneidende, scheinbar improvisierte Dialoge mit einem perfekten Zusammenspiel des Ensembles, eine bewegliche Kameraführung, lange Einstellungen und ein kreativer Schnitt von Bild und Ton verleihen den Filmen einen dokumentarischen Charakter und wurden zum Markenzeichen des Regisseurs.

Auch in den Filmen Michael Ritchies verbergen sich hinter simplen Plots genau beobachtete Milieustudien, welche die Schwächen und Marotten der Protagonisten und ihrer Umwelt ins Lächerliche ziehen. Charakteristisch sind lange Szenenfolgen ohne Dialog, die oft in halbdokumentarischer Form gedreht sind. Die daraus entstehenden Szenen erscheinen manchmal so realistisch, daß sie peinlich berühren. *The Candidate* (1972, *Bill McKay – der Kandidat*) nimmt die Wahlkampagne eines liberalen Politikers zum Anlaß für eine bissige Satire auf den Politzirkus, in *Smile* (1975, *Lauter nette Mädchen*) bildet ein Schönheitswettbewerb den Rahmen für eine Demaskierung der Kleinstadtmentalität, *The Bad News Bears* (1976, *Die Bären sind los*) benutzt die Geschichte einer unorthodoxen Kinder-Baseball-Mannschaft und ihres trinklustigen Trainers für eine realistische Studie des Lebens in den Vor- und Kleinstädten. *Semi-Tough* (1978, *Zwei ausgebuffte Profis*) verbindet eine Dreiecksgeschichte über zwei Football-Profis und eine gemeinsame Freundin mit der klassischen Erfolgsstory eines Football-Teams, um die zeitgenössische Begeisterung für ominöse Gurus und Wunderheiler, esoterische Heilslehren und magische Fetische, Selbsterfahrungs-Workshops und den modischen Psycho-Jargon der Lächerlichkeit preiszugeben. In *An Almost Perfect Affair* (1979, *Perfekter Seitensprung*) bildet die Liebesaffäre eines jungen amerikanischen Filmemachers und der Gattin eines italienischen Produzenten den Rahmen für einen Einblick in die Selbstdarstellungs- und Profilierungsmethoden von Stars und Nachwuchskünstlern auf den Filmfestspielen in Cannes.

Ein auffälliges Merkmal vieler Komödien der Zeit ist ein respektloser und anarchistischer Sinn für Humor, mit dem Zeiterscheinungen und Stereotypen karikaturistisch überzeichnet und bloßgestellt werden. Dieses Phänomen hatte seinen Ursprung in der Popkultur der sechziger Jahre, deren Lebensgefühl Filme wie *What's New, Pussycat?* (1965, *Was gibts Neues, Pussy*) wiedergeben, wo die absurde Komik der Marx-Brothers wiederbelebt und diese mit zeitgemäßen Zutaten angereichert wird. Das Drehbuch stammt von Woody Allen und enthält bereits die charakteristischen absurden Elemente und überspannten, besessenen Typen seiner späteren Filme, wie *Take The Money and Run* (1969), *Bananas* (1971), *Everything You Always Wanted to Know About Sex* (1972, *Was Sie schon immer über Sex wissen wollten*), oder *Sleeper* (1973, *Der Schläfer*). Eine ähnliche absurde Situationskomik und derselbe respektlose Sinn für Humor, findet sich unter anderem in den Filmen von Mel Brooks, in Altmans *Brewster McCloud* und *M.A.S.H.* oder in Ashbys *Harold and Maude* und *The Last Detail* (1973, *Das letzte Komando*).

less of journalistic ethics. Even people's discontent and protests are commercialized and packaged in meaningless phrases and gestures that thwart any real change. George Roy Hill's satire *Slap Shot* (1977) looks at the way sport is transformed into a mere commercial show by the media's hunger for sensation. The film centres around an unsuccessful ice hockey team that is afraid of being disbanded. Things change when the manager employs three new players who distinguish themselves by their brutality and turn every match into a fight. The team is acclaimed by the press and fans, and finally even wins the championship. But it is still disbanded, because it is financially advantageous for the woman who owns it to write off the loss.

Realization of the media's power in image-building, which had built up as a result of the television debates between politicians introduced in the sixties, strengthened awareness of the unholy alliance between the media and politics, a theme addressed by *Being There* (1979) by Hal Ashby and *H.E.A.L.T.H.* (1979) by Robert Altman. *Being There* tells the story of Mr. Chance, an elderly man who has worked all his life as gardener in a rich household. When his employer dies he comes into contact with the outside world for the first time in his life. An accident leads to a connection with a rich married couple who introduce him to good society. Although he cannot read or write, and his view of the world is extremely simple and limited, his habit of addressing every subject in terms of gardening, the only craft he knows anything about, is seen as wisdom. He is finally made an advisor to the American President because of his ability to reduce complex matters to commonplaces. *H.E.A.L.T.H.* is a political satire about elections to the board of a health organization of the same name in which the candidates are shown to be hypocritical, career-addicted intriguers and the election as a meaningless media fuss. Robert Altman reveals the hollowness of the worlds of show-business and politics in *Nashville* (1975). He shows, in a kaleidoscopic, tragi-comic story about 24 people whose paths cross over a period of five days, how eminent people and the lower ranks alike will do anything at all to survive in the mass-media dominated stronghold of Country and Western music, showing how the dominance of commerce in show-business and the superficiality of politics produce a meaningless and unreal world that is sold as the American dream.

Like most of Altman's films, the episodic form of *H.E.A.L.T.H.* and *Nashville* gives them the quality of milieu studies in which an ironic commentary is combined with sharp social criticism. Altman's protagonists are strange oddities or social outsiders like the eponymous hero of *Brewster McCloud* (1970), a young man experimenting with a flying machine at Houston aerodrome and murdering anyone who stand in the way of his plans, or the two gamblers in *California Split* (1974) who are chasing the big win in the gambling halls and casinos of San Francisco and Reno. These anti-heroes' behaviour is marked by loss of reality and alienation, underlined by the distanced view taken by the uninvolved observer. Style characteristics like overlapping, apparently improvised dialogue allied with perfect ensemble playing, fluent camerawork, long shots and creative picture and sound editing give these films a documentary character and became the director's trade mark.

Michael Ritchie's films also have simple plots concealing precisely observed milieu studies that push the weaknesses and fads of the leading characters and the people around them to ridiculous lengths. Characteristic features are long sequences of scenes without dialogue, often shot in semi-documentary form. The footage produced often seems so realistic that they are embarrassingly moving. *The Candidate* (1972) makes a liberal politician's election campaign a basis for a biting satire on the political circus, in *Smile* (1975) a beauty contest provides the framework for unmasking small town morality, and *The Bad News Bears* (1976) uses the story of an unorthodox children's baseball team and their hard-drinking trainer for a realistic study of life in the suburbs and small towns. *Semi-Tough* (1978) combines a triangular story about two professional footballers and their shared girl-friend with a classic football team success story in order to ridicule contemporary enthusiasm for unsavoury gurus and miracle healers, esoteric doctrines of salvation and magic fetishes, self-knowledge workshops and modish psycho-jargon. In *An Almost Perfect Affair* (1979) a love affair between a young American film-maker and the wife of an Italian producer forms the framework for a look at the self-presentation and profiling methods used by stars and young artistes at the Cannes Film Festival.

One striking feature of many comedies of this period is a disrespectful and anarchistic sense of humour, used to caricature and lay bare contemporary phenomena and stereotypes. This originated in sixties pop culture. Films like *What's New, Pussycat?* (1965) reflect its sense of life, reviving the absurd comedy of the Marx Brothers and enriching it with up-to-date ingredients. The book is by Woody Allen and already contains the characteristic absurd elements and extreme, obsessive types featured in his later films like *Take the Money and Run* (1969), *Bananas*

Dramen – Porträts einer kranken Gesellschaft

Angesichts des Anspruchs einer ernsthaften und kritischen Auseinandersetzung mit der amerikanischen Realität war das Drama naturgemäß ein wichtiges Genre des neuen Hollywood. In klassischen Hollywood-Filmen ging es dabei in der Regel um die Konfrontation gegensätzlicher Wertvorstellungen und Verhaltensweisen, repräsentiert durch unterschiedliche Charaktere. Diese lief auf die Bestätigung der traditionellen, »guten« amerikanischen Werte hinaus, häufig in Form einer Versöhnung der Gegensätze. Die Struktur des Dramas erlaubte in weitaus größerem Maße als andere Genres die psychologische Durchdringung der Charaktere und die Offenlegung sozialer Konflikte. Eine gängige Form war das Familienmelodram, dessen Charakteristika dem Milieu der amerikanischen Kleinfamilie entsprangen.

Auffallend an den Dramen der siebziger Jahre ist dagegen, daß sie mehr wie eine Bestandsaufnahme einer sozialen Situation wirken. Sie beschreiben die Defekte der Gesellschaft und decken Konflikte auf, bieten jedoch keinerlei oder, wenn doch, dann nur unbefriedigende Lösungen an. Formal beinhaltet das in der Regel eine Abweichung von der klassischen Erzählstruktur, dem Prinzip der Einführung, Zuspitzung und glücklichen oder tragischen Lösung eines klar definierten Konflikts zugunsten einer offenen, episodenhaften oder assoziativen Erzählweise. Auf diese Art sind die Dramen des neuen Hollywood oberflächlich und oft nur durch ihre tragische Grundstimmung als solche erkennbar. Entgegen den klassischen Konventionen wird der dramatische Konflikt nicht durch die Konfrontation von Individuen entwickelt, sondern durch die Beschreibung eines sozialen Milieus und die Betonung des Widerspruchs zwischen Individuum und Gesellschaft.

Viele Dramen der ersten Welle New Hollywoods sind eine Selbstdarstellung der Gegenkultur. Sie beschäftigen sich mit der Protestbewegung, der Rockszene, der Hippiekultur und dem Drogenkonsum. Die ersten Filme, die den sozialen Protest ernsthaft thematisierten, standen unter dem Eindruck der Verschärfung des Konflikts im Jahre 1968. Haskell Wexlers *Medium Cool*, der 1968 als Eigenproduktion entstand und im folgenden Jahr nur unter Schwierigkeiten in die Kinos kam, schildert die Liebesgeschichte eines Fernsehkameramanns und einer jungen Witwe vor dem Hintergrund der Unruhen anläßlich des Parteitags der Demokraten 1968 in Chicago. Mit Stuart Hagmans *The Strawberry Statement* (*Blutige Erdbeeren*) und Richard Rushs *Getting Straight* kamen 1969 die ersten beiden Filme über die Revolte an den amerikanischen Universitäten in die Kinos. Im Mittelpunkt von *The Strawberry Statement* steht ein junger, unpolitischer Student, der sich zunächst aus Neugier der Besetzung der Columbia Universität im

112. Verna Bloom (Eileen) und Robert Forster (John Cassellis) in *Medium Cool* von Haskell Wexler, 1968.
113. Bruce Davison (Simon) und Kristin Van Buren (Meg) in *Blutige Erdbeeren* von Stuart Hagman, 1969.

112. Verna Bloom (Eileen) and Robert Forster (John Cassellis) in *Medium Cool* by Haskell Wexler, 1968.
113. Bruce Davison (Simon) and Kristin Van Buren (Meg) in *The Strawberry Statement* by Stuart Hagman, 1969.

(1971), *Everything You Always Wanted to Know About Sex* (1972) or *Sleeper* (1973). Similarly absurd situation comedy and the same disrespectful sense of humour is also to be found in the films of Mel Brooks, in Altman's *Brewster McCloud* and *M.A.S.H.* or in Ashby's *Harold and Maude* and *The Last Detail* (1973).

Dramas – portraits of a sick society

Given the desire to examine American realities seriously and critically, the drama was naturally an important genre in New Hollywood. Classical Hollywood films of his kind are usually about a confrontation between conflicting values and behaviour, represented by a variety of characters. This tended to lead to confirmation of traditional »good« American values, frequently by reconciling conflicts. The structure of the drama, to a much greater extent than other genres, made it possible to analyse the characters' psychology penetratingly and to reveal social conflicts. A popular form was the family melodrama, whose characteristics originated from the milieu of the American nuclear family.

The striking feature of the seventies dramas on the other hand is that they seem more as though they are taking stock of a social situation. They identify defects in society and reveal conflicts, but do not offer solutions, or at best unsatisfactory ones. Formally this means departure from the classical narrative structure, the principle of the introduction, heightening and happy or sad solution to a clearly defined conflict, in favour of an open, episodic or associative narrative method. This means that New Hollywood dramas are superficially recognizable as such only because of their tragic basic mood. The dramatic conflict runs counter to the classical conventions by developing not from confrontation between individuals, but from the description of a social milieu and emphasis on the contradictions between individuals and society.

Many dramas from the first wave of New Hollywood are self-presentations by the alternative culture. They deal with protest movements, the rock scene, hippie culture and drug use. The first films to address social protest seriously were triggered by the sharpening of the conflict in 1968. Haskell Wexler's *Medium Cool*, made in 1968 as an independent production, and shown in cinemas the following year only with difficulty, is about a television cameraman's love for a young widow, set against the background of the riots at the Democratic Party Congress in Chicago in 1968. Stuart Hagman's *The Strawberry Statement* and Richard Rush's *Getting Straight*, both 1969, were the first two films about the revolt in the American universities to reach the cinemas. *The Strawberry Statement* is built around a young, apolitical student who

Jahre 1968 anschließt, sich dort in ein Mädchen verliebt, durch das er weiter in das Geschehen hineingezogen wird, und schließlich durch seine Erfahrungen mit dem Vorgehen von Polizei und Universitätsleitung zum politischen Aktivisten wird. In einer Mischung aus ironischer Distanz und echter Betroffenheit vermittelt der Film perfekt das Zeitgefühl und die Stimmung an den Universitäten Ende der sechziger Jahre. *Getting Straight* handelt von einem Universitätsstudenten, der sich vor dem Abschluß befindet und vor der Entscheidung steht, sich in der Protestbewegung zu engagieren oder über die Erziehung der jüngeren Generation eine Veränderung zu bewirken. *The Revolutionary* (1970) von Paul Williams ist eine Studie über einen College-Studenten, der allmählich in den politischen Aktivismus hineingezogen wird. Jack Nicholson durchleuchtet in seinem Regiedebüt *Drive, He Said* (1971) den zunehmenden Prozeß der Entfremdung eines Basketballspielers an einem College, während Michelangelo Antonionis *Zabriskie Point* (1970) alle wesentlichen Elemente der Filme über die Gegenkultur der Zeit vereint: den politischen Protest an den Universitäten, Drogenkonsum, freie Liebe und die Flucht in die Natur.

Die Drogenproblematik greift unter anderem Paul Williams in *Dealing: Or the Berkeley-to-Boston Forty-Brick Lost-Bag Blues* (1972, *Heißer Stoff für Boston*) auf, einem Film über einen Harvard-Studenten, der mit Drogen dealt, seine Freundin in seine Geschäfte hineinzieht und nach ihrer Verhaftung durch die Erpressung eines korrupten Polizisten ihre Freilassung erreichen kann. Weitaus kritischer setzt sich Jerry Schatzbergs *The Panic in Needle Park* (1971, *Panik im Needle Park*), in dem Al Pacino seine erste Hauptrolle spielt, mit der Drogenszene rund um den sogenannten Needle Park in New York auseinander. Im Mittelpunkt steht ein junges Paar, das mit Diebstählen, Betrug, Drogenhandel und Prostitution seine Sucht finanziert und dessen Leben sich zwischen der Gefahr einer Überdosis schlechten Stoffes und der Angst vor der Arrestzelle abspielt. *Believe in Me* (1971) von Stuart Hagman handelt von der Drogenabhängigkeit einer Karrierefrau in East Village. Bill Norton verbindet in *Cisco Pike* (1972) die Drogenproblematik mit einer Milieustudie der Rockmusik- und Gegenkulturszene von Los Angeles. Kris Kristofferson, einer der bekanntesten Folkrocksänger der Zeit, spielt einen heruntergekommenen drogenabhängigen Rockmusiker und Kleindealer, der von einem korrupten Polizisten dazu erpreßt wird, eine größere Menge Marihuana für ihn zu verkaufen. Im Gegensatz zu *Easy Rider*, wo der Joint Ausdruck des Gemeinschaftsgefühls und Mittel der Bewußtseinserweiterung ist, konzentriert sich die Darstellung in diesen Filmen auf den allmählichen Abstieg und den moralischen Verfall durch die Drogenabhängigkeit. Damit distanziert sie sich von der Verherrlichung des Drogenkonsums, wie er in der sechziger Jahren vorherrschte.

Die allgemeine Politisierung weckte auch Interesse an der frühen Entwicklung der Arbeiterbewegung. *The Molly Maguires* (1970, *Verflucht bis zum jüngsten Tag*) von Martin Ritt spielt vor dem Hintergrund der Arbeitskämpfe irischstämmiger Bergarbeiter in Pennsylvania in den siebziger Jahren des 19. Jahrhunderts. 1971 drehte der Schwede Bo Widerberg *Joe Hill*, ein Sozial-

114. *Getting Straight* von Richard Rush, 1969.
115. Al Pacino (Bobby) und Kitty Winn (Helen) in *Panik im Needle Park* von Jerry Schatzberg, 1971.

114. *Getting Straight* by Richard Rush, 1969.
115. Al Pacino (Bobby) and Kitty Winn (Helen) in *The Panic in Needle Park* by Jerry Schatzberg, 1971.

joins the sit-in at Columbia University in 1968 out of curiosity at first, then finally becomes a political activist as a result of his experiences of actions taken by the police and the university authorities. The film's mixture of ironic distance and genuine dismay perfectly conveys the mood of the day and the atmosphere in the universities in the late sixties. *Getting Straight* is about a university student who is about to graduate and has to decide whether to commit himself to the protest movement or to bring about a change in the education of the younger generation. *The Revolutionary* (1970) by Paul Williams is a study of a college student who is gradually drawn into political activism. In his directorial début *Drive, He Said* (1971), Jack Nicholson sheds light on the increasing alienation of a basketball player at a college, while Michelangelo Antonioni's *Zabriskie Point* (1970) brings together all the essential elements of contemporary alternative culture: political protest at the universities, drug use, free love and escapes into nature.

Paul Williams looks at drugs problems among other things in *Dealing: Or the Berkeley-to-Boston Forty-Brick Lost-Bag Blues* (1972), a film about a Harvard student who deals drugs and involves his girl-friend in the business. When she is arrested he is able to get her released by blackmailing a corrupt policeman. Jerry Schatzberg's *The Panic in Needle Park* analyses the drug scene in the so-called Needle Park in New York much more critically, with Al Pacino in his first leading role. It centres around a young couple who finance their addiction by theft, fraud, drug-dealing and prostitution and whose life is lived out between fear of the danger of an overdose of bad gear and fear of being arrested. *Believe in Me* (1971) by Stuart Hagman deals with the drug addiction of a career woman in East Village. In *Cisco Pike* (1972), Bill Norton combines drugs problems with a milieu study of rock music and the alternative scene in Los Angeles. Kris Kristofferson, one of the best-known folk-rock singers of the period plays a down-and-out drug-dependent rock musician and small-time dealer who is blackmailed by a corrupt policeman into selling a large quantity of marihuana for him. Unlike *Easy Rider*, where the joint expresses a feeling of community and consciousness-raising, these films concentrate on gradual decline and moral degeneration as a result of drug addiction, this distancing themselves from the glorification of drug use predominant in the sixties.

Alongside all this, the generally increased involvement in politics aroused interest in the early days of the labour movement. *The Molly Maguires* (1970) by Martin Ritt is set against the background of Pennsylvania miners of Irish origin involved in labour conflicts in the 1870s. In 1971 the Swede Bo Widerberg made *Joe Hill*, a social drama about the life of the Swedish emigrant who becomes a trade union leader in America and ends up innocent in the electric chair. The title song of the film was provided by the folk-singer Joan Baez, one of the most eminent female protest activists. *Bound for Glory* (1976) by Hal Ashby shows in ballad-like form how the legendary protest singer Woody Guthrie, an alternative culture icon, hitch-hiked from Oklahoma to Los Angeles and finally to New York in the thirties. This paints a realistic picture of the USA at the time of the great depression, of poor people's struggles to survive, but also of their soli-

drama über das Leben des schwedischen Auswanderers, der in Amerika zum Gewerkschaftsführer wird und unschuldig auf dem elektrischen Stuhl endet. Den Titelsong zu dem Film lieferte die Folksängerin Joan Baez, eine der prominenten Aktivistinnen der Protestbewegung. *Bound for Glory* (1976, *Dieses Land ist mein Land*) von Hal Ashby schildert in balladenhafter Form, wie der legendäre Protestsänger Woody Guthrie, eine Ikone der Gegenkultur, in den dreißiger Jahren von Oklahoma nach Los Angeles und schließlich nach New York trampte. Dabei entwirft er ein realistisches Bild der USA zur Zeit der großen Depression, des Überlebenskampfes der Armen, aber auch ihrer Solidarität und Hoffnung auf eine bessere Zukunft. In diesen Filmen ging es weniger um die Rückbesinnung auf eine kämpferische Tradition als um deren nostalgische Verklärung, denn das gängige Bild der bestehenden Gewerkschaften war geprägt von Korruption, illegalen Machenschaften und der Verwicklung in die kriminellen Aktivitäten der Bosse.

Außerdem beschäftigten sich einige Filme mit einem dunklen Kapitel der amerikanischen Geschichte, der Kommunistenverfolgung der fünfziger Jahre. *The Way We Were* (1973, *Cherie Bitter*) von Sydney Pollack behandelt das Thema im Rahmen einer Liebesgeschichte zwischen einer kommunistischen Aktivistin jüdischer Abstammung und einem konservativen Sunnyboy, die sich trotz ihrer Differenzen zueinander hingezogen fühlen und heiraten. Doch durch die Einführung von Hollywoods schwarzer Liste und den Beginn der McCarthy-Ära Anfang der fünfziger Jahre verschärfen sich ihre weltanschaulichen Gegensätze, was schließlich zu ihrer Trennung führt. In *The Front* (1976, *Der Strohmann*) von Martin Ritt stellt Woody Allen einen Kellner dar, der sich aus Geldnöten bereit findet, für einen befreundeten Drehbuchautor und zwei weitere Autoren, die auf der schwarzen Liste stehen, beim Verkauf ihrer Drehbücher an das Fernsehen den Strohmann zu spielen. Zunächst läuft alles bestens, doch dann gerät er selbst ins Visier der Ermittler der Zensurbehörden und muß seine Haltung definieren. Den Einfluß der Kommunistenverfolgung der fünfziger Jahre auf die Protestgeneration der sechziger untersucht Sidney Lumet in seinem Film *Daniel* (1983), der direkten Bezug auf die historische Affäre um Julius und Ethel Rosenberg nimmt. Im Mittelpunkt steht ein unpolitischer Student, der durch den Selbstmordversuch seiner politisch aktiven Schwester motiviert wird, sich mit seinen Kindheitserlebnissen auseinanderzusetzen, und beginnt, sich dem Schicksal seiner Eltern zu stellen, die 1953 als angebliche sowjetische Spione hingerichtet wurden.

Dieser Film, für dessen Realisierung Lumet zehn Jahre lang kämpfen mußte, ist Teil eines Trends der Hinwendung zum Sozial- und Politdrama, der Ende der siebziger Jahre begann und bis in die achtziger Jahre hinein reichte. Neues Interesse an der Auseinandersetzung mit der Arbeiterbewegung offenbaren *Blue Collar* (1978), die erste Regiearbeit von Paul Schrader, und *Norma Rae* (1979) von Martin Ritt. *Blue Collar* untersucht die Realität der amerikanischen Arbeiter, ihre Vorstellungen und Wünsche an das Leben und die realen Möglichkeiten zu deren Verwirklichung. Im Mittelpunkt stehen drei befreundete Arbeiter einer Autofabrik, die ihre finanziellen Probleme durch den Raub der Gewerkschaftskasse lösen wollen und dabei auf Beweise für illegale Machenschaften der Funktionäre stoßen. Es sickert durch, wer den Diebstahl begangen hat, einer von ihnen wird umgebracht, die anderen retten sich, indem sie ihr Wissen an verschiedene Seiten verkaufen. Schließlich sind alle miteinander verfeindet. *Norma Rae* erzählt die Geschichte einer unpolitischen Arbeiterin in einer Baumwollspinnerei in North Carolina, die sich durch den Einfluß eines Gewerkschaftsaktivisten zu einer politisch aktiven Frau wandelt und sich an die Spitze des Kampfes der Arbeiter um bessere Arbeitsbedingungen stellt. Der Film ist der einzige über das Thema, der ein optimistisches Ende hat, während bei allen anderen das Establishment letzten Endes siegt, wie im Fall von *Silkwood* (1983) von Mike Nichols, dessen Handlungsmuster ähnlich ist. Der Film basiert auf der wahren Geschichte von Karen Silkwood, einer Arbeiterin in einer Plutoniumfabrik, die zufällig auf Hinweise für absichtliche Manipulationen bei der Materialprüfung von Plutoniumbrennstäben stößt, daraufhin beginnt, sich in der Gewerkschaft zu engagieren, und schließlich unter ungeklärten Umständen ums Leben kommt, als sie gerade dabei ist, Beweise zu beschaffen. Mit den Möglichkeiten der Durchsetzung liberaler Politik beschäftigt sich *Brubaker* (1980) von Stuart Rosenberg, ein Projekt Robert Redfords, der darin auch die Hauptrolle spielte. Der Film handelt von einem Strafvollzugsexperten, welcher in den sechziger Jahren im Auftrag eines liberalen Gouverneurs angeworben wird, um auf einer Gefängnisfarm Reformen durchzuführen, dabei jedoch auf einen Sumpf an Korruption und den Widerstand der örtlichen Autoritäten stößt, auf deren Druck hin er schließlich entlassen wird.

All diese Filme sind in mehr oder weniger starkem Maße von der Erkenntnis des Scheiterns getragen. Der Enthusiasmus und das revolutionäre Hochgefühl der sechziger Jahre sind der Resignation und dem Gefühl der Ohnmacht gegenüber einem korrupten Machtapparat gewi-

116. Kris Kristofferson (Cisco Pike) und Karen Black (Sue) in *Cisco Pike* von Bill Norton, 1972.
117. Sean Connery (Jack Kehoe), Richard Harris (James McParlan / McKenna) und Anthony Costello (Frank McAndrew) in *Verflucht bis zu zum jüngsten Tag* von Martin Ritt, 1970.
118. David Carradine (Woody Guthrie) in *Dieses Land ist mein Land* von Hal Ashby, 1976.

116. Kris Kristofferson (Cisco Pike) and Karen Black (Sue) in *Cisco Pike* by Bill Norton, 1972.
117. Sean Connery (Jack Kehoe), Richard Harris (James McParlan / McKenna) and Anthony Costello (Frank McAndrew) in *The Molly Maguires* by Martin Ritt, 1970.
118. David Carradine (Woody Guthrie) in *Bound for Glory* by Hal Ashby, 1976.

darity and hope for a better future. These films were less concerned with looking back at a fighting tradition than in transfiguring it nostalgically, as the current image of the existing trade unions was one of corruption, illegal machinations and involvement in the bosses' criminal activities.

As well as this, some films concerned themselves with a dark chapter of American history, the persecution of the Communists in the fifties. *The Way We Were* (1973) by Sydney Pollack treats the theme in the context of a love story involving a Communist activist of Jewish descent and a conservative golden boy who feel attracted to each other and marry despite their differences. But the introduction of the Hollywood black list and the start of the McCarthy era in the early fifties heightens the contrasts in their attitudes, and they finally separate. In *The Front* (1976) by Martin Ritt, Woody Allen plays a waiter who is so short of money that he is prepared to play the front man for a screenplay writer who is his friend and two other authors who are on the black list in selling their screenplays to television. At first everything goes well, but he is then targeted himself by the censorship authority's investigators and has to define his attitude. Sidney Lumet examined the influence of fifties Communist persecution on the sixties protest generation in his film *Daniel* (1983), which relates directly to the historical affair involving Julius and Ethel Rosenberg. This centres around an apolitical student who is led by his politically motivated sister's suicide attempt to try to come to terms with his childhood experiences and starts to face up to the fate of his parents, who were executed as alleged Soviet spies in 1953.

This film, for which Lumet had to fight ten years to realize, is part of a trend towards social and political drama that started in the late seventies and continued into the eighties. New interest in the labour movement is shown in *Blue Collar* (1978), Paul Schrader's directorial début, and *Norma Rae* (1979) by Martin Ritt. *Blue Collar* examines the realities of the American workers' existences, their ideas and what they want from life, and their chances of actually bringing this about. It centres around three friends working in a car factory who intend to solve their financial problems by stealing from trade union funds, which makes it clear to them that the officials have been indulging in corrupt practices. The truth about the theft gets out, one of the friends is killed and the others save themselves by selling their knowledge to various parties, ending up as enemies. *Norma Rae* tells the story of an apolitical woman working in a North Carolina cotton mill who becomes politically active because of the influences of a female trade union activist and leads the workers in their fight for better conditions. The film is the only one on this subject with an optimistic ending. The establishment wins in all the others, as in Mike Nichols's *Silkwood* (1983), which has a similar plot. The film is based on the true story of Karen Silkwood, a worker in a plutonium factory who chances across suggestions of deliberate manipulation in the checking of material for plutonium fuel rods. She is prompted to commit herself to the trade union, and finally loses her life in unexplained circumstances just as she is about to find proof. *Brubaker* (1980) by Stuart Rosenberg is a project by Robert Redford, who also played the leading role, dealing with the possibilities of implementing liberal policies. The

chen. Den Verlust der Illusionen spiegelt auch die große Zahl von Filmen wider, die sich mit der Demontage des Mythos von Amerika als dem Land der unbegrenzten Möglichkeiten befassen. Modellfälle des fehlgeschlagenen amerikanischen Traums zeigen unter anderem John Schlesingers *Midnight Cowboy* (1969) und *The Day of the Locust* (1975, *Der Tag der Heuschrecke*), *They Shoot Horses, Don't They*? von Sydney Pollack, *The King of Marvin Gardens* (1972, *Der König von Marvin Gardens*) von Bob Rafelson und *Days of Heaven* (1978, *In der Glut des Südens/Tage des Himmels*) von Terrence Malick. Der Held aus *Midnight Cowboy*, ein naiver junger Mann aus der Provinz, hält sich für einen »echten« Mann, den die Frauen unwiderstehlich finden. Angetan mit einem Cowboykostüm reist er nach New York, wo er sein Geld als Liebhaber reicher alter Frauen verdienen will. Doch in der Großstadt muß er feststellen, daß die Werte, die er zu repräsentieren glaubt, von niemandem mehr ernstgenommen werden und er als lächerliche Gestalt betrachtet wird. Schließlich landet er auf der untersten Stufe der sozialen Leiter und lernt durch die Freundschaft mit einem homosexuellen, tuberkulosekranken Gelegenheitsdieb, sich der Wirklichkeit zu stellen. *The Day of the Locust* schildert die Erlebnisse eines jungen Screendesigners, der 1938 nach Hollywood kommt und die Niederungen der Traumstadt kennenlernt. Am Beispiel einer jungen Möchte-Gern-Schauspielerin zeigt der Film das materielle und seelische Elend, die Egozentrik, Menschenfeindlichkeit und kalte Berechnung hinter der glänzenden Oberfläche. Am Ende steht ein surreales Höllenszenarium entfesselter, amoklaufender Massen, die zur Metapher für den moralischen Verfall und den Realitätsverlust werden, den die Scheinwelt Hollywoods in den Menschen bewirkt. Die Titelfigur von *The King of Marvin Gardens* ist der windige Jason Staebler, der einen hochtrabenden Plan nach dem anderen verfolgt, um schnell reich zu werden. Für ihn ist stellt sich das Leben als ein Monopolyspiel mit Spielgeld dar. Begeht man Fehler, bleibt dies ohne reale Konsequenzen. Die Ironie liegt darin, daß das Spielfeld Marvin Gardens nicht wirklich existiert und Jason sich somit auf eine Fiktion bezieht, wenn er sich selbst als König von Marvin Gardens bezeichnet. Durch die Konfrontation mit seinem introvertierten, bedächtigen Bruder, den er als Strohmann für ein angeblich todsicheres Geschäft gewinnen will, offenbart sich, daß er der einzige ist, der das Leben als ein Spiel betrachtet, das gewonnen werden kann, während alle anderen längst resigniert haben. *They Shoot Horses, Don't They?* beschreibt einen der Tanzmarathons, wie sie in der Depressionszeit der dreißiger Jahre üblich waren. Er zeigt, wie die Teilnehmer, getrieben von der Hoffnung, mit dem Gewinn des Preises für kurze Zeit der drückenden Armut zu entkommen oder für den Film entdeckt zu werden, unvorstellbare Qualen auf sich nehmen. Dabei zieht er Parallelen zum American Way of Life: Die Devise, daß angeblich nur die Besten und Ausdauerndsten gewinnen, während die anderen auf der Strecke bleiben, wird Lügen gestraft, als sich am Ende herausstellt, daß es überhaupt keine Gewinner geben wird, sondern nur Verlierer und Überlebende, da die Unterhaltskosten der Teilnehmer während des Wettbewerbs von der Siegerprämie abgezogen werden. *Days of Heaven* von Terrence Malick schildert den aussichtslosen Kampf dreier jungener Leute, zu Wohlstand und einem sorgenfreien Leben zu kommen. Der junge Gelegenheitsarbeiter Bill, seine Geliebte Abby und seine kleine Schwester Linda ziehen in den Jahren vor dem Ersten Weltkrieg aus Chicago in den Süden und verdingen sich bei einem Farmer in Texas als Erntehelfer. Als sich durch die Heirat Abbys mit dem Farmer die Gelegenheit bietet, an eine große Erbschaft heranzukommen, ergreifen sie die Chance. Die Dinge entwickeln sich jedoch anders als erwartet und münden in einer tragischen Auseinandersetzung zwischen den beiden Männern, bei der Bill den Farmer tötet und schließlich nach einer regelrechten Treibjagd von der Polizei erschossen wird. *American Gigolo* (1980, *Ein Mann für gewisse Stunden*) von Paul Schrader durchleuchtet die Degradierung des Menschen zur Ware. Der gutaussehende Julian Kaye, gespielt von Richard Gere, hat sich vom Strichjungen zum Luxus-Callboy hochgearbeitet. Er verkehrt in der High Society von Los Angeles, seine Kundinnen schätzen seine Gesellschaft und entlohnen ihn reichlich für seine Zuwendung. Als er jedoch unter Mordverdacht gerät, weigert sich die Frau, mit der er zusammen war, ihm ein Alibi zu geben, seine vermeintlichen Freunde wenden sich von ihm ab, und es wird deutlich, daß er nichts weiter ist als ein Luxusartikel und Statussymbol in einer seichten Scheinwelt.

Den Mangel an realen Zukunftsaussichten in einer feindseligen Gesellschaft erkunden Filme über Jugendbanden, wie Stanley Kubricks *A Clockwork Orange* (1971), Philip Kaufmans *The Wanderers* (1979), Walter Hills *The Warriors* (1979) und Francis Ford Coppolas *Rumblefish* (1983) und *The Outsiders* (1983, *Die Outsiders*). Der vielschichtigste und mit Abstand schockierendste dieser Filme ist *A Clockwork Orange*, in dem Kubrick das Bild einer gefühlskalten, sterilen Konsum- und Mediengesellschaft voller Brutalität entwirft, deren Produkt die »Droogs« sind, eine

119. Robert Redford (Henry Brubaker) in *Brubaker* von Stuart Rosenberg, 1980.
120. Sally Field (Norma Rae) in *Norma Rae* von Martin Ritt, 1979.
121. Meryl Streep (Karen Silkwood) in *Silkwood* von Mike Nichols, 1983.

119. Robert Redford (Henry Brubaker) in *Brubaker* by Stuart Rosenberg, 1980.
120. Sally Field (Norma Rae) in *Norma Rae* by Martin Ritt, 1979.
121. Meryl Streep (Karen Silkwood) in *Silkwood* by Mike Nichols, 1983.

film is about an expert on the penal system who is recruited by a liberal governor to carry out reforms on a prison farm. However, he is drawn into a morass of corruption and resistance from the local authorities, and he is finally dismissed as a result of pressure from them,

All these films are carried to a greater or lesser extent by the acknowledgement of failure. The enthusiasm and revolutionary elation of the sixties have given way to resignation and feelings of impotence in the face of a corrupt power structure. This loss of illusions is also reflected in the large number of films demolishing the myth of America as the land of unlimited possibilities. Model cases showing the American dream coming to nothing include John Schlesinger's *Midnight Cowboy* (1969) and *The Day of the Locust* (1975), (1969, *They Shoot Horses*, *Don't They*) by Sydney Pollack, *The King of Marvin Gardens* (1972) by Bob Rafelson and *Days of Heaven* (1978) by Terrence Malick. The hero of *Midnight Cowboy*, a naïve young provincial, sees himself as a »real« man whom women find irresistible. Wearing a cowboy costume, he travels to New York, where he intends to earn a living as a lover to rich old women. But in the city he is forced to recognize that the values he thinks he represents are not taken seriously by anyone, and he is treated as a ridiculous figure. Finally he ends up on the bottom rung of the social ladder and learns to face reality from a homosexual, tubercular opportunist thief. *The Day of the Locust* describes the experiences of a young screen designer who comes to Hollywood in 1938 and gets to know the dream city's low life. The film takes a young would-be actor to show the material and psychological misery, the egocentricity, misanthropy and cold calculation behind the glistening surface. In finishes up with a surreal, hellish scenario of unfettered masses running amok, a metaphor for the moral decay and loss of reality that Hollywood's unreal world brings about in people. The eponymous hero of *The King of Marvin Gardens* is the dubious Jason Staebler, who pursues one high-flown, get-rich-quick plan after another. He sees life as a game of monopoly, with play money and no real consequences if you make mistakes. The irony lies in the fact that Marvin Gardens is the only square in American Monopoly that does not really exist; Jason is thus drawing on fiction when he calls himself the King of Marvin Gardens. Confrontation with his introverted, thoughtful brother, whom he wants to act as front man for an apparently sure-fire deal, reveals that he is the only person who regards life as a game that can be won, while all the others have long since given up. *They Shoot Horses, Don't They?* describes a dance marathon of the kind that used to be held in the thirties depression. It shows how the participants, driven by the hope of escaping from driving poverty for a time by winning the prize, or of being discovered for the movies, subject themselves to unimaginable tortures, thus drawing parallels with the American way of life: the notion that only the best and those with the most stamina win, while all the others are left behind, is shown to be hollow when it finally turns out that there will not be any winners at all, but only losers and survivors, as the participants' living expenses during the competition are deducted from the

Jugendbande, für die Einbruch, Raub, Vergewaltigung und das Zusammenschlagen ihrer Opfer ein Ritual darstellen, das zu einem perfekten Abend gehört. Als der fünfzehnjährige Anführer der Bande von der Polizei gefaßt wird, willigt er ein, sich einer Therapie zu unterziehen, die jeden Antrieb zu Sexualität und Gewalt auslöscht. Nach seiner vorzeitigen Freilassung erweist er sich bei Angriffen als unfähig zur Gegenwehr und wird nun seinerseits zum hilflosen Opfer der Gewalt. Dieses Dilemma enthält eine bitterböse Kritik an der skrupellosen Manipulation, Instrumentalisierung und Brutalisierung des Individuums. Die Suche nach Idealen und einer Lebensperspektive von Jugendlichen aus den Armenvierteln der Städte thematisieren *The Wanderers*, *The Warriors*, *Rumblefish* und *The Outsiders*. Angesichts einer beängstigenden, feindseligen Realität, in der Gewalt zum täglichen Überlebenskampf gehört, schließen sich die Jugendlichen auf der Suche nach Geborgenheit, Solidarität und einem trügerischen Machtgefühl in Banden zusammen und geraten damit in eine selbstzerstörerische Spirale der Gewalt, die zwangsläufig tragisch endet.

Der Konflikt zwischen Gesellschaft und Individuum wird häufig dargestellt als aussichtsloser Kampf des Individuums gegen ein übermächtiges System, das seine Freiheit beschränkt und seine Individualität zu zerstören sucht. Den Prototyp des Rebellen gegen ein reglementiertes Leben, das keinerlei persönlichen Freiraum mehr zuläßt, verkörpert Paul Newman in *Cool Hand Luke* (1967, *Der Unbeugsame*) von Stuart Rosenberg. Der Held wird wegen der Beschädigung einer Parkuhr zu zwei Jahren Haft auf einer Gefängnisfarm verurteilt. Obwohl die Häftlinge fair behandelt werden, solange sie sich unterordnen, empfindet er die Gefängnisregeln als unerträglich. Immer wieder unternimmt er Fluchtversuche, wird jedoch jedes Mal gefaßt und bestraft, bis ihn die Gefängnisaufseher schließlich nach einem letzten Ausbruch töten. Die gleiche rebellische Haltung repräsentieren die Protagonisten von *One Flew Over The Cuckoo's Nest* (1975, *Einer flog über das Kuckucksnest*) von Milos Foreman und *Lenny* (1974) von Bob Fosse. In *One Flew Over The Cuckoo's Nest* verkörpert Jack Nicholson einen anarchistischen Helden, der sich als geistesgestört ausgibt, um dem Gefängnis zu entkommen, und in eine Nervenklinik eingeliefert wird, wo er für seine Mitpatienten Pokerpartien, Basketballspiele und einen Angelausflug organisiert, um etwas Leben in die tödliche Eintönigkeit zu bringen. Die Betreuer sehen jedoch die Ordnung gestört und versuchen, seinen Geist systematisch durch Bestrafung zu brechen, was ihnen am Ende gelingt, indem sie ihn mit Elektroschocks in ein geistiges Wrack verwandeln. *Lenny* schildert das bewegte Leben des provokanten, ständig vom Gefängnis bedrohten Stand-Up-Komikers Lenny Bruce, der in den fünfziger und sechziger Jahren eine Kultfigur der intellektuellen Bohème war und schließlich an einer Überdosis Heroin starb.

Allgemein ist das Menschenbild vieler Dramen des New Hollywood von der Überzeugung geprägt, daß die anonyme, urbane Massengesellschaft verstörte, kaputte Menschen hervorbrächte. Häufig geht es um Identitätskrisen und Entfremdung. Alan Pakula schildert in *The*

122. William Atherton (Tod Hackett) in *Der Tag der Heuschrecke* von John Schlesinger, 1975.
123. Jane Fonda (Gloria Beatty) und Michael Sarrazin (Robert Syverton) in *Nur Pferden gibt man den Gnadenschuß* von Sydney Pollack, 1969.

122. William Atherton (Tod Hackett) in *The Day of the Locust* by John Schlesinger, 1975.
123. Jane Fonda (Gloria Beatty) and Michael Sarrazin (Robert Syverton) in *They Shoot Horses, Don't They?* by Sydney Pollack, 1969.

prize. *Days of Heaven* by Terrence Malick presents three young people's hopeless struggle to achieve prosperity and a care-free life. The young casual worker Bill, his lover Abby and his little sister Linda move to the South from Chicago in the years before the First World War, and go to help with the harvest on a farm in Texas. When Abby's marrying the farmer offers the chance of a large legacy, they take the opportunity. But things turn out differently from their expectations and lead to a tragic conflict between the two men in which Bill kills the farmer and is finally shot dead after a regular witch-hunt by the police. *American Gigolo* (1980) by Paul Schrader shows how people can be degraded to the status of goods. The good-looking Julian Kaye, played by Richard Gere, has worked his way up from being a rent-boy to the role of luxury escort. He operates in Los Angeles high society, his female clients enjoy his company and reward him well for his attention. But when he is suspected of murder, the woman he was with refuses to give him an alibi, his supposed friends desert him and it becomes clear that he is nothing more than a luxury item and status symbol in a shallow, illusory world.

Films about youth gangs like Stanley Kubrick's *A Clockwork Orange* (1971), Philip Kaufman's *The Wanderers* (1979), Walter Hill's *The Warriors* (1979) and Francis Ford Coppola's *Rumblefish* (1983) and *The Outsiders* (1983) explore the lack of real prospects for the future in a hostile society. The most complex and by far the most shocking of these is *A Clockwork Orange*, where Kubrick paints a picture of an emotionally cold, sterile consumer and media fraught with brutality. This produces the »Droogs«, a youth gang for whom burglary, theft, rape and beating up their victims is a ritual that is part of a good night out. When the fifteen-year-old leader of the gang is caught by the police he agrees to undergo a therapy that eliminates any drives towards sex or violence. After his early release, he proves unable to defend himself when attacked, and now becomes a hopeless victim of violence himself. This dilemma contains venomous criticism of the way in which individuals are manipulated, instrumentalized and brutalized. *The Wanderers*, *The Warriors*, *Rumblefish* and *The Outsiders* are about young people in the poor districts of cities searching for ideals and a view of life. Given a frightening, hostile reality, in which violence is part of the daily struggle for survival, the young people form gangs in their search for security, solidarity and a false sense of power and thus get into a self-destructive spiral of violence that inevitably ends tragically.

The conflict between the individual and society is often presented as the individual's hopeless struggle against an unduly powerful system that limits his freedom and threatens to destroy his individuality. The prototype of a rebel against a regimented life leaving absolutely no personal scope is played by Paul Newman in *Cool Hand Luke* (1967). The hero is sentenced to two years on a prison farm for damaging a parking meter. Although the inmates are treated fairly as long as they conform, he finds the prison regime intolerable and constantly tries to escape, but he is captured and punished every time, until the prison warders finally kill him after

Sterile Cuckoo (1969, *Pookie*) die unglückliche Liebesgeschichte zwischen einer jungen Außenseiterin, die sich verzweifelt nach Zuwendung sehnt, und einem schüchternen Neuankömmling an ihrer Schule. *A Safe Place* (1971, *Ein Zauberer an meiner Seite*) von Henry Jaglom handelt von einem jungen Mädchen, das sich weigert, erwachsen zu werden, und sich in Tagträume über ihre Kindheit flüchtet, bis es schließlich Traum und Wirklichkeit nicht mehr unterscheiden kann. Robert Altman drehte in Kanada das düstere Psychodrama *That Cold Day in the Park* (1969, *Ein kalter Tag im Park*), in dem eine vereinsamte Frau sich einen Studenten in die Wohnung holt und ihn dort gefangen hält. In *Images* (1972, *Spiegelbilder*) verfolgt Altman das Thema weiter, indem er eine verstörte junge Frau in den Mittelpunkt stellt, in deren Kopf sich Vergangenheit und Gegenwart, Realität und Phantasie zunehmend vermischen. Eine eigenwillige Untersuchung der Möglichkeiten der weiblichen Emanzipation stellt Altman in *Three Women* (1977) an. In diesem sehr komplexen und vielschichtigen Film mit einer traumartigen, surrealen Bildersprache beschreibt er die Entfremdung in einer konsumorientierten Überflußgesellschaft und die Abhängigkeits- und Machtverhältnisse dreier Frauen, die am Ende eine neue Solidarität entwickeln, der Männerwelt den Rücken kehren und ihren eigenen, gemeinsamen Lebensstil finden. Alan Rudolphs *Welcome to L. A.* (1977, *Willkommen in Los Angeles*), eine Studie des Lebensstils rund um die Musikindustrie in Los Angeles, entlarvt die Isolation und Beziehungsunfähigkeit der Menschen, die sie durch eine rastlose Jagd nach beruflichem Erfolg und sexuellen Abenteuern kompensieren, während die Protagonistin seines Films *Remember My Name* (1978, *Du wirst noch an mich denken*) eine merkwürdige, psychisch aus dem Lot geratene Frau ist, die nach einer langen Gefängnisstrafe wegen des Mordes an der Geliebten ihres damaligen Mannes zurückkehrt und beginnt, ihn zu verfolgen und in sein Leben einzudringen, um seine neue Ehe zu zerstören. Die Helden dieser Filme wirken in ihrer Weltfremdheit, Vereinsamung und Entfremdung manchmal lächerlich, oft anrührend, sie erregen Mitgefühl und Verständnis, sind jedoch keine starken Identifikationsfiguren, wie sie im klassischen Hollywood üblich waren.

Weitaus zwiespältiger noch stellt sich eine andere Variante des Antihelden von New Hollywood dar, welche in der Tradition der innerlich zerrissenen, illusionslosen Figuren steht, die Paul Newman ab Anfang der sechziger Jahre mit seinen Rollen in *The Hustler* (1961, *Haie der Großstadt*) von Robert Rossen oder *Hud* (1963, *Der Wildeste unter Tausend*) von Martin Ritt prägte. Deren Charakter unterscheidet sich in wesentlichen Punkten von den Filmrebellen der fünfziger Jahre, wie sie Montgomery Clift in *From Here to Eternity* (*Verdammt in alle Ewigkeit*), Marlon Brando in *The Wild One* (*Der Wilde*) oder James Dean in *Rebel Without Cause* (*... denn sie wissen nicht, was sie tun*), darstellten. Ihnen gemeinsam ist das Gefühl der Entfremdung von einer Umwelt, die sie als feindselig empfinden. Doch während die Antihelden der fünfziger Jahre Opfer eines unfairen, korrupten Systems sind und darum kämpfen, ihren eigenen moralischen Prinzipien treu zu bleiben, verkörpert Newman in *The Hustler* und *Hud* Männer, die kei-

124. Richard Gere (Bill) und Brooke Adams (Abby) in *In der Glut des Südens / Tage des Himmels* von Terrence Malick, 1978.
125. Frances Bergen (Mrs. Laudner) und Richard Gere (Julian Kaye) in *Ein Mann für gewisse Stunden* von Paul Schrader, 1980.
126. Malcolm McDowell (Alex DeLarge) in *A Clockwork Orange* von Stanley Kubrick, 1971.
127. Matt Dillon (Rusty-James) und Mickey Rourke (»Motorcycle Boy«) in *Rumblefish* von Francis Ford Coppola, 1983.

124. Richard Gere (Bill) and Brooke Adams (Abby) in *Days of Heaven* by Terrence Malick, 1978.
125. Frances Bergen (Mrs. Laudner) and Richard Gere (Julian Kaye) in *American Gigolo* by Paul Schrader, 1980.
126. Malcolm McDowell (Alex DeLarge) in *A Clockwork Orange* by Stanley Kubrick, 1971.
127. Matt Dillon (Rusty-James) und Mickey Rourke (»Motorcycle Boy«) in *Rumblefish* by Francis Ford Coppola, 1983.

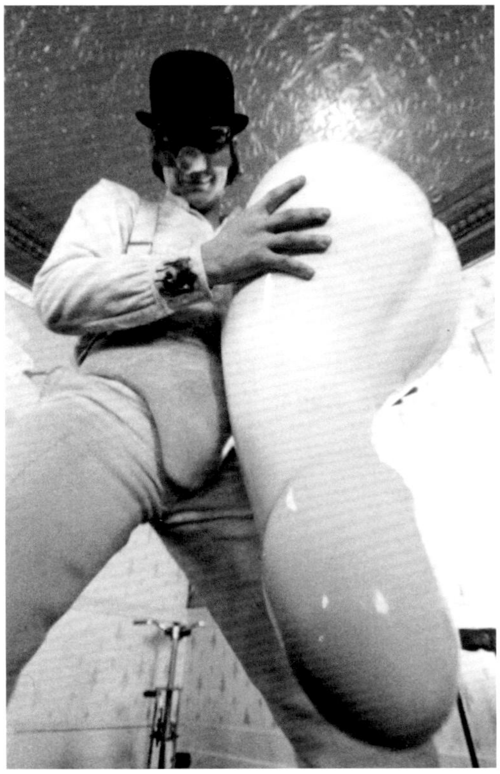

a final outbreak. The leading figures in *One Flew Over the Cuckoo's Nest* (1975) by Milos Forman and *Lenny* (1974) by Bob Fosse also represent this rebellious attitude. In *One Flew Over the Cuckoo's Nest* Jack Nicholson plays an anarchistic hero who pretends to be mentally disturbed in order to get out of prison and is sent to a psychiatric hospital where he arranges poker games, basketball and a fishing trip for his fellow patients in order to introduce some life into the deadly monotony. But the staff see this as running counter to order and try to break his spirit by systematic punishment, which finally succeeds, as electric shock treatment makes him into a nervous wreck. *Lenny* presents the whirlwind life of the provocative comedian Lenny Bruce, who is constantly threatened with prison. He was a cult figure of intellectual bohemians in the fifties and sixties, and finally died of a heroine overdose.

Generally speaking, the image of humanity in many New Hollywood dramas is shaped by the conviction that anonymous, mass urban society produces damaged people. Very frequently this involves identity crises and alienation. In *The Sterile Cuckoo* (1969), Alan Pakula presents an unhappy love story about a young outsider who is desperate for affection and a shy new arrival at her school. *A Safe Place* (1971) by Henry Jaglom deals with a young girl who refuses to grow up, taking refuge in daydreams about her childhood until she can finally no longer distinguish between dreams and reality. Robert Altman shot the gloomy melodrama *That Cold Day in the Park* (1969) in Canada; this shows a lonely woman taking a student into her home and holding him prisoner. Altman develops this theme further in *Images* (1972) by focusing on a damaged young woman who increasingly confuses past and present, reality and fantasy. Altman sets up an unusual examination of the possibilities for female emancipation in *Three Women* (1977). This is a very complex and multi-layered film using a dreamlike, surreal pictorial language. It describes the three women's alienation in a consumer-oriented affluent society, and their dependencies and power relationships. They ultimately develop a new solidarity, turn their back on the male world and find a common life-style of their own. Alan Rudolph's *Welcome to L.A.* (1977), a life-style study of the L.A. music industry, reveals people's isolation and inability to form relationship, making up for this by a ceaseless search for professional success and sexual adventure. The leading woman in his film *Remember my Name* (1978) is a remarkable, psychologically unstable woman who comes back after a long prison sentence for the murder of her former husband's mistress. She starts to pursue him and force her way into his life in order to destroy his new marriage. The leading figures in these films are sometimes ridiculous, sometimes moving in their unworldliness, isolation and alienation, they arouse sympathy and understanding, but they are not strong identification figures of the kind usual in classical Hollywood.

Another variant on the New Hollywood anti-hero is much more contradictory. These are in the tradition of figures who are inwardly at odds with themselves but without illusions as established by Paul Newman from the early sixties with his roles in *The Hustler* (1961) by Robert

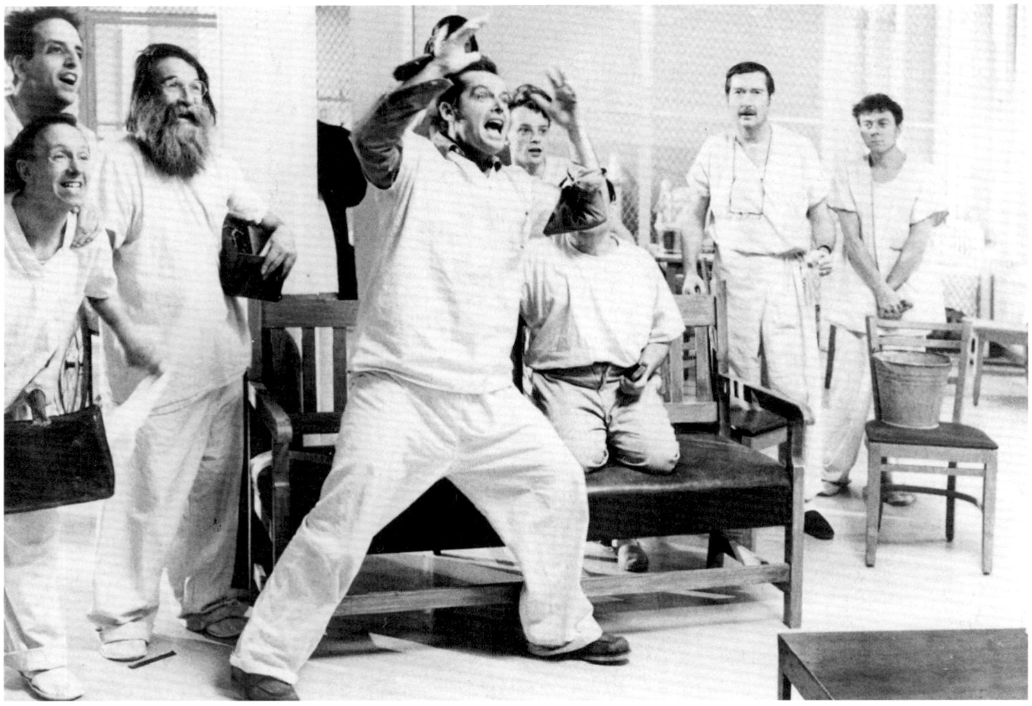

nerlei Moralkodex haben, sondern einfach unfähig zur Kommunikation mit anderen sind. Dieser Typ des Antihelden ist ein rebellischer, selbstbezogener Zyniker, der alle, die versuchen, sich ihm anzunähern, vor den Kopf stößt und schließlich allein bleibt. Aus seinem desillusioniertem Verhalten spricht Enttäuschung von einer Gesellschaft, in der die Suche nach einem sinnvollen Leben vergeblich erscheint. Ein ähnliches Verhalten zeigt Robert Dupea aus Bob Rafelsons *Five Easy Pieces* (1970). Er ist ein Mann, der keinen Platz in der amerikanischen Gesellschaft der siebziger Jahre findet, ein entwurzelter Mensch und selbstbezogener Egoist, zu einer wirklichen Bindung unfähig. Seine Haltung kann Verständnis und Mitleid erregen, weil sein innerer Konflikt nachvollziehbar ist, aber kaum Sympathie. Das gleiche gilt für die Hauptfigur von *Downhill Racer* (1969) von Michael Ritchie. Darin spielt Robert Redford einen jungen Skirennläufer aus einfachen Verhältnissen, der skrupellos seinen sportlichen und kommerziellen Aufstieg verfolgt, dabei seine Wurzeln und alle moralischen Prinzipien hinter sich läßt und zum verhaßten Einzelgänger wird.

Martin Scorsese schuf seine eigene Version des Antihelden, die des falschen Heiligen, welche er mit der Gestalt des Charlie aus *Mean Streets* (1973) einführte. Charlie ist zutiefst durchdrungen von katholischen Wertbegriffen, die ihn seine Existenz als Kleingangster und seine heimliche sexuelle Beziehung zu seiner Cousine als Sünde empfinden lassen. Er sehnt sich nach Vergebung und erwählt als Objekt der Sühne seinen leichtsinnigen Freund Johnny Boy, indem er es sich zur Aufgabe macht, ihm aus allen Schwierigkeiten herauszuhelfen, wobei sich seine Rettungsaktionen jedoch als fatal erweisen. Ähnliche Merkmale zeigt der Held von *Taxidriver* (1975). Auch er hat ein zwiespältiges Verhältnis zum Sex. Seine Freizeit verbringt er in Pornokinos, doch ist die Prostitution für ihn Teil des Schmutzes der Stadt, den es ihn auszurotten drängt. Schließlich ernennt er sich selbst zum Retter der zwölfjährigen Prostituierten Iris, die keinerlei Bedürfnis hat, gerettet zu werden. Mehr noch als Charlie ist er ein Niemand, der davon träumt, zum Erlöser zu werden. Diese Helden verachten sich selbst, sie leben auf der Schattenseite der Gesellschaft und sehnen sich danach, ins Licht zu treten. Ein weiterer von Scorseses Antihelden ist der Boxer Jake La Motta, auf dessen Biographie *Raging Bull* (1980, *Wie ein wilder Stier*) beruht. Der Film zeigt eine Abfolge von Kämpfen im Ring. Vorrangig handelt er jedoch nicht vom Boxen, sondern von einem Mann, dessen Verhalten von Gewalttätigkeit, Brutalität und Unbeherrschtheit geprägt ist. Dahinter verbergen sich enorme Schuldgefühle und Minderwertigkeitskomplexe. Die Bestrafung im Ring bedeutet für ihn eine Art Beichte, Buße und Absolution. Sein Masochismus nährt die Wut, die ihn an die Spitze gebracht hat, zerstört aber auch die Beziehung zu den Menschen, die ihm am nächsten stehen, und treibt ihn in die Vereinsamung, mit der sein Niedergang beginnt.

Die Zwiespältigkeit der Helden läßt die Dramen des neuen Hollywood weitaus komplexer erscheinen als die klassischen Vertreter des Genres, zumal sie oft mit Elementen anderer Genres

128. Jack Nicholson (Randle Patrick McMurphy) in *Einer flog über das Kuckucksnest* von Milos Forman, 1975.
129. Tuesday Weld (Susan / Noah) and Orson Welles (Magician) in *Ein Zauberer an meiner Seite* von Henry Jaglom, 1971.
130. Paul Newman (Lucas »Luke« Jackson) in *Der Unbeugsame* von Stuart Rosenberg, 1967.
131. Geraldine Chaplin (Emily) and Anthony Perkins (Neil Curry) in *Du wirst noch an mich denken* von Alan Rudolph, 1978.

128. Jack Nicholson (Randle Patrick McMurphy) in *One Flew Over The Cuckoo's Nest* by Milos Forman, 1975.
129. Tuesday Weld (Susan / Noah) and Orson Welles (Magician) in *A Safe Place* by Henry Jaglom, 1971.
130. Paul Newman (Lucas »Luke« Jackson) in *Cool Hand Luke* by Stuart Rosenberg, 1967.
131. Geraldine Chaplin (Emily) and Anthony Perkins (Neil Curry) in *Remember My Name* by Alan Rudolph, 1978.

Rossen or *Hud* (1963) by Martin Ritt. These characters are fundamentally different from the film rebels of the fifties as portrayed by Montgomery Clift in *From Here to Eternity*, Marlon Brando in *The Wild One* or James Dean in *Rebel Without Cause*. They share a sense of alienation from their environment, which they feel to be hostile. But while the anti-heroes of the fifties were victims of an unfair, corrupt system and fought to remain faithful to their own moral principles, Newman, in *The Hustler* and *Hud* plays men who have no moral code but are simply incapable of communicating with other people. This type of anti-hero is a rebellious, self-centred cynic who offends everyone who tries to approach him and finally remains alone. His disillusioned behaviour suggests disappointment with a society in which it seems pointless to try to find a meaningful life. Robert Dupea from Bob Rafelson's *Five Easy Pieces* (1970) shows a similar attitude. He is a man who cannot find a place in seventies American society, a man without roots and a self-centred egoist, incapable of real bonding. He is able to attract understanding and pity because his inner conflict makes sense, but not sympathy. The same is true of the main character in *Downhill Racer* (1969) by Michael Ritchie. Here Robert Redford plays a young skier from a humble background who unscrupulously pursues sporting and commercial success, leaving all his roots and moral principles behind and becoming a hated loner.

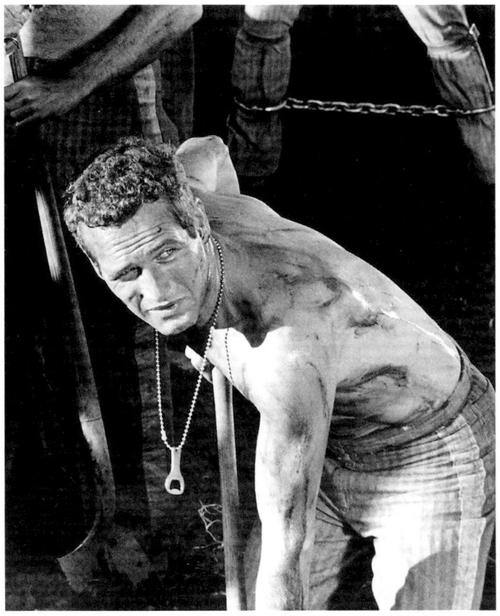

Martin Scorsese created his own version of the anti-hero, that of the false saint, introduced with the character of Charlie in *Mean Streets* (1973). Charlie is deeply imbued with Catholic values, which make him see his existence as a small-time gangster and his secret sexual relationship with his cousin as a sin. He longs for forgiveness and chooses his frivolous friend Johnny Boy as a means of atonement by trying to rescue him from his difficulties, but his campaign turns out to have fatal consequences. The hero of *Taxi Driver* (1975) has similar characteristics. He too has an ambivalent attitude to sex. He spends his free time in porn cinemas, but for him prostitutes are part of the scum of city that he sees it as his duty to eradicate. He finally takes it upon himself to rescue a 12-year-old prostitute called Iris, who does not want to be rescued. Even more than Charlie, he is a nobody who dreams of becoming a redeemer. These heroes despise themselves, they live on the shady side of society and long to come out into the light. Another of Scorsese's anti-heroes is the boxer Jake la Motta, on whose biography *Raging Bull* (1980) is based. The film shows a sequence of fights in the ring, but it is not mainly about boxing, but about a man whose behaviour is violent, brutal and uncontrolled. All of this conceals enormous feelings of guilt and inferiority complexes. For him, punishment in the ring is a kind of confession, repentance and absolution. His masochism feeds the fury that has taken him to the top, but also destroys his relationship with the people closest to him and drives him into the isolation that is the start of his downfall.

The ambiguous quality of the heroes makes the New Hollywood dramas much more complex than their classical predecessors, especially as they are often mixed with elements of other genres like ideas from gangster films in *Mean Streets* and *Taxi Driver*, or from the sports

vermischt werden wie mit denen des Gangsterfilms im Fall von *Mean Streets* und *Taxidriver* oder denen des Sportfilms in *Raging Bull*, im Grunde aber Gesellschafts- oder Charakterstudien sind. Das gleiche gilt für Sidney Lumets *Serpico* (1973) und *Prince of the City* (1981), die im Polizeimilieu spielen und Elemente des Kriminalfilms enthalten. Im Mittelpunkt steht jedoch nicht den Konflikt zwischen Gangster und Gesetz, sondern der Gewissenskonflikt ihrer Protagonisten, der durch die Konfrontation der korrupten gesellschaftlichen Institutionen und der eigenen Wertmaßstäbe entsteht. *Serpico* erzählt in straffem Dokumentarstil die Geschichte eines jungen Polizisten. Dieser weigert sich, bei der allgemein verbreiteten Korruption unter seinen Kollegen mitzuwirken, und wird darüber zum geächteten Außenseiter. *Prince of the City* durchleuchtet differenziert die Problematik eines bestechlichen Polizisten, der sich entschließt, mit einer Untersuchungskommission gegen Polizeikorruption zusammenzuarbeiten, und dabei immer mehr zum Opfer einer Maschinerie wird, die keinerlei Hemmungen hat, ihn fallenzulassen, wenn sich dies als nötig erweisen sollte. Die Korruption der Justiz greift Lumet in *The Verdict* (1982, *The Verdict – Die Wahrheit und nichts als die Wahrheit*) auf, einem klassischen Gerichtsdrama, in dem Paul Newman einen heruntergekommenen Anwalt spielt, der seit Jahren in einer persönlichen und beruflichen Krise steckt und durch sein Engagement in einem Schadenersatzfall seine Würde zurückerobert. Das Justizsystem wird hier als Instrument im Dienste der Reichen und Mächtigen gegen die Schwachen entlarvt. Im Gegensatz zu den klassischen Dramen, die zwar auch die dunklen Seiten der amerikanischen Gesellschaft aufdeckten, doch die Fehlentwicklungen am Ende korrigierten und so die Überlegenheit des bestehenden Wertesystems bestätigten, stellt Lumet die Polizei und Justiz als unheilbar krank dar. Sowohl in *Serpico* als auch in *Prince of the City* wird deutlich, daß die Behörden die Korruptionsvorwürfe nur halbherzig verfolgen, um dem Druck der Öffentlichkeit Genüge zu tun, während in *The Verdict* die Gerechtigkeit nur deshalb siegen kann, weil sich die Geschworenen über die juristischen Regeln hinwegsetzen.

Das Thema des klassischen Familienmelodramas greifen dagegen nur wenige Filme auf, und wenn dann behandeln sie den Zerfall der Familie, wie Robert Bentons *Kramer vs. Kramer* (1979), die Geschichte eines Ehemanns, dessen Frau ihn und ihren kleinen Sohn verläßt, weil sie sich in ihrer Ehe unglücklich und unausgefüllt fühlt. Nach anfänglichen Schwierigkeiten wandelt er sich vom Workaholic zu einem fürsorglichen, verständnisvollen Vater. Doch dann taucht seine Exfrau wieder auf und verlangt das Sorgerecht für den Jungen. Paul Schraders *Hardcore* (1979, *Hardcore – Ein Vater sieht rot*) beschreibt die Suche eines angesehenen Geschäftsmannes aus einer streng religiösen, kalvinistischen Gemeinde nach seiner halbwüchsigen Tochter, die sich während eines Ausflugs ihrer Kirchengruppe absetzt und im Rotlichtmilieu von Los An-

132. Robert De Niro (Travis Bickle) und Jodie Foster (Iris) in *Taxi Driver* von Martin Scorsese, 1975.
133. Dustin Hoffman (Ted Kramer) und Justin Henry (Billy Kramer) in *Kramer vs. Kramer* von Robert Benton, 1979.
134. Robert De Niro (Jake La Motta) in *Wie ein wilder Stier* von Martin Scorsese, 1980.
135. Al Pacino (Frank Serpico) in *Serpico* von Sidney Lumet, 1973.

132. Robert De Niro (Travis Bickle) and Jodie Foster (Iris) in *Taxi Driver* by Martin Scorsese, 1975.
133. Dustin Hoffman (Ted Kramer) and Justin Henry (Billy Kramer) in *Kramer vs. Kramer* by Robert Benton, 1979.
134. Robert De Niro (Jake La Motta) in *Raging Bull* by Martin Scorsese, 1980.
135. Al Pacino (Frank Serpico) in *Serpico* by Sidney Lumet, 1973.

film in *Raging Bull*, but essentially they are social or character studies. The same applies to Sidney Lumet's *Serpico* (1973) and *Prince of the City* (1981), which are set in a police milieu and contain elements of the detective film. The key feature, however, is not the conflict between gangsters and the law, but their leading characters' conflicts of conscience, which derive from confrontation between corrupt social institutions and the characters' own values. *Serpico* uses a tight documentary style to tell the story of a young policeman. He refuses to involve himself in the corruption that is widespread among his colleagues, which makes him into a despised outsider. *Prince of the City* is a sophisticated examination of the problems faced by a policeman who is susceptible to bribery. He decides to work with an enquiry into police corruption, and thus increasingly becomes the victim of a machinery that has no compunction about dropping him if this seems necessary. Lumet takes up the corruption of justice in *The Verdict* (1982), a classic courtroom drama in which Paul Newman plays a down-and-out lawyer who has been in a state of professional and personal crisis for years, and regains his dignity by committing himself to a damages case. Here the justice system is revealed to be an instrument serving the rich and powerful. Unlike classical dramas, which did reveal the darker sides of American society, but also corrected the fault at the end, thus revealing the superiority of the existing system of values, Lumet presents justice and the police as incurably sick. Both *Serpico* and *Prince of the City* show clearly that the authorities only pursue accusations of corruption enough to satisfy public pressure, while in *The Verdict* justice succeeds only because the jury disregard the legal rules.

Only a few dramas take up the feel of the classic family melodrama, and if they do they deal with the breakdown of the family, as in Robert Benton's *Kramer vs. Kramer* (1979), the story of a married man whose wife leaves him and their little son because she feels unhappy and unfulfilled in the marriage. After some early difficulties he changes from a workaholic to a caring, understanding father. But then his ex-wife turns up and demands custody of the boy. Paul Schrader's *Hardcore* (1979) describes the search by a highly regarded businessman from a strictly religious, Calvinistic community for his teenage daughter, who runs away during a trip with her church group and disappears in the red-light district of Los Angeles because she cannot stand her father's strict moral rules and lack of approachability.

The only director to address the classic themes of marriage and family in all his films, though always focusing on middle-class neuroses and points of view, is John Cassavetes. In *Faces* (1968) he dissects the marital crisis of a middle-class couple, condensed down to the events of a single night in which both risk breaking out of their unsatisfactory relationship and those of the next morning, when they come back, and the alienation arising from having been through something different that they know they will never find in their accustomed lives. *Husbands* (1970) shows marriage from the man's point of view. After a friend's funeral, three middle-aged men take a spontaneous trip to London and try to escape from age and death, responsibility

geles untertaucht, weil sie die strikten moralischen Regeln und die Unnahbarkeit ihres Vaters unerträglich findet.

Der einzige Regisseur, der sich in fast allen seinen Filmen mit den klassischen Themen Ehe und Familie beschäftigte, dabei allerdings vor allem die Konflikte und Neurosen des Mittelstands ins Blickfeld rückt, ist John Cassavetes. In *Faces* (1968, *Gesichter*) seziert er die Ehekrise eines Mittelstandspaares, kondensiert auf die Ereignisse einer Nacht, in der beide den Ausbruch aus ihrer unbefriedigenden Beziehung wagen, und des darauffolgenden Morgens, als sie zurückkehren, und die Entfremdung durch das Erlebnis von etwas anderem gewachsen ist, von dem sie wissen, daß sie es in ihrem gewohnten Leben nicht finden werden. *Husbands* (1970, *Ehemänner*) schildert die Ehe aus der Sicht der Männer. Nach der Beerdigung eines Freundes unternehmen drei Ehemänner mittleren Alters einen spontanen Ausflug nach London und versuchen, durch einen Rückfall in ihr Junggesellenleben vor Alter und Tod, Verantwortung und einem festgelegten Leben zu fliehen, um danach mangels anderer Perspektiven wieder zu ihren Familien zurückzukehren. *A Woman Under the Influence* (1974) erzählt die erschütternde Geschichte der Ehefrau eines Arbeiters und Mutter von drei Kindern, die verzweifelt bemüht ist, die an sie gestellten Anforderungen zu erfüllen, und in ihrem Übereifer, es allen recht zu machen, immer wieder peinliche Szenen provoziert. Schließlich läßt ihr Mann sie unter dem Druck seiner mäkeligen Mutter in eine Nervenklinik einweisen. Nach sechs Monaten kehrt sie scheinbar geheilt nach Hause zurück, doch es zeigt sich, daß ihre Angst, Fehler zu begehen, durch das Trauma, von ihrem Mann im Stich gelassen worden zu sein, noch zugenommen hat. *Love Streams* (1984) befaßt sich mit den Nachwirkungen einer gescheiterten Ehe. Im Mittelpunkt des Films steht das Geschwisterpaar Sarah und Robert, gespielt von Gena Rowlands und John Cassavetes, die beide eine Krise durchleben. Erneut geht es um die verzweifelte Suche nach Liebe sowie die Schwierigkeit, tragfähige Beziehungen einzugehen und Verantwortung zu übernehmen. Auf die Angst vor dem Älterwerden kommt Cassavetes in *Opening Night* (1977, *Die erste Vorstellung*) zurück. Gena Rowlands verkörpert die Bühnenschauspielerin Myrtle Gordon, die in eine Krise gerät, als sie die Hauptrolle in einem Stück übernimmt, das von den Problemen einer alternden Frau handelt. Sie weigert sich einzusehen, daß das Altern eine Frage ist, die auf die Lebenshaltung, das Handeln und die Träume eines Menschen Einfluß hat, wie es die Autorin vertritt. Der Film endet mit einer typischen Cassavetes-Szene: Myrtle erscheint am Abend der Premiere volltrunken im Theater und verwandelt mit Unterstützung ihres Partners die große endgültige Auseinandersetzung in eine Farce. Die Problematik löst sich in einem albernem Spiel auf, in dem beide sich und dem Publikum beweisen, daß sie weder alt, noch gesetzt, noch resigniert sind.

Wie hier verhindert Cassavetes durch Dialogwitz, Showeinlagen, Musikszenen, vor allem aber durch die Betonung des oftmals Paradoxen der Bemühungen, über den eigenen Schatten zu springen, daß seine Filme ins Melodramatische abkippen. Eine bemerkenswerte Szene, in der die Verzweiflung den Ausdruck des Tragikomischen erhält, findet sich in *Love Streams*, wo Gena Rowlands in eine Zoohandlung geht und eine ganze Menagerie kauft, darunter zwei Ponies, eine Ziege, Enten, Hühner und einen Hund, sie in ein Taxi stopft und ihrem Bruder bringt, da sie meint, all sein Unglück beruhe darauf, daß er niemanden habe, den er lieben und um den er sich kümmern könne. Dieser Versuch, eine praktische Lösung zu finden und irgendwie zur Normalität zurückzukehren, beruht auf der Erkenntnis der Ausweglosigkeit der Situation. Die Zerfallserscheinungen von Ehe und Familie sind offensichtlich. Es steht außer Zweifel, daß die Familie aufgehört hat, als Grundpfeiler des »American Way of Life« zu funktionieren, weil die traditionelle Rollenverteilung aufgebrochen ist und Sehnsüchte nach Liebe, Toleranz, Vertrauen, gegenseitiger Verantwortung und Achtung freigelegt worden sind, die sie nur ungenügend erfüllen kann.

136. Gena Rowlands (Sarah Lawson) und John Cassavetes (Robert Harmon) in *Love Streams* von John Cassavetes, 1984.

136. Gena Rowlands (Sarah Lawson) and John Cassavetes (Robert Harmon) in *Love Streams* by John Cassavetes, 1984.

and a rigidly fixed life by going back to their bachelor existence, but then return to their families because of a lack of other prospects. *A Woman Under the Influence* (1974) tells the shattering story of the wife of a worker and mother of three children who tries desperately to meet the demands made on her and constantly provokes embarrassing scenes because she is so keen to do everything right. Finally her husband has her put in a psychiatric hospital, under pressure from his carping mother. After six months she comes home, apparently cured, but it turns out that her fear about making mistakes has become even greater because of the trauma of being left in the lurch by her husband. *Love Streams* (1984) deals with the effects of a failed marriage. At the centre of the film are Sarah and Robert, a brother and sister who are both undergoing a crisis; they are played by Gena Rowlands and John Cassavetes. Once more the theme is a desperate search for love, the difficulty of entering into viable relationships and taking responsibility. Cassavetes returns to fear of growing older in *Opening Night* (1977). Gena Rowlands plays the stage actress Myrtle Gordon, who gets into a crisis when she takes on the leading role in a play and dealing with older women's problems. She refuses to accept that ageing is a question that influences people's attitude to life, actions and dreams, as suggested by the author. The film ends with a typical Cassavetes scene: Myrtle turns up at the theatre completely drunk on the first night, and with the support of her partner turns the great final conflict into a farce. The problems dissolve into a stupid game in which both prove to themselves and the audience that they are not old or set in their ways, and have not given up.

As is the case here, Cassavetes is able to use witty dialogue, show set-pieces, musical scenes but above all emphasis on paradoxical efforts to change one's spots to stop his films sliding into melodrama. A remarkable scene in which despair achieves tragi-comic status takes place in *Love Stream*. Gena Rowlands goes into a pet shop and buys a whole menagerie, including two ponies, a goat, ducks, hens and a dog, stuffs them into a taxi and takes them to her brother because she thinks all his unhappiness stems from the fact that he has no one to love and care for. This attempt to find a practical solution and return to normality in some way is based on recognizing that there is no way out of the situation. The signs of marital and family decay are obvious. There is no doubt that the family has ceased to be the pillar of the »American Way of Life«, because the traditional role distribution has broken down, revealing a longing for love, tolerance, trust, mutual responsibility and esteem that it cannot fulfil adequately.

Verdienste und Grenzen

Betrachtet man die Abweichungen New Hollywoods von den klassischen Konventionen, so kristallisiert sich ein grundlegender Unterschied heraus: Während das alte Hollywood die bestehende soziale Ordnung und ihre Institutionen, die ihr zugrundeliegenden Werte und das Selbstbild der Amerikaner bestätigte, untermauerte und zum Teil erst prägte, ziehen die Filmemacher des neuen Hollywood all dies grundsätzlich in Zweifel. Ihre Filme sind geprägt vom Geist der siebziger Jahre, einem Jahrzehnt der verzweifelten Suche nach einer besseren Welt, deren Scheitern vorprogrammiert war. Die Ideale der Gegenkultur der sechziger Jahre waren an der rauhen Wirklichkeit zerschellt. Zurück blieben Wut und Trauer über den Verlust des amerikanischen Traums, für den das Establishment verantwortlich gemacht wurde. Diese Weltsicht schlägt sich sowohl in den Filmen nieder, die erkennbar mit den klassischen Genreformeln brechen, als auch in jenen, die sie im wesentlichen beibehalten und variieren. Sie äußert sich im offenen oder versteckten Angriff auf die amerikanischen Institutionen und die offizielle Politik, in der bissigen Kritik am »American Way of Life«, in der Demontage der Mythen und Legenden, in der Vorliebe für Antihelden, im Verzicht auf ein Happy-End, in der Lust an der Provokation durch schockierende Sex- oder Gewaltszenen und im Verstoß gegen die Sehgewohnheiten und in der Unterwanderung der Genreerwartungen. Und aus ihr resultieren die Andersartigkeit, die Faszination und die beunruhigende Kraft, die auch heute noch von vielen Filmen jener Zeit ausgeht. Der fortschrittliche Gehalt von New Hollywood liegt in dem Bemühen, dem idealisierten Bild Amerikas, wie es die alten Hollywoodfilme zeigten, eine realistische und differenzierte Sichtweise gegenüberzustellen und gesellschaftliche Konflikte offenzulegen. Wird jedoch versucht, Lösungen anzubieten, die über die klassischen Konfliktlösungen der Versöhnung der Gegensätze oder des Sieges über das Böse durch eine direkte Aktion hinausgehen, so manifestiert sich eine nostalgische Sehnsucht nach dem festgefügten Wertgefüge und den überschaubaren sozialen Beziehungen früherer Zeiten. Das heißt, in dieser Hinsicht unterscheiden sich die Filme des neuen Hollywood nicht wesentlich von denen des alten. Überhaupt ist Nostalgie eine verbreitete Erscheinung im amerikanischen Kino der siebziger Jahre. Sie äußert sich im Kult des romantischen Außenseiters, in der Verklärung des traditionellen Moralkodexes des Westens oder in Filmen, die einen wehmütigen Rückblick auf die scheinbar heile Welt amerikanischer Kleinstädte der fünfziger und sechziger Jahre enthalten, wie *The Last Picture Show* (1970) von Peter Bogdanovich und *American Graffiti* (1973) von George Lucas. Ihren deutlichsten Ausdruck findet sie in dem Phänomen der sogenannten Nostalgiefilme, wie *Nickelodeon* (1976) von Peter Bogdanovich oder *The Great Waldo Pepper* (1975, *Tollkühne Flieger*) von George Roy Hill, die beide auf eine Pionierzeit zurückblicken, die der Filmindustrie und der Fliegerei, und mit Wehmut feststellen, daß diese vom großen Abenteuer zum Geschäft geworden sind.

Der Hang zur Nostalgie reflektiert den Bewußtseinsstand der Gegenkultur, deren Suche nach Alternativen sich unter dem Einfluß der Hippiekultur vor allem auf die Vergangenheit und nach innen richteten. Dieser Umstand begünstigte die Rückkehr zum alten Gesellschaftsbild und damit den Niedergang von New Hollywood, als sich in der zweiten Hälfte der siebziger Jahre das politische Klima in den USA allmählich wandelte. Nach dem Rücktritt Nixons im August 1974 begann unter den Präsidentschaften von Gerald Ford und Jimmy Carter die Wiederherstellung des Vertrauens in die offiziellen Institutionen, die sich offensichtlich als stark genug erwiesen hatten, der Korruption Einhalt zu gebieten. Zugleich fand eine Aufarbeitung des Traumas statt, das der Vietnamkrieg ausgelöst hatte. Die Krise des amerikanischen Selbstbewußtseins begann abzuklingen. Gleichzeitig litten die Amerikaner zunehmend unter innenpolitischen Problemen. Wachsende Inflation, Rezession, Arbeitslosigkeit und die Energiekrise sorgten für eine wirtschaftliche Instabilität, für die man die zögerliche Amtsführung Carters verantwortlich machte. Die Folge waren eine konservative Wende und der Ruf nach dem starken Mann. Diese Entwicklung schlug sich 1980 in der Wahl Ronald Reagans zum Präsidenten nieder, der mit dem Versprechen antrat, für eine Erneuerung des amerikanischen Selbstbewußtseins zu sorgen. Er forderte eine Rückbesinnung auf traditionelle Werte und die Wiederherstellung der internationalen Führungsposition der USA durch eine Politik der Stärke. Auf die gesellschaftliche Desintegration der siebziger Jahre folgte eine neue Phase der Integration.

Die Filmindustrie reagierte darauf, indem sie wieder verstärkt auf die klassischen Formeln setzte, die nie vollständig ihre Gültigkeit verloren hatten, wie der kommerzielle Erfolg von Katastrophenfilmen *The Towering Inferno* (1974, *Flammendes Inferno*) etwa, oder *The Hindenburg* (1975, *Die Hindenburg*), konventionellen Musicals, wie *Funny Lady* (1975) und *A Star is Born*

137. Charles Martin Smith (Terry »The Toad« Fields), Richard Dreyfuss (Curt Henderson), Harrison Ford (Bob Falfa), Cindy Williams (Laurie Henderson) und Ron Howard (Steve Bolander) in *American Graffiti* von George Lucas, 1973.

137. Charles Martin Smith (Terry »The Toad« Fields), Richard Dreyfuss (Curt Henderson), Harrison Ford (Bob Falfa), Cindy Williams (Laurie Henderson) and Ron Howard (Steve Bolander) in *American Graffiti* by George Lucas, 1973.

Merits and limitations

If we look at New Hollywood's departures from the classical conventions, one fundamental difference soon becomes very clear: classical Hollywood used to confirm and underpin the existing social order and its institutions, and indeed helped to shape them to an extent, but the New Hollywood film-makers challenge them on principle. Their films are imbued with the spirit of the seventies, a decade of desperate searching for a better world, which was doomed to failure. The sixties alternative culture ideals had been dashed to pieces on the rocks of harsh reality. What remained was rage and regret about the loss of the American dream, and the establishment was held responsible for this. This world view is clearly apparent in those films that clearly break with the classical genre formulae and also in those that essentially hold on to them, with variations. It is expressed in open or concealed attacks on American institutions and official policies, in fierce criticism of the »American Way of Life«, in the dismantling of myths and legends, in the preference for anti-heroes, in the lack of happy endings, in delight at provocation by shocking scenes of sex and violence, in breaking normal visual conventions and in undermining the expectations placed in the genre. And it releases the different qualities, the fascination and the disturbing power that these films still exude today. The progressive element of New Hollywood lies in its efforts to set a realistic and sophisticated way of looking at things against old Hollywood's idealized vision of America and to take the lid of the social conflicts. But as soon as any attempt is made to offer solutions that go beyond the classic conflict solutions of conciliation or defeating evil by direct actions, then there is a sense of a nostalgic longing for the firmly established values and manageable social relationships of earlier times. In other words, these New Hollywood films are not very much different from the classical products. Nostalgia was anyway a widespread phenomenon in the American cinema of the seventies. It comes to the surface in the cult of the romantic outsider, in the transfiguration of the traditional moral code of the West or in films that cast a melancholy glance at the apparently perfect world of small-town America in the fifties and sixties, like *The Last Picture Show* (1970) by Peter Bogdanovich and *American Graffiti* (1973) by George Lucas. It is expressed most clearly in the phenomenon of so-called nostalgia films like *Nickelodeon* (1976) by Peter Bogdanovich or *The Great Waldo Pepper* (1975) by George Roy Hill. Both of these go back to a pioneering period, of the film industry or of flying, and regretfully point out that these have changed from great adventures into mere commerce.

This inclination to nostalgia reflects the alternative culture, which started its search under the influence of hippie culture, and thus looked above all at the past and inwards. This state of af-

(1976), oder von den Boxerfilmen *Rocky I* (1976) und *Rocky II* (1979) zeigte. Andererseits blieben auch die Filmemacher des neuen Hollywood vom Stimmungsumschwung in den USA nicht unbeeinflußt. In der zweiten Hälfte der siebziger Jahre plädieren immer mehr Filme, darunter so erfolgreiche, wie *Kramer vs. Kramer*, *American Gigolo*, *Urban Cowboy*, *Heaven Can Wait* oder *9 to 5*, für die Versöhnung der Gegensätze als Möglichkeit der Konfliktlösung. In dieselbe Richtung weisen *All the President's Men* und *The China Syndrome*, die trotz ihrer harschen Gesellschaftskritik letztlich die Fähigkeit der Amerikaner zur Bewältigung der sozialen Konflikte bestätigen. Gleichzeitig beschäftigen sich viele Filme mit der Aufarbeitung der gesellschaftlichen Umbrüche der sechziger Jahre und der daraus entstandenen nationalen Desintegration. *Coming Home*, *The Deer Hunter* und *Apocalypse Now* legten zwar einerseits die unverheilten Wunden des Vietnamkriegs offen, leisteten damit aber auch einen wichtigen Beitrag zur Bewältigung des Traumas der Niederlage in Vietnam. Sozialkritische Filme, wie *Blue Collar*, *Norma Rae* und *Brubaker,* verweisen nicht nur auf die Grenzen, sondern auch auf die Möglichkeiten einer sozialen Veränderung innerhalb der bestehenden gesellschaftlichen Institutionen. Eine ganze Reihe von Filmen, darunter *The Return of the Secaucus 7* (1980, *Rückkehr nach Secaucus*) von John Sayles, *Four Friends* (1981, *Vier Freunde*) von Arthur Penn und *The Big Chill* (1983, *Der große Frust*) von Lawrence Kasdan, beschäftigen sich mit den gescheiterten Hoffnungen der sechziger Jahre oder liefern einen nostalgisch verklärten Rückblick auf die Beat- und Hippiebewegung, wie der Musicalfilm *Hair* (1979) von Milos Forman, oder *Heart Beat* (1980, *Herzschläge*) nach der Autobiographie von Carolyn Cassady, der Witwe eines der Begründer der Beat-Bewegung, und bezogen so Distanz zu einem bewegten Kapitel der amerikanischen Geschichte. Von da aus war es nur noch ein kleiner Schritt zu typisch amerikanischen Erfolgsstories, wie *The Right Stuff* (1983, *Der Stoff, aus dem die Helden sind*) von Philip Kaufman oder *Places in The Heart* (1984, *Ein Platz im Herzen*) von Robert Benton oder der Bestätigung der Überlegenheit des »American Way of Life« in Paul Mazurskys *Moscow on the Hudson* (1983, *Moskau in New York*). Daneben weisen diese Filme eine ausgeprägte Neigung zur Nostalgie auf, die sich im Gegensatz zu den siebziger Jahren, wo die Sehnsucht nach der Zeit der offenen Grenzen einherging mit der melancholischen Erkenntnis von deren unwiederbringlichem Verlust, in der Sentimentalisierung und Romantisierung der Vergangenheit äußert und damit zur Realitätsflucht einlädt. Derselbe Grundton ist auch in den Achtziger-Jahre-Filmen von Coppola zu erkennen, die allesamt in der Vergangenheit spielen und diese unkritisch verklären.

Diese Filme ordnen sich dem allgemeinen Trend unter, die traditionellen Wertvorstellungen und Institutionen zu bestärken, dessen Ausdruck Filme wie *Coalminer's Daughter* (1980, *Nashville Lady*), *Private Benjamin* (1980, *Schütze Benjamin*), *On Golden Pond* (1981, *Am goldenen See*), *An Officer and a Gentleman* (1982, *Ein Offizier und Gentleman*) und *Terms of Endearment* (1983, *Zeit der Zärtlichkeit*) sind. Deren Erfolg zeigt, daß die sozialen Verlierer und rebellischen Außenseiter des neuen Hollywood der Vergangenheit angehören. Im Mittelpunkt stehen hier charakterfeste, tatkräftige und optimistische Durchschnittsmenschen, die sich gegen alle Widerstände durchsetzen und damit die Gültigkeit des amerikanischen Traums beweisen. Zur gleichen Zeit leiteten Politdramen wie *Cuba* (1979, *Explosion in Kuba*) von Richard Lester, *Reds* (1981) von Warren Beatty und *Missing* (1981, *Vermißt*) von Costa-Gavras eine Tendenz ein, soziale Konflikte in fremde Länder zu verlagern, die sich später in Filmen wie *Ghandi* (1982) von Richard Attenborough, *Under Fire* (1983, *Unter Feuer*) von Roger Spottiswood, *The Killing Fields* (1984, *Killing Fields – Schreiendes Land*) von Roland Joffé und *Salvador* (1986) von Oliver Stone fortsetzte.

Darüber hinaus gab New Hollywood den Anstoß zu wichtigen Trends, welche die Rückkehr zum Eskapismus der Achtziger begünstigten. Der Erfolg von *American Graffiti* zog eine Welle von Filmen nach sich, die einen sentimentalen Blick auf die heile Welt von Kindheit und Jugend in den fünfziger und sechziger Jahren werfen. Zudem inspirierte er die außerordentlich erfolgreiche Teenagerkomödie *Animal House* (1978, *Ich glaub', mich tritt ein Pferd*) von John Landis, die im Collegemilieu derselben Zeit spielt, allerdings im Gegensatz zu ihrem Vorläufer auf eine Abfolge von derben Späßen und absurden Gags setzt, die zum Markenzeichen für die Highschool-Komödien der achtziger Jahre wurden. Gleichzeitig erlebten die »Teenieslasher«-Filme in der Nachfolge von *Carrie* und *Halloween* ihre große Zeit. Im Unterschied zu ihren Vorbildern arbeiteten sie vor allem mit gruseligen Spezialeffekten und plakativer Gewalt. An die Tradition der Rockfilme knüpfte *Saturday Day Night Fever* (1977, *Nur Samstag Nacht*) an und löste die Diskowelle aus, die in den nachfolgenden Jahren eine Serie von seichten Tanzfilmen hervorbrachte.

138. Ryan O'Neal (Leo Harrigan) in *Nickelodeon* von Peter Bogdanovich, 1976.
139. Bo Svenson (Axel Olsson) and Robert Redford (Waldo Pepper) in *Tollkühne Flieger* von George Roy Hill, 1975.

138. Ryan O'Neal (Leo Harrigan) in *Nickelodeon* by Peter Bogdanovich, 1976.
139. Bo Svenson (Axel Olsson) and Robert Redford (Waldo Pepper) in *The Great Waldo Pepper* by George Roy Hill, 1975.

fairs favoured a return to the old vision of society and thus the decline of New Hollywood when in the second half of the seventies the political climate in America gradually changed. After Nixon's resignation in August 1974, trust in official institutions started to be restored under Gerald Ford and Jimmy Carter, as the institutions had obviously proved themselves to be strong enough to resist corruption. At the same time, the trauma of the Vietnam War started to be reappraised. The crisis of American self-confidence started to fade. At the same time, the Americans suffered increasingly from internal political problems. Rising inflation, recession, unemployment and the energy crisis created economic instability, and this was blamed on Jimmy Carter's indecisive leadership. This development led in 1980 to the election of Ronald Reagan as president. He came to power with a promise to renew American self-confidence, promoting a return to traditional values and the restoration of the USA's leading international position through the politics of strength. A new phase of integration followed the social disintegration of the seventies.

The film industry reacted to this by relying strongly on classical formulae again. They had never completely lost their validity, as can be seen from the commercial success of disaster movies like *The Towering Inferno* (1974) or *The Hindenburg* (1975, conventional musicals like *Funny Lady* (1975) and *A Star is Born* (1976) or the boxing films *Rocky* (1976) and *Rocky II* (1979). The New Hollywood film-makers were also not immune to the change of mood in the USA. In the second half of the seventies, more and more films, including very successful ones like *Kramer vs. Kramer*, *American Gigolo*, *Urban Cowboy*, *Heaven Can Wait* or *9 to 5* pleaded for the reconciliation of conflicts as a problem-solving possibility. *All the President's Men* and *The China Syndrome* point in the same direction: despite their harsh social criticism they ultimately confirm America's ability to manage social conflict. At the same time, a lot of films reappraise the social upheaval of the sixties and the national disintegration that arose from this. *Coming Home*, *The Deer Hunter* and *Apocalypse Now* did reveal the unhealed wounds of Vietnam, but they also made an important contribution to coming to terms with defeat in that war. Socially critical films like *Blue Collar*, *Norma Rae* and *Brubaker* do not just identify limitations, they also indicate possibilities for social change within the existing institutions. A whole series of films, including *The Return of the Secaucus 7* (1980) by John Sayles, *Four Friends* (1981) by Arthur Penn and *The Big Chill* (1983) by Lawrence Kasdan address the failed hopes of the sixties or provide a nostalgically transfigured look back at the Beat and hippie movement, like the musical *Hair* (1979) by Milos Forman or *Heart Beat* (1980), based on the autobiography of Carolyn Cassady, the widow of one of the founders of the Beat movement, thus distancing themselves from a lively chapter of American history. From there it was only a small step to typical American success stories like *The Right Stuff* (1983) by Philip Kaufman or *Places in the Heart* (1984) by Robert Benton, or Paul Mazursky's *Moscow on Hudson* (1984), which confirmed the superiority of the »American Way of Life«. These films also show a marked tendency to nostalgia. Unlike the seventies, when a nostalgic longing for the days of open borders went hand in hand with a melancholy recognition of irreplaceable loss, it was now expressed by sentimentalizing and romanticizing the past, thus inviting an escape from reality. The same basic tone is also to be found in Coppola's eighties films, which are all set in the past and glorify it uncritically.

These films fit in with the general trend of reinforcing traditional values and institutions, as expressed by films like *Coalminer's Daughter* (1980), *Private Benjamin* (1980), *On Golden Pond* (1981), *An Officer and a Gentleman* (1982) and *Terms of Endearment* (1983). Their success shows that New Hollywood's social losers and rebellious outsiders are a thing of the past. All these films are built around energetic, optimistic, ordinary people with strong characters who succeed against all the odds and thus prove the validity of the American dream. At the same time, political dramas like *Cuba* (1979) by Richard Lester, *Reds* (1951) by Warren Beatty and *Missing* (1981 by Costa-Gavras introduce a tendency to shift social conflict to foreign countries, which continued later in films like *Ghandi* (1982) by Richard Attenborough, *Under Fire* (1983) by Roger Spottiswood, *The Killing Fields* (1984) by Roland Joffé and *Salvador* (1986) by Oliver Stone.

As well as this, New Hollywood initiated some important trends that worked in favour of the eighties return to escapism. The success of *American Graffiti* led to a wave of films that took a sentimental look at the perfect world of childhood and youth in the fifties and sixties. It also inspired the extraordinarily successful teen comedy *Animal House* (1978) by John Landis, which is set in the college milieu of the period. Unlike its predecessors, it relies on a series of coarse jokes and absurd gimmicks that were to become the hallmark of the high-school comedies of

Die bedeutsamste Entwicklung setzte George Lucas' *Star Wars* (1977) in Gang, ein Film, der bewußt für jugendliche Zuschauer konzipiert war. Handlung und Darstellung stützen sich auf eine Mischung aus modernem Comicstrip und uralten Konventionen des Märchens, das bereits dem klassischen Hollywood als Grundlage für die verschiedenen Genres diente. Das Ergebnis sind eindimensionale Charaktere, die klare Unterscheidung von Gut und Böse und ein simpler Plot, der durch Spezialeffekte in eine phantasievolle und neuartige Form gebracht wird, die Modernität vorspiegelt. Dieses Rezept prägte nicht nur die zukünftigen Science-fiction-Filme, sondern auch andere Genres wie den Kriminalfilm, den Kriegsfilm und den Horrorfilm. Insbesondere wurde es zum gängigen Muster eines der populärsten Genres der achtziger Jahre, des Actionfilms, dessen typische Helden Comicstrips entsprungen zu sein scheinen und mit dem innerlich zerrissenen, auf moralische Integrität bedachten Actionhelden der siebziger Jahre wenig gemeinsam haben, sondern Nachfolger einer Abart des Antihelden sind, der in den sechziger Jahren entstand: der kaltblütige, berechnende, hochqualifizierte Profi, der seinen Job frei von allen moralischen Bedenken versieht. Nach dem durchschlagenden Erfolg von *Rambo* (1982) entstand eine Welle von Actionfilmen, in welchen amerikanische Elitekämpfer zur Befreiung von Kriegsgefangenen nach Vietnam zogen und das amerikanische Überlegenheitsgefühl wiederherstellten, indem sie quasi nachträglich den Krieg gewannen. *Star Wars* zog außerdem eine Flut von Fantasyspektakeln nach sich, unter denen das erfolgreichste die *Indiana-Jones*-Trilogie war, für die sich Steven Spielberg und George Lucas zusammenschlossen.

Diese Trends wurden von einer Reihe anderer Filmemacher, deren Namen mit New Hollywood verbunden sind, mitgetragen. John Boorman, der sich bereits nach *Deliverance* (1971) Fantasystoffen zugewendet hatte, drehte den brillant photographierten historischen Abenteuerfilm *Excalibur* (1981) und das Dschungelabenteuer *The Esmerald Forrest* (1985, *Der Smaragdwald*). John Milius lieferte den Fantasy-Actionfilm *Conan the Barbarian* (1982, *Conan, der Barbar*), in dem Arnold Schwarzenegger, einer der Superstars der Achtziger, seine erste Hauptrolle spielte. Brian De Palma, der sich, wie Spielberg und Lucas, vorwiegend für eine Erneuerung der Genres interessierte, machte eine Reihe von mehr oder minder erfolgreichen Psychothrillern und klassischen Gangsterfilmen, durch die seine Karriere neuen Auftrieb erhielt. Andere Filmemacher versuchten, sich an das neue Klima anzupassen, ohne ihren künstlerischen Anspruch aufzugeben. Alan J. Pakula, Philip Kaufman, Milos Forman, Robert Benton und Sydney Pollack konnten sich als Regisseure anspruchsvoller Mainstream-Filme etablieren, griffen darin allerdings Stoffe auf, die jeden sozialkritischen Kommentar vermeiden oder die konservativen Wertvorstellungen bestätigen. Trotz einiger großer Erfolge ging ihre Produktivität in den Achtzigern allerdings merklich zurück. Leichter fiel die Anpassung offensichtlich Komödienregisseuren, wie Paul Mazursky und Michael Ritchie, die in ihren Filmen die Sozialkritik immer mehr durch einen versöhnlichen Ton oder wie in den Chevy-Chase-Filmen von Ritchie durch alberne Gags ersetzten. Mike Nichols hatte nach einer Flaute in seiner Karriere 1983 ein Comeback mit *Silkwood*, einem von der Thematik und Weltsicht her für die Zeit eher untypischen Drama. Danach drehte er einige harmlose Gesellschaftskomödien, von denen *Working Girl* (1988, *Die Waffen der Frauen*) am erfolgreichsten war. Zwei der ehedem vielversprechendsten Talente des neuen Hollywood, Bob Rafelson und Michael Cimino, konnten wieder im Filmgeschäft Fuß fassen. Rafelson kehrte 1981 für *The Postman Always Rings Twice* (*Wenn der Postmann zweimal klingelt)* zu seiner Zusammenarbeit mit Jack Nicholson zurück und hatte nach zehn Jahren erstmals wieder einen kommerziellen Erfolg, während Cimino mit *The Year of the Dragon* (1985, *Im Jahr des Drachen*) seinen beschädigten Ruf teilweise wiederherstellte. Beide reichten jedoch nicht wieder an ihren früheren Ruhm heran. Ähnlich erging es Francis Ford Coppola, der von seinem Mythos als Superstar zehrte und trotz des finanziellen Desasters von *One from the Heart* (1982) und *Cotton Club* (1984) in den achtziger Jahren insgesamt acht Filme drehte, jedoch mit keinem auch nur annähernd an seine Erfolge der siebziger Jahre anknüpfen konnte. Im Gegensatz zu Coppola, der unentschieden zwischen seinen künstlerischen Visionen und kommerziellen Zugeständnissen schwankte, hielt Martin Scorsese an seinen persönlichen Projekten fest und schaffte es, seinen Ruf als einer der kreativsten und talentiertesten Regisseure Hollywoods zu festigen. Größere Erfolge konnte er aber erst wieder mit *The Color of Money* (1986, *Die Farbe des Geldes*) und *The Last Temptation of Christ* (1988, *Die letzte Versuchung Christi*) verbuchen, mit denen er von seinem gewohnten Metier der kritischen Gesellschafts- und Charakterstudien abwich. Ein weiterer Regisseur, der sich weitgehend treu blieb, war Sidney Lumet, dessen Reputation bis in die fünfziger Jahre zurückreichte. Er drehte in den achtziger Jahren zehn Filme und behielt dabei seine bewährte Mischung aus Sozial- und Charakterstudien, Gesellschaftssatiren und psychologischen Dramen bei, die auch sein Werk der siebziger Jahre kennzeich-

140. Darth Vader (David Prowse) in *Krieg der Sterne* von George Lucas, 1977.

140. Darth Vader (David Prowse) in *Star Wars* by George Lucas, 1977.

the eighties. At the same time the »Teenieslasher« films triggered by *Carrie* and *Halloween* enjoyed a heyday, relying unlike their forerunners on grisly special effects and eye-catching violence. *Saturday Night Fever* (1977) picked up on the rock film tradition and started the disco wave that was to produces a series of shallow dance films in subsequent years.

George Lucas's *Star Wars* (1977) was to launch the most important development. It is a film consciously conceived for younger audiences. The plot and performances were built around a mixture of the modern comic-strip and ancient fairy-tale conventions that classical Hollywood had already used as the basis for various genres. The result was one-dimensional characters, a clear distinction between good and evil and a simple plot, presented in an imaginative and innovative form by the use of special effects, giving a sense of modernity. This recipe did not just affect future science-fiction films, but also other genres like detective films, war films and horror films. It became the accepted pattern in actions films in particular, one of the most popular genres in the eighties. Here the typical heroes seem to have emerged from comic strips. They have nothing in common with the inwardly shattered but morally intact action heroes of the seventies. They are successors to a variety of the anti-hero who emerged in the sixties: the cold-blooded, calculating, highly qualified professional who does his job free of all moral scruples. The breakthrough success of *First Blood* (1982) was followed by a wave of action films in which élite American forces went to Vietnam to liberate prisoners of war and to restore the American sense of superiority by winning the war retrospectively, as it were. *Star Wars* also triggered a flood of fantasy spectacles, of which the most successful was the *Indiana Jones trilogy*, a joint venture by Steven Spielberg and George Lucas.

A series of other film-makers whose names are linked with New Hollywood were also involved in these trends. John Boorman, who had turned to fantasy material immediately after *Deliverance* (1971), made the brilliantly photographed historical adventure film *Excalibur* (1981) and the jungle adventure *The Emerald Forest* (1985). John Milius came up with the fantasy action film *Conan the Barbarian* (1982), in which Arnold Schwarzenegger, one of the superstars of the eighties, played his first leading role. Brian De Palma, who like Spielberg and Lucas was mainly interested in the renewal of the genre, made a series of more or less successful psycho-thrillers and classical gangster films which gave a new boost to his career. Other film-makers tried to adapt to the new climate without abandoning their artistic credentials. Alan J. Pakula, Philip Kaufman, Milos Forman, Robert Benton and Sydney Pollack established themselves as directors of ambitious mainstream films, but used material that avoided any social comment or confirmed conservative values. Despite some major successes, their productivity declined noticeably in the eighties. Comedy directors like Paul Mazursky and Michael Ritchie obviously found it easier to adapt, increasingly replacing social criticism in their films with a conciliatory tone or ridiculous gimmicks, as in Ritchie's Chevy Chase films. After a low point in his career, Mike Nichols made a comeback in 1983 with *Silkwood*, a drama that fell outside the pattern of

net, konnte allerdings seine Erfolgsserie jener Zeit nicht wiederholen. Eine Ausnahmeerscheinung bildete Woody Allen, dessen treue und umfangreiche Fangemeinde ihm ermöglichte, in gewohnter Produktivität seine persönlichen Themen weiterzuverfolgen.

Die Karriere anderer Filmemacher des neuen Hollywood ging steil bergab, weil sie Schwierigkeiten hatten, sich dem Zeitgeschmack anzupassen. Hal Ashby drehte nach seinem letzten großen Erfolg *Being There* (1979, *Willkommen Mr. Chance*) noch fünf Filme, bevor er 1988 starb, wählte dafür aber Stoffe, die weder an sein vorheriges Niveau heranreichten noch beim Publikum ankamen. William Friedkin erregte mit seinen zwiespältigen, düsteren Actionthrillern *Cruising* (1980) und *To Live and Die in L.A.* (1985, *Leben und Sterben in L.A.*) zwar noch einmal Aufmerksamkeit, scheiterte damit jedoch an den Kinokassen und beschränkte sich daraufhin auf die Arbeit beim Fernsehen. Der Ruhm von Peter Bogdanovich begann bereits nach seinem letzten größeren Erfolg mit *Paper Moon* (1973) zu verblassen. Nachdem er einen Flop nach dem anderen geliefert hatte, widmete er sich schließlich ab 1979 nur noch kleineren Produktionen, die geringe Resonanz hatten. In den neunziger Jahren arbeitet er überwiegend für das Fernsehen. George Roy Hill zog sich nach einer kommerziellen Pechsträhne, die 1975 mit *The Great Waldo Pepper* einsetzte, Ende der achtziger Jahre ganz aus dem Filmgeschäft zurück. James Bridges konnte nach dem Erfolg von *The China Syndrome* und *Urban Cowboy* seinen nächsten Film, *Mike's Murder* (1982), nur unter Schwierigkeiten auf den Markt bringen, und erlebte 1985 mit *Perfect* ein Fiasko, von dem er sich bis zu seinem Tod 1993 nicht mehr erholte.

Ein wichtiger Faktor, der den Niedergang von New Hollywood beschleunigte, war das Wiederaufleben des Blockbuster-Syndroms in der Folge von *Star Wars* und anderen Megahits. Die Filmgesellschaften konzentrierten sich daraufhin wieder auf konventionelle Produkte für ein Massenpublikum und waren kaum noch an intelligenten Stoffen interessiert, deren Realisierung ein nur kleines Budget erfordert hätte. Dies bewirkte, daß sich Filmemacher, die nicht bereit waren, Konzessionen zu machen, ganz oder teilweise aus dem Hollywood-Mainstream zurückzogen. So lieferte Stanley Kubrick, der zwischen 1968 und 1975 eine für ihn ungewöhnliche Produktivität an den Tag gelegt hatte, in den folgenden zwölf Jahren nur zwei Filme ab. Schlesinger arbeitete überwiegend in Europa, wo er unter anderem bei einer Reihe von Operninszenierungen Regie führte. Sam Peckinpah drehte bis zu seinem Tod im Jahre 1984 nach *Convoy* (1978) nur noch einen Film. John Cassavetes brachte in den achtziger Jahren lediglich zwei Filme heraus, davon eine Auftragsarbeit, ehe er 1989 nach längerer Krankheit starb. Robert Altman, Arthur Penn, Paul Schrader, Alan Rudolph und Jerry Schatzberg richteten sich mit kleineren Produktionen am Rande des Hollywood-Mainstreams ein.

Für einige der Filmemacher wendete sich das Blatt Anfang der neunziger Jahre. Robert Altman gelang mit *The Player* (1992) und *Short Cuts* (1993) ein Comeback, Francis Ford Coppola hatte wieder Erfolg mit *The Godfather: Part III* (1990, *Der Pate: Teil III*), William Friedkin kehrte erfolgreich ins Filmgeschäft zurück, Brian De Palma konnte sich endlich im Bereich der Blockbuster etablieren, Martin Scorsese erlebte einen neuen Höhepunkt seiner Karriere und so eigenwillige Filmemacher, wie Alan Rudolph, Arthur Penn und Paul Schrader, fanden in Hollywood wieder offene Türen. Gleichzeitig begann ein Kult um das neue Hollywood der siebziger Jahre, das, angesichts der Flut von stereotypen Großproduktionen mit simplen Plots der achtziger und neunziger Jahre, zum letzten Goldenen Zeitalter des amerikanischen Films erklärt wurde. Die wichtigsten Vertreter von New Hollywood verehrt man mittlerweile als Meisterregisseure, und viele Filme, die seinerzeit ein Flop waren, werden aufgrund ihrer Kreativität und Originalität neu gewürdigt.

its times in terms of its theme and world view, then made a few harmless social comedies of which *Working Girl* (1988) was the most successful. Two of New Hollywood's previously most successful talents, Bob Rafelson and Michael Cimino, were able to gain a foothold in the film business again. Rafelson worked with Jack Nicholson again in 1981 on *The Postman Always Rings Twice*, and enjoyed a commercial success after almost ten years, while Cimino partially repaired his damaged reputation with *Year of the Dragon* (1985). Neither of them came close to their former fame, however. Francis Ford Coppola followed a similar pattern. He lived on his myth as a superstar, and despite two financial disasters, *One from the Heart* (1982) and *Cotton Club* (1984) he made a total of eight films in the eighties, but none of them even came close to his successes in the seventies. In contrast with Coppola, who lurched uncertainly between his artistic vision and concessions to commercial pressure, Martin Scorsese clung on to his personal projects and managed to secure his reputation as one of Hollywood's most creative and talented directors. But he was not to notch up major successes until *The Color of Money* (1986) and *The Last Temptation of Christ* (1988), which took him away from his usual métier of critical social and character studies. Another director who largely remained true to himself was Sidney Lumet, whose reputation went back to the fifties. He made ten films in the eighties, retaining the tried-and-tested mixture of social and character studies, social satire and psychological drama that also characterized his sixties dramas, but he was not able to repeat his successes of that period. Woody Allen was an exception here: his faithful and extensive community of fans made it possible for him to pursue his personal themes at the usual level of productivity.

Other New Hollywood film-makers' careers went rapidly downhill because they had difficulty in adapting to the taste of the times. After his last major success, *Being There* (1979), Hal Ashby made five more films before his death in 1988, but chose material for them that did not match up to his former achievements, and did not appeal to the public either. William Friedkin attracted attention again with his ambiguous, dark action thrillers *Cruising* (1980) and *To Live and Die in L.A.* (1985), but they failed at the box office, and after that he restricted himself to television work. Peter Bogdanovich's fame started to pale immediately after his last major success *Paper Moon* (1973). After making one flop after the other, he finally turned exclusively to small-scale productions that met with little response after 1979, and largely worked for television in the nineties. George Roy Hill left the film industry altogether in the late eighties after a run of commercial bad luck starting with *The Great Waldo Pepper* in 1975. James Bridges, after the success of *The China Syndrome* (1979) and *Urban Cowboy* (1980) had great difficulty in getting his next film, *Mike's Murder* (1982), on to the market at all, and *Perfect* (1985) was such a fiasco that he had not recovered from it by the time he died in 1993.

One important factor that accelerated the decline of New Hollywood was the revival of the blockbuster syndrome after *Star Wars* and other mega-hits. The film companies continued to concentrate on conventional products for a mass audience and took next to no interest in intelligent material that only needed a low budget. This meant that film-makers who were not prepared to make concessions withdrew completely or partially from mainstream Hollywood. So Stanley Kubrick, who had been unusually productive for him from 1968 to 1975, made only two films in the next twelve years. Sam Peckinpah made only one film after *Convoy* (1978) before he died in 1984. Schlesinger worked mainly in Europe, where he was responsible for a number of opera productions, among other things. John Cassavetes brought out only two films in the eighties, of which one was commissioned, before dying in 1989 after a long illness. Robert Altman, Arthur Penn, Paul Schrader, Alan Rudolph and Jerry Schatzberg set themselves up with small-scale productions on the fringes of mainstream Hollywood.

Things changed for some film-makers in the early nineties. Robert Altman made a successful comeback with *The Player* (1992) and *Short Cuts* (1993), Francis Ford Coppola was successful again with *The Godfather: Part III* (1990), William Friedkin returned successfully to the film industry and Brian De Palma finally established himself in the blockbuster field. Martin Scorsese's career reached another peak and even highly individual film-makers like Alan Rudolph, Arthur Penn and Paul Schrader found open doors in Hollywood again. At the same time a seventies New Hollywood cult started: it was pronounced the last golden age of the American film, given the flood of stereotypical mega-productions with simple plots in the eighties and nineties. The major representatives of New Hollywood are now celebrated as master directors, and many films that flopped at the time are starting to be acknowledged for their creativity and originality.

Ausgewählte Literatur

Balio, Tino (Hrsg.), *The American Film Industry*, Madison 1976.

Bernardoni, James, *The New Hollywood: What the Movies did with the new Freedoms of the Seventies*, Jefferson, North Carolina, 1991.

Bertelsen, Martin, *Roadmovies und Western: Ein Vergleich zur Genre-Bestimmung*, Ammersbek bei Hamburg 1991.

Biskind, Peter, *Easy Riders, Raging Bulls. Wie die Sex & Drugs & Rock'n Roll-Generation Hollywood rettete*, Hamburg 2000.

Brode, Douglas, *The Films of the Sixties*, New York 1980.

Cook, David, *Lost Illusions: American Cinema in the Shadows of Watergate and Vietnam, 1970–1979*, New York 2000.

Dittmar, Linda und Gene Michaud (Hrsg.), *From Hanoi to Hollywood. The Vietnam War in American Film*, New Brunswick und London 1990.

Hillier, Jim, *The New Hollywood: A Movie Book*, London 1992.

Jacobs, Diane, *Hollywood Renaissance*, New York und London 1977.

Kolker, Robert Philipp, *A Cinema of Loneliness*, New York 1980.

Lev, Peter, *American Films of the '70s: Conflicting Visions*, Austin 2000.

Lewis, Jon, *Whom God Wishes to Destroy ... : Francis Coppola and the New Hollywood*, Durham 1995.

Litwak, Mark, *Reel Power: the Struggle for Influence and Success in the New Hollywood*, New York 1986.

Madsen, Axel, *The New Hollywood: American Movies in the '70s*, New York 1975.

Man, Glenn, *Radical Visions: American Film Renaissance, 1967–1976*, Westport 1994.

Monaco, James, *American Film Now*, New York 1979.

New Hollywood, mit Beiträgen von Hans C. Blumenberg u. a., München und Wien 1976.

Pye, Michael, und Lynda Myles, *The Movie Brats. How the Film Generation took over Hollywood*, New York 1979.

Ray, Robert B., *A Certain Tendency of the Hollywood Cinema, 1930–1980*, Princeton, New Jersey, 1985.

Reinecke, Stefan, »Hollywood goes Vietnam. Der Vietnamkrieg im US-amerikanischen Film«, in: *Aufblende. Schriften zum Film*, Bd. 5, Marburg 1993.

Schatz, Thomas, *Old Hollywood/New Hollywood: Ritual, Art, And Industry*, Ann Arbor, Michigan, 1983.

Thompson, Kristin, *Storytelling in the New Hollywood. Understanding Classical Narrative Technique*, Cambridge, Mass., 1999.

Thomsen, David, *Overexposures: The Crisis in American Filmmaking*, New York 1981.

Weiss, Ulli, *Das neue Hollywood. Francis Ford Coppola, Steven Spielberg, Martin Scorsese*, München 1986.

Wood, Robin, *Hollywood from Vietnam to Reagan*, New York 1986.

Selected bibliography

Balio, Tino (ed.), *The American Film Industry*, Madison, 1976.

Bernardoni, James, *The New Hollywood: What the Movies did with the new Freedoms of the Seventies*, Jefferson, North Carolina, 1991.

Bertelsen, Martin, *Roadmovies und Western: Ein Vergleich zur Genre-Bestimmung*, Ammersbek near Hamburg, 1991.

Biskind, Peter, *Easy Riders, Raging Bulls. Wie die Sex & Drugs & Rock'n Roll-Generation Hollywood rettete*, Hamburg, 2000.

Brode, Douglas, *The Films of the Sixties*, New York, 1980.

Cook, David, *Lost Illusions: American Cinema in the Shadows of Watergate and Vietnam, 1970–1979*, New York, 2000.

Dittmar, Linda und Gene Michaud (ed.), *From Hanoi to Hollywood. The Vietnam War in American Film*, New Brunswick and London, 1990.

Hillier, Jim, *The New Hollywood: A Movie Book*, London, 1992.

Jacobs, Diane, *Hollywood Renaissance*, New York and London, 1977.

Kolker, Robert Philipp, *A Cinema of Loneliness*, New York, 1980.

Lev, Peter, *American Films of the '70s: Conflicting Visions*, Austin, 2000.

Lewis, Jon, *Whom God Wishes to Destroy ... : Francis Coppola and the New Hollywood*, Durham, 1995.

Litwak, Mark, *Reel Power: the Struggle for Influence and Success in the New Hollywood*, New York, 1986.

Madsen, Axel, *The New Hollywood: American Movies in the '70s*, New York, 1975.

Man, Glenn, *Radical Visions: American Film Renaissance, 1967–1976*, Westport, 1994.

Monaco, James, *American Film Now*, New York, 1979.

New Hollywood, with contributions by Hans C. Blumenberg and others, Munich and Vienna, 1976.

Pye, Michael, and Lynda Myles, *The Movie Brats. How the Film Generation took over Hollywood*, New York, 1979.

Ray, Robert B., *A Certain Tendency of the Hollywood Cinema, 1930–1980*, Princeton, New Jersey, 1985.

Reinecke, Stefan, »Hollywood goes Vietnam. Der Vietnamkrieg im US-amerikanischen Film«, in: *Aufblende. Schriften zum Film*, vol. 5, Marburg, 1993.

Schatz, Thomas, *Old Hollywood/New Hollywood: Ritual, Art, And Industry*, Ann Arbor, Michigan, 1983.

Thompson, Kristin, *Storytelling in the New Hollywood. Understanding Classical Narrative Technique*, Cambridge, Mass., 1999.

Thomsen, David, *Overexposures: The Crisis in American Filmmaking*, New York, 1981.

Weiss, Ulli, *Das neue Hollywood. Francis Ford Coppola, Steven Spielberg, Martin Scorsese*, Munich, 1986.

Wood, Robin, *Hollywood from Vietnam to Reagan*, New York, 1986.

Index